H.M.S. WARSPITE

This book is dedicated to the Officers and Men of the last Commission of the 7th *Warspite* 1937–1944

Captain S. W. Roskill D.S.C., R.N.

H.M.S. Warspite

The Story of a Famous Battleship

Futura Publications Limited

A Futura Book

First published in Great Britain in 1957
by William Collins & Sons Ltd
First Futura Publications edition 1974

The text of H.M.S. *Warspite* has been approved by
The Lords Commissioners of the Admiralty

ISBN 0 8600 71723
Printed in Great Britain by
Hazell Watson & Viney Ltd
Aylesbury, Bucks

Futura Publications Limited
49 Poland Street,
London W1A 2LG

ACKNOWLEDGMENTS

I WOULD first of all thank the Lords Commissioners of the Admiralty for their generous permission to make use of their records, and the heads of the many Admiralty Departments whom I have importuned for information. All have put themselves to great trouble on my behalf, and without their help this book could never have been written.

Secondly I must acknowledge my debt to the many officers and men who served in or were connected with the last *Warspite*, who have lent me documents, diaries and photographs, and have read and criticised my drafts. Under this heading I would especially mention the help I have received from Admiral of the Fleet Lord Chatfield, P.C., G.C.B., O.M., K.C.M.G., C.V.O., Admiral of the Fleet Viscount Cunningham of Hyndhope, K.T., G.C.B., O.M., D.S.O., Admiral The Hon. Sir Reginald Plunket-Ernle-Erle-Drax, K.C.B., D.S.O., Vice-Admiral Sir Humphrey T. Walwyn, K.C.M.G., K.C.S.I., C.B., D.S.O., Admiral Sir Victor A. C. Crutchley, V.C., K.C.B., D.S.C., Admiral Sir Douglas B. Fisher, K.C.B., K.B.E., Admiral Sir Herbert A. Packer, K.C.B., C.B.E., Vice-Admiral M. H. A. Kelsey, C.B., D.S.C., Rear-Admiral W. S. Chalmers, C.B.E., D.S.C., Rear-Admiral Sir Charles E. Madden, Bart., C.B., and Messrs. Daniel Reardon, E. A. Ogden, J. Fidler and W. Lawes of the last *Warspite's* company.

I would also thank Commander G. Hare, D.S.C., R.N., for his assistance with research, Colonel T. M. Penney for help with the maps, all of which have been drawn by Mr. D. K. Purle, Dr. Charles Talbot for advice on the derivation of the ship's name, Major L. F. Ellis, C.V.O., C.B.E., D.S.O., M.C., for allowing me to exploit his expert knowledge regarding the Normandy landings of 1944, and Professor Christopher Lloyd, M.A., for historical criticisms. The Editors of the *Western Morning News* and *Daily Mirror* have allowed me access to their files. The Directors of the Public Records Office and of the National Maritime Museum have found me documents and illustrations. The Editor of *The Sea Cadet* has allowed me to reprint " The Subject," and Messrs. John Murray & Co. have been equally generous regarding " The Old Lady." The Secretary of the Marine Society has helped with the history of the " Training Ship

ACKNOWLEDGMENTS

Warspite," and the Wolverhampton Metal Company, Ltd., has provided information regarding the breaking up of the 7th *Warspite*. Extracts from official documents and certain photographs, which are Crown copyright, are published by kind permission of the Controller, H.M. Stationery Office.

For permission to reproduce the illustrations my thanks are due to: Her Majesty's Stationery Office for Nos. 3, 4, 5 and 7; the National Maritime Museum for Nos. 1 and 2; the Imperial War Museum for Nos. 11, 12 and 13; the *Daily Mirror* for Nos. 6 and 14; and Rear-Admiral Sir Charles Madden for Nos. 8, 9 and 10.

Any book which purports to be a serious contribution to history must contain references adequate to satisfy a critical public, and for the earlier part of the book I have endeavoured to meet that need. But I felt that where a great many of the references are, as in the case of the 7th *Warspite*, contained in unpublished Admiralty documents it would be of little help to include them; since the critical reader cannot have access to them until the day comes when they are transferred to the Public Record Office. I have therefore felt it preferable to omit all references to unpublished sources, even though I realise the dangers and disadvantages of doing so. Other sources are numbered in the text and can be referred to in Appendix G.

S. W. R.

Blounce, South Warnborough
February, 1957

FOREWORD

*By Admiral of the Fleet, Viscount Cunningham
of Hyndhope*
K.T., G.C.B., O.M., D.S.O., ETC.

I AM glad that the story of the 7th and last *Warspite* has
been written, and not only because she was my flagship
in the Mediterranean from 1939 to 1941. Many good
books have been written about the part of the smaller
ships—destroyers, submarines, corvettes and coastal craft
—in the recent war; but as far as I know this is the only
one which gives an account of a big ship's entire life, and
of her fighting record in both world wars. It is all too
easy to forget that the work of the smaller ships depended
greatly on the power of the main fleets behind them.
Though it is true that the composition of those fleets has
changed out of all recognition during our lifetime, their
function has remained unaltered. We relearnt this old
lesson very forcibly in 1942, when losses and the heavy
calls from other theatres left us without a battle fleet in
the Mediterranean; and we very nearly lost our grip on
the whole Middle East theatre in consequence.

But *Warspite* was more than just one unit in one main
fleet. In the first place her fighting record is unique in
modern times, spanning as it does both Jutland in 1916
and Normandy in 1944. Between those dates she was
present at many famous fights, and I learn now that in the
course of her long career she wore out no less than three
complete sets of 15-inch guns. Many times did those guns

of hers hit the enemy hard; and in return she was many times damaged by her enemies; but she had great vitality, and was always repaired in time to renew the fight. All ships have personalities, but *Warspite's* was highly original. She always had a touch of feminine capriciousness about her. She was liable to take a dislike to her consorts and collide with them; she was not unknown to leave her proper element to taste the feeling of the land. She was always something of an anxiety to those who commanded her; for she had a will of her own, and they never knew when she would take it into her head to do something quite uncalled for and unexpected, such as turning a complete circle on her own. She learnt that embarrassing manœuvre at Jutland, and she never forgot it. Her stubborn, wilful, lovable character never changed, and right to the end her wheel had to be handled with caution lest her incalculable sense of humour should be aroused. At the last, when her life was almost extinct, she showed a final flicker of those same qualities when she threw off her tugs and preferred the Cornish coast to a ship-breaker's yard. And who can blame her?

She was a great ship, and the last of a famous line which bore her name. Although one may hope that not many years will pass before the name is revived, the 7th *Warspite* is as secure of her niche in her country's history as she is in the memories of those who served in her.

Cunningham of Hyndhope

THE SUBJECT

You say you have no subject
 And your brushes all have dried;
But come to Marazion
 At the ebbing of the tide,

And look you out to seaward,
 Where My Lady battle-scarred
Hugs the rock that is more welcome
 Than the shameful breaker's yard.

Paint her there upon the sunset
 In her glory and despair
With the diadem of victory
 Still in flower upon her hair.

Let her whisper as she settles
 Of her blooding long ago
In the mist that mingles Jutland
 With the might of Scapa Flow.

Let her tell you, too, of Narvik
 With its snowy hills, and then
Of Matapan, Salerno
 And the shoals of Walcheren;

And finally of Malta,
 When along the purple street
Came in trail the Roman Navy
 To surrender at her feet.

Of all these honours conscious
 How could she bear to be
Delivered to the spoiler
 Or severed from the sea?

So hasten then and paint her
 In the last flush of her pride
On the rocks of Marazion
 At the ebbing of the tide.

BY LIEUTENANT-COMMANDER R. A. B. MICHELL
H.M.S. Warspite, 1939-42

CONTENTS

CONTENTS

LIST OF MAPS

INTRODUCTION

" The Ship's Book contains particulars regarding the ship from the date when she was ordered to be built till finally removed from the Navy List."

Admiralty instructions on flyleaf of the 7th ' Warspite's ' Ship's Book

IT IS not so much a book as an enormous file of documents. In the case of *Warspite* it is about a foot thick. To a landsman it would not only appear totally devoid of sentiment (which it is), but it would not convey the slightest hint of the romance of a great ship's life; but on a sailor, and especially on one who served in the ship to which the book belonged, its dry pages have a very different effect. To him a ship was, and will always remain a living entity. He served her, and became part of her; and she unconsciously became a part of himself. So it is that when such a ship's record comes again, even after an interval of many years, into the hands of one of her company, its pages evoke countless memories and seem vibrant with the life that was once hers.

I first saw *Warspite's* Ship's Book in 1936 when I joined her in Portsmouth Dockyard, where she was completing a big reconstruction. I was then concerned only with the entry in it of the changes made in her armaments, but I did glance at the folio which told a little of the history of her ancestors. I realised then, if I had not realised before, the fame of her name and the continuity of the fighting tradition which, with scarcely a break, she and her six predecessors had maintained during more than three centuries of service in the Royal Navy.

Twenty years later in a basement room in the Admiralty on a bitingly cold winter's evening, I again had the book in my hands. I started turning the pages over idly, and I saw the first entry:

Warspite (Name as per Admiralty Order S.3981/12).
Battleship.
Ordered to be built. Programme 1912-13.
Laid Down, 31st October, 1912.
Launched, 26th November, 1913.

I went on turning the pages until I came to the last entry:

Final Disposal of Ship.
Approved to scrap, 31st July, 1946. (S.M.B.A. 2671/46).

I am not ashamed to admit that the last entry caused me a deep pang of sorrow, as though I was reading the epitaph on the grave of a much-loved friend—as indeed I was. I put a match to the fire in that cold basement room, and when it had brought some warmth into the darkness of the evening, and into the passing darkness of my thoughts, I sat before it with the book on my knees. I did not notice the passage of the hours as I went on turning its many pages, for they were immensely evocative of the ship herself, and of the officers and men, now scattered far and wide, who had served in her with me. It was then that this story was born, for I was determined that she should have a fuller, and possibly a finer epitaph than the laconic order "Approved to scrap"; and the purpose of this book is no more than to tell the story of her ancestors, and then to record a little of what happened during the thirty-four years between the first and the last entry in her Ship's Book.

It was, I think, in the spring of 1937, on *Warspite's* quarterdeck in Malta harbour, that Captain Victor Crutchley* remarked to me: "After all, this ship exists only to carry those eight big guns." His words, though casually spoken, struck me very forcibly, for not only was I her Gunnery Officer at the time, but my Captain's service and experience had been very different from that gained in the school in which I had done my specialist training. He was, in fact, a very fine example of the "salt horse" officer whom, in between wars, the Navy was inclined to belittle or neglect. He had won his Victoria Cross in the second attempt to block Ostend on the 10th May, 1918, and had done much of his service in small ships. Yet his remark made it plain that he at any rate had no doubts at all regarding the function of the ship which then wore his pendant. I glanced up at the burnished muzzles and the shining, crested tampions of the great guns above us, and knew quite well that Crutchley had left half his remark unspoken. "And," he might have gone on, "it is your job to see that their complicated machinery (of which I know nothing) works perfectly, and that the five hundred or so officers and men who man and control them are every one of them masters of their craft." That then was the purpose towards which we worked for more than two years, and then just before war came, I was called to other duties, and had to turn "my" big guns over to other hands. But I knew by that time that the tool we had fashioned would not fail when the test came; for *Warspite* was the finest ship in which I ever served. I never saw her again after I left her, for the war took me to waters far distant from those in which she covered herself with glory; but I have never forgotten her and never shall.

* Now Admiral Sir Victor Crutchley, V.C., K.C.B., D.S.C.

In some quarters it had, long before the last war, been all too loudly proclaimed that the big-gun ship was an expensive, useless survival from a long-past era. Perhaps it may now be true that we shall never build such ships again. I do not know. What I do know is that in *Warspite* and her four sisters the art of the big ship and big gun designer reached its zenith; that the three decades of her life covered two of the fiercest sea struggles in which Britain has ever been involved; that we ultimately emerged victorious and with unviolated shores from both those struggles; and that, no matter how great was the contribution of other arms and services, those victories could never have come to pass without the few big-gun ships we possessed. It may well prove that this book is part of their Requiem; but if that is so let us at least admit the quality and performance of the ships which have passed for ever, acknowledge the debt we owe to those who designed and built them, to those who manned and fought them; and admit with Wordsworth that:

" Men are we, and must grieve when even the shade
Of that which once was great has passed away."

This then is the story not of all the big-gun ships that ever thundered their salvos to rend the inoffending sea ten or twelve miles away, but of one of them. When the *Queen Elizabeth* was flagship of the Mediterranean Fleet she had as much of beauty as there was of past history, and now of future hope, in her name. *Barham*, *Valiant* and *Malaya* all had individual character and did great deeds. But *Warspite* became the most famous of her class, for her name will always be connected not only with Jutland, which she shares with three of her sisters, but with Narvik, Calabria, Tripoli, the evacuation from Crete, Matapan, the peril to Ceylon in 1942, Salerno's beaches and Normandy's tremendous landings. Four times in her long career did she suffer grievous damage at her enemies' hands, but each time she was repaired to renew the fight. Small wonder that by 1945 she was worn out! She and her sisters may not have possessed that wonderful combination of strength, speed and beauty that was the lovely but ill-fated *Hood's*; but no one who saw the 1st Battle Squadron moored in the sun of peacetime Valletta harbour, or plunging through Atlantic seas in war, can deny that they, too, had beauty—the beauty of strength and of character. I never knew one of her class to be other than a happy and successful ship; nor can it be doubted that the thousands upon thousands who served in them were proud of that service, and that those who survive remain so to this day. It is, in fact, to some of those who served with me in *Warspite* that this book owes its life; for when I was asked to write about a ship, and allowed to choose my subject, they were insistent upon what it should be. But we must leave her story to unfold itself in due time, and return to the beginning—to the origin of her name, and to the service of her forebears.

S. W. R.

CHAPTER ONE

The First Two Ancestors

1596-1715

> "War's spite, indeed, and we to do him right—
> Will call the ship he fought in the "'War's-Spite.'"
>
> *Words put into Queen Elizabeth I's mouth*
> *by Thomas Heywood in a play published in 1605*

EVEN TO-DAY the derivation of the name remains rather obscure. There is, however, no doubt at all that it dates from the time of the first Elizabeth, and was first used as a ship's name during her wars with Spain. The old English word "spight" is a contraction of "despight," which expressed contempt, or contemptuous defiance. If used as a verb (and it could be used in many other ways as well) it meant "to treat with contempt." In documents written before the spelling of English had been codified the name took many forms such as Warspight, Wastspight or Warspitt. The first variation seems to have been the most common until early in the eighteenth century, when the spelling took its modern form. The intention of the name is therefore abundantly clear. It expressed contempt for and defiance of Elizabeth's enemies. Its spirit is exactly the same as that of her famous speech to the troops assembled at Tilbury under Essex on 9th August, 1588, when the Armada was in the Channel: "I think foul scorn that Parma or Spain, or any Prince of Europe, should dare to invade the borders of my realm." The last

Warspite inherited something of that same spirit through her official crest, which shows "a ship's gun (*circa* 1600) in gold on a green field," and in her motto, "*Belli dura despicio*" ("I despise the hardships of war").

The word "spight," however, had a second and quite different meaning in Elizabethan times. It was also the colloquial name of the green woodpecker, or "yaffle" as countrymen call the bird to-day. No clue has been found to suggest that any of the early *Warspites* connected their ship's name with the woodpecker; but quite apart from the phonetic similarity of "Warspite" and "Woodspite," it would certainly not have been inappropriate had they done so. A connection between a warship whose guns were intended to punch holes in the wooden hulls of her adversaries, and a bird which drives holes into trees with a beak of astonishing strength, though fanciful, might well have appealed to sailors.* What is certain is that early in the career of the last *Warspite*, before the Admiralty produced crests and mottos for all ships of the Royal Navy, the woodpecker was adopted as the ship's unofficial crest. This took place while Captain F. Clifton-Brown was in command (May, 1920-May, 1922, see Appendix B.), and one of his officers remembers that he went to great trouble over its selection and design.† Nor did the issue by the Admiralty of the official crest a short time later result in the displacement of the woodpecker. Her guns continued right to the end to carry it on their tampions, and her boats wore it on their bows, what time the official crests

---

* The etymology of "spight" (woodpecker) is totally different from that of "despight" (to treat with contempt). The former also appears in old documents as Speight, Specht and Speicht., e.g. Douglas, Aeneid, VII, IV, 91 (1513) "Ane byrd . . . with sprutlit wingis, clepit a speicht wyth us, quhilk in Latyne hect Picus Marcyus." It is fairly certain that the spight was the green woodpecker and not one of the other varieties of the species. Ray, Willoughby's Ornithology, 135, says "The green woodpecker or Woodspite, called also the Rainfowl, High-Heo and Hew-hole."

† From Rear-Admiral W. S. Chalmers, C.B., C.B.E., who was First Lieutenant of *Warspite* under Captain Clifton-Brown.

remained disregarded in the Gunner's and Bosun's store-rooms; and her company always gave the name of "Woodpeckers" to certain of their activities such as the ship's dance band.* Though it is certainly the case that the Admiralty crest and motto convey the true spirit of her name, the fact that sailors considered the woodpecker a more attractive symbol than the squat Elizabethan cannon probably explains why the former survived so long, and in defiance of heraldry.

But to turn from conjecture to fact, the creation of the "Royal Navy" as a service ready at all times to carry out the wishes of the Government can confidently be attributed to Henry VIII (1509-1547); but he owed much to the manner in which his father had fostered the ship-building industry, and overseas trade. Henry VII did not, however, have ships designed specifically for fighting purposes. Privately owned ships were merely hired for purposes of war whenever the need arose, and there was little distinction between cargo vessels and combat ships. Nor did the ship-of-war acquire different characteristics from the trading ship for another 150 years.

It was the threat of a powerful French fleet in the Channel which first directed Henry VIII's attention to the need for a fighting navy. His father's modest fighting fleet was greatly expanded, the supporting shore organisation needed to administer and maintain it was created, and in his wars with France he showed a clear understanding of the use of a navy both defensively against invasion and offensively to carry his troops overseas. Fighting tactics were, however, still virtually non-existent and the larger warships or "galleons" did not become the "line-of-

---

* When the 7th *Warspite* was at Alexandria during the 1939-45 war the code message which was passed to recall her officers and men to the ship in emergency was "Mr. Woodpecker is required by his wife." (Admiral Sir Douglas Fisher to the author, September 1955.)

battle ships" (whence descends our modern title of "battleship") until the Commonwealth generals introduced the disciplined movements of military formations into the fleet in the mid-seventeenth century. It is none the less reasonable to trace the origins of the battleship to Henry VIII's development of the fighting fleet, and it is certain that it was due to his understanding of the sea and encouragement of the fighting navy that his daughter inherited both a navy and the elements of a naval strategy.

Elizabeth I continued the development of the fighting ship, and especially the smaller, faster "race-built" galleons. She took a lively interest in the fortunes of her fleet, and she and Hawkins totally reconstructed the older ships. Seven new galleons were also added to the 22 which she had inherited. None the less, and in spite of her wars with Spain, there were periods during her reign when the fleet was badly neglected. The first *Warspite*, which was launched in about March, 1596, was one of the few ships built by Elizabeth. She appears in a very early "Navy List" printed in 1603, the year of Elizabeth I's death, among the twenty-eight galleons which "her Majesty left at her death." She is there shown as a ship of 600 tons, but other records suggest that she was in fact some fifty tons larger. Her armament was thirty-six guns, and her complement is shown as only "12 men in harbour" but "300 men at sea." Of the latter 190 were mariners, thirty were "gunners" and eighty are classed as "sailors."[1] It should perhaps be explained that in the sixteenth century "mariners" were those of the crew who manned the guns and fought the ships, while "sailors" were concerned only with working the sails. After 1700 "sailors" were generally referred to as "seamen."

Warspite very soon saw active service, for in June of

the year of her launching she took part in Essex's expedition of 150 ships carrying 10,000 men sent by Elizabeth to attack Philip II's great naval base and stronghold of Cadiz. Her captain was one of the most famous seamen of all time, Sir Walter Raleigh. Because *Warspite* was also Rear-Admiral of the Fleet*, she led one of the four squadrons into which the expedition was organised, and she was in the van for the actual assault. Not the least interesting side of the story of the capture of Cadiz lies in the rivalry between Essex, who was Elizabeth's favourite at the time, and Raleigh, whose recent secret wedding to Bessie Throgmorton had brought him into disfavour with his royal mistress. The two courtiers seem to have been determined by their conduct the one to retain and the other to regain the Queen's favour.

Raleigh's account of the forcing of the harbour has survived. "With the first peep of day," he wrote, "I weighed anchor and bare with the Spanish fleet, taking the start of all ours at a good distance. . . . I was first saluted by the Fort called 'Philip,' afterwards by the ordnance on the curtain, and lastly by all the galleys, in good order. To show scorn for all which, I answered first the fort and afterwards the galleys, to each piece a blurr with a trumpet, disdaining to shoot one piece at any one of all of those esteemed dreadful monsters."[2] The Spanish galleys were forced to retire higher up the harbour, and as they passed the *Warspite*, Raleigh "bestowed a benediction amongst them."

But besides impressing the Queen by his leadership and gallantry Sir Walter was also bent on avenging the death of his friend Sir Richard Grenville in the *Revenge*, and he made for the two great Spanish ships *St. Philip*

---

* In Elizabethan times the title "Admiral" applied to the ship, and not to the officer flying his flag in her.

and *St. Andrew*, which had been present at the fight off the Azores five years earlier.

" I must," he continued, not very modestly, " without glory, say for myself, that I headed single in the head of all. No other ship pushed up as far forward as the *Warspite*. . . . For almost three hours the *Warspite* continued in action, and the volleys of cannon and culverin came as thick as if it had been a skirmish of musketeers. . . . I laid out a warp by the side of the *Philip* to shake hands with her." The nearest English ships, the *Repulse* and the *Lion*, followed suit. On that the *St. Philip* and the three galleons nearest her " all let slip and ran aground, tumbling into the sea heaps of soldiers, so thick as if coals had been poured out of a sack . . . some drowned and some sticking in the mud."

The result was that the *St. Philip* and *St. Thomas* were burnt ; but the *St. Mathew* and *St. Andrew* " were recovered with our boats 'ere they could get out to fire themselves." Finally, says Raleigh, whose chivalry was as Elizabethan as his fighting spirit, " Ourselves spared the lives of all after the victory." The soldiers then landed, captured the city of Cadiz and held it for a fortnight. The destruction executed among the Spanish Fleet was so complete that Medina Sidonia despondently reported to his master " Neither ship, nor fleet, nor Cadiz remains " ; and Philip knew that his ambitions were, at any rate temporarily, frustrated. He died two years later.

There are certain not very well substantiated reports that the first *Warspite* was not a success as a warship, and the fact that the sum of £712 was spent on repairing her in 1598 has been mentioned in support of them. It would, however, have been surprising if, after Raleigh's determined handling of her in Cadiz harbour, she had not needed refitting. It seems almost certain that the criticisms of the ship originated from Raleigh himself. He considered her heavily over-gunned, and her lively movements in a seaway caused him a good deal of apprehension.[3]

After the destruction of Cadiz, Elizabeth continued to send raiding squadrons out from England to seize the Spanish treasure fleets from the Indies. In 1597 the *Warspite*, still under Raleigh, took part in Essex's expedition to the Azores, organised for that purpose. Raleigh captured Fayal by a combined operation ; but all the treasure fleet except two ships slipped safely past the English squadrons. Nor was another expedition in which *Warspite* took part three years later any more successful.

In between these two attempts to catch the treasure ships, *Warspite* had in 1599 joined the force known as the " Channel Guard," whose function it was to protect our shipping in the narrow seas. It is interesting to recall that when in 1940 Britain was faced by similar perils, the name Channel Guard was revived, and given to the anti-aircraft gunners who took our convoys through the narrow seas.[4]

In 1601 *Warspite* fought in another action against the Spaniards. On reports being received that they were sending an expedition to support the Desmond rebellion in Ireland, Admiral Sir Richard Leveson was appointed " Captain-General and Admiral of certain of Her Majesty's ships to serve against the Spaniards lately landed in Ireland."[5] Early in December he forced his way into the harbour of Kinsale, and after a severe fight destroyed the whole Spanish fleet. *Warspite* remained with Leveson for his expedition to the coast of Spain in 1602. The powerful fleet of nine English and twelve Dutch ships was ordered " to infest the Spanish coast," but the Dutch were late in joining the admiral, and he sailed without them on the 19th March. Vice-Admiral Sir William Monson stayed behind to await his dilatory allies, but the Queen told him to follow Leveson at once with what he had, because she had word that "the silver ships were arrived at Terceira" (in the Azores). Her Majesty certainly took the liveliest interest in the replenishment of her treasury at the expense of her Spanish brother-in-law. In this case the intelligence on which she acted was correct, but the treasure ships had sailed again before Monson joined Leveson. The latter could do nothing with the few ships he had, and thus the opportunity was missed. "If the Hollanders," commented Monson bitterly, "had kept touch according to promise, and the Queen's ships had been fitted out with care, we had made Her Majesty mistress of more treasure than any of her progenitors ever enjoyed."[6]

Not till the end of May, 1602, did Monson and Leveson meet, and then various causes combined to prevent the latter from retaining his full strength. On the 2nd June with only the *Warspite* and four other ships still in company, he did, however, find a Spanish squadron consisting of a large carrack (the *San Valentino*) and eleven galleys in Cezimbra Bay, near Lisbon. In spite of the strength of the defences Leveson decided to attack next morning. He led his squadron in the *Warspite*, and had intended to anchor her as close as possible to the carrack; but his plan went awry, due apparently to mismanagement by the ship's Master. In consequence *Warspite* drifted out of the bay, and Leveson had to shift to the *Dreadnought* in order to continue to direct the battle. None the less, after an all-day fight the entire enemy force was captured or destroyed; and the carrack proved to be one of the richest prizes captured during the Elizabethan wars. She was valued at a million ducats. The success offered some compensation to Leveson for having missed the treasure fleet.[7]

The great attack on Cadiz in 1596 was soon followed by the death of Philip II and, in 1603, by that of Elizabeth.

The turn of the century saw the passing of an era. James I quickly brought the Spanish war to an end, and the Navy at once experienced one of those downward cycles of neglect which have been so marked a feature of the years following every one of England's major wars. With Charles I on the throne, and in spite of the fact that the Navy was in a sorry state both materially and morally, little was done to prepare for the plain approach of war with France and Spain. In March, 1627, France signed a treaty with Spain. The opportunity for which Richelieu had been waiting had come.

In England, in spite of the decay of the fleet and the emptiness of the treasury, an expedition was organised to go to the support of the Huguenots in western France. Buckingham was pretentiously commissioned as " Admiral, Captain General, and Governor of the King's Royal Fleet intended to be set out to sea for the recovery of the rightful patrimony of the Prince Elector, and my brother-in-law." On 11th June, King Charles inspected the fleet, from Portsmouth, and visited several ships including the *Warspite*. On the 27th eighty-four ships, carrying upwards of 10,000 men, sailed from Stokes Bay. The fleet was ill-led, ill-trained and ill-equipped. Though the initial landings were successful, everything then went wrong. On 29th October Buckingham re-embarked his force. One historian of the period says " Want of victuals, incompetency in the supreme command, lack of unity among the chief officers, deficiency in material, an inadequate intelligence department, all these were strikingly in evidence in this terrible disaster."[8] Though the parallel must not be carried too far, it may justly be remarked that the Norwegian expeditions of 1940, in which the last *Warspite* took part, contain lessons regarding the conduct of combined operations similar to those suggested by the failure at La Rochelle in 1627.[9]   It was the last occasion on which the first *Warspite* saw active service, and a career which had started at Cadiz on a note of high accomplishment thus ended on one of utter failure among the rocks and reefs of Biscay's shores.   In 1634 she was cut down to a hulk for harbour service.

But the disaster at La Rochelle brought little or no improvement to naval affairs in England. While the Thirty Years' War (1618-48) raged over Europe, disunity at home was moving steadily towards the outbreak of civil war in 1642. There was, however, one country which prospered greatly in both industry and commerce at this time. Dutch explorers were opening up new lands, Dutch colonies were established in the East and in the West; and they had also made themselves masters of the carrying trade of the world. Finally in 1648, by the Peace of Westphalia, the United Provinces threw off the hated Spanish yoke. Here, once England's schism had been healed, were fruitful grounds for a clash between the two countries who had joined hands against Spain in the previous century. As soon as the Commonwealth government felt strong enough the Navigation Act, which was a calculated attack on Dutch carrying trade, was passed, and " letters of marque " were issued to privateers enjoining action against Dutch ships on the high seas. The Commonwealth had meanwhile been rebuilding the neglected Navy, and had greatly improved the pay and conditions of its men; and, more important even than these changes, it had won the loyalty of two very fine fighting men—Robert Blake and George Monk.

The First Dutch War did not actually break out until 1652, by which time many of the fruits of a wiser administration than that of the early Stuarts were ripe for harvesting. Apart from the improvements in the Navy's material and moral well-being, and from the rise of a new generation of great seamen, the period saw a revolution in naval tactics. For Blake and Monk, both soldiers of the Commonwealth by training and experience, brought to their new element the disciplined formations and movements which they had used to such good effect on land. Line-ahead now became the normal fighting formation, and indeed remained so right down to the present century. The happy-go-lucky gallantry of the Elizabethan admirals was replaced by rigid manœuvres intended to bring the greatest gun-power to bear simultaneously on one part of the enemy fleet.

There was no *Warspite* in the fleet while Blake, Monk and Penn fought their many fierce actions with Tromp, de Ruyter and Evertzen during the First Dutch War, so we need only note that the struggle ended by the Dutch accepting virtually all the English demands, including the right to the " Sovereignty of the Seas." The Restoration of 1660 brought more changes in the Navy. The number of English warships and the cost of equipping and maintaining them had increased so greatly, that it had become anomalous for them to continue the private property of the Monarch, and impossible for him to meet such a commitment. It was therefore both rational and economically necessary for the warships to become a charge on the State, and henceforth they were designated ships of the " Royal Navy." Steps were also taken to recruit and train youths to carry the responsibilities of its officers. In the realm of tactics the first " Fighting Instructions," which owed much to Blake's experience and wisdom, were issued ; while in that of discipline and administration the legal code known as " The Articles of War " was drawn up. That same code holds good to this day ; and the splendid rhetoric of its preamble has proved an inspiration to many generations of British seamen. The opening words will stand repeating. " It is upon the Navy under the good Providence of God that the safety, honour and welfare of this Realm do chiefly depend."

Such was the background to the revival of *Warspite*'s name in 1666. She was a third-rate, of 898 tons and sixty-four guns. There is an interesting minute in Pepys' naval papers about the improvements made in the design of new ships, including *Warspite*, at this time. It shows the deep interest of " the busy little Secretary " in technical as well as administrative matters, and how his influence penetrated to all branches of the naval service. " In the years '63 and '64," he recorded, " the Dutch and French built another sort of ships with 2 decks which carried 60 to 70 guns, and were so contrived that they carried their lower guns 4 foot from the water, and to stow 4 months provision ; whereas our frigates from the Dunkirk-built, which were narrower and sharper, carried their guns but little more than 3 foot from the water, and but 10 weeks provision, which was to be avoided. Observing this A. D. [Sir Anthony Deane] built the *Rupert* and *Resolution*, Mr. Shish the *Cambridge*, Mr. Johnson [shipbuilder of Blackwall, later Sir Henry Johnson] the *Warspight*, Mr. Castle the *Defiance*. The two latter were by contract with the commissioners of the Navy bound to carry 6 months provision ; and their guns to lie 4½ foot from the water. This was another great step and improvement to our Navy." [10]

With a king who, for all his faults and weaknesses, was sincerely devoted to the service of which he was the the effective as well as titular head, and the genius of Samuel Pepys already making itself felt as Clerk of the Acts (i.e. secretary and junior member of the Navy Board) in the Navy Office, the new era seemed full of promise.

Yet it ended in disaster and disgrace. The Second Dutch War became inevitable when in 1665 the English seized the Dutch Settlement of New Amsterdam, and renamed it New York. The first pitched battle was fought off Lowestoft in that same year, and in June, 1666, Monk, now Duke of Albemarle, fought de Ruyter in the "Four Days' Battle"—one of the greatest sea fights of all time. The new *Warspite* had only just been launched at Blackwall, and missed the battle. She was, however, ready in time for the next clash, which took place on St. James's Day (25th July), 1666. There Albemarle, with eighty-one ships, inflicted on de Ruyter's slightly superior fleet the most crushing defeat of all this long series of stubbornly contested battles. We know that *Warspite* was serving in Albemarle's own Red Squadron, that she came off comparatively lightly in the matter of casualties, and that she grappled successfully with two Dutch fireships which attempted to close her. Her captain was Robert Robinson, who had already greatly distinguished himself in the Four Days' Battle in the *Elizabeth*. He was therefore " promoted to the *Warspite* of sixty-four guns, in which he also had an opportunity, which he did not neglect, of signalising himself during the two actions fought in that year (i.e. 1666) between the English and Dutch fleets."[11] Although Captain Robinson's accounts of some of his sea fights have survived, that for the St. James's Day battle is not among them; nor can details of *Warspite*'s part be found from other sources. The contemporary ballads, however, at least give a clear idea of " the ferocious exultation " in which these battles with the Dutch were fought.[12]

In September, 1666, *Warspite* played a leading part in the capture off Dungeness of the French ship *Rubis*, of 900 tons and fifty-four guns. The Frenchman had been in a squadron sent by Louis XIV to join the Dutch fleet, but became detached from her consorts and ran into an English force. She was evidently a valuable prize, for a letter from Dover tells us that she was " a very fine vessell allmost as great as the *Royall Soveraigne*," and that the *Warspite* and another ship first intercepted her.[13] In December of that year Robinson sailed from home as commodore of a squadron of five of the smaller ships of the line, including *Warspite*, to protect an important convoy of about sixty ships with naval stores from the Baltic. He encountered an equal Dutch force in the North Sea, and on a wild and stormy Christmas morning fought a brilliant action in which he not only defended his charges successfully, but captured the entire enemy force. The fight started off the Dogger Bank and ended that evening within sight of the church spires of Holland, where the Dutch commodore surrendered. Robinson then triumphantly made harbour on the Suffolk coast with " the Dutch colours hanging and the King's flying."

Captain Robinson's account of his Christmas Day battle in defence of the convoy reads remarkably like one of the many similar actions of the recent war, when from the Arctic to the Mediterranean, British cruisers and destroyers again and again, as Robinson described in 1666, " formed themselves between the enemy and the convoy," and then vigorously attacked the would-be assailants. He must have been a fine seaman and a determined leader, and his *Warspite*, for all that her crew was raw and reduced by sickness, had certainly inherited the fighting qualities of her Elizabethan ancestor.

After the victory of St. James's Day Charles II, harassed by debts and unable to curb his own extravagances, laid up the main strength of the fleet at Chatham. The seamen's " tickets " on which they should have been able to draw their arrears of pay were dishonoured—and many of them went over to the Dutch. In June, 1667, de Ruyter, guided by British seamen, sailed up the Thames to Chatham, burnt several ships and carried off our largest battleship, the *Royal Charles*, to Holland. Luckily, and thanks largely to the exertions of Albemarle, half the fleet survived. *Warspite* was not among the ships in Chatham at the time, and so emerged unscathed from a tragic and shameful episode in English history. Peace was signed at Breda a month later, on terms which show all too clearly how the victory of St. James's Day was thrown away by the disgrace in the Thames estuary.

The five brief years of peace which followed did something to restore the shattered morale of the Navy. In 1670 Charles II signed a secret treaty, the terms of which do him no credit, with Louis XIV. By it he virtually hired the Royal Navy to Louis in return for French gold. The fleet was mobilised in April, and *Warspite*'s name appears under the command of " Captain and Rear-Admiral " Sir John Kempthorne, who had already commanded her on the Downs Station since 1668. Very soon he was relieved by that same Captain Robert Robinson who had already handled her with such distinction in the Second Dutch War.

Soon after mobilisation the English and French fleets concentrated at Portsmouth, and then with about 100 ships moved to Solebay (Southwold Bay) on the Suffolk coast. Albemarle had died in 1669, and the Duke of York (soon to become James II) was in command of the fleet.

Warspite, still commanded by Robinson, was serving in the Earl of Sandwich's Blue Squadron. On 28th May, 1672, the Allied fleet was surprised while at anchor by the approach of de Ruyter from the east. Sandwich and James put to sea at once, but the French squadron hauled away on the opposite tack, and never entered the fight. De Ruyter sent a small force to contain the French ships, and flung his main strength against the English centre. Sandwich in the *Royal James* fought magnificently, but was soon beset by the fire-ships which his adversary sent down upon him. The *Warspite* supported her admiral most loyally, fended off two fire-ships herself and was about to answer Sandwich's appeal for help when the *Royal James* blew up. De Ruyter then withdrew. Though he carried off no prizes he had crippled the English fleet. For his part in the fight Robinson was knighted.

That the Solebay battle was no victory for the British is shown by the fact that a squadron including *Warspite* was sent to guard the Thames estuary, " and to annoy the enemy should he come up."[14] Doubtless memories of 1667 had revived; but this time such fears were groundless, because the invasion of Holland by Louis XIV's army brought crisis to the young Republic, and de Ruyter was forced to act defensively. He withdrew into the Scheldt estuary, and declined to be enticed out to engage in a pitched battle. *Warspite*, in which Captain Richard White had now relieved Sir Robert Robinson, was in Vice-Admiral Sir John Harman's Red Squadron of the fleet under Prince Rupert which waited for de Ruyter off the Scheldt estuary in 1673. Two skirmishes, called the First and Second Battles of Schooneveld, took place there on 28th May and 4th June.[15] They produced no important results, but in the second of them *Warspite*'s captain was killed.

After the second skirmish off the Scheldt the fleet had to return to England for repairs. Then Rupert took his ships along the coast of Holland, acting as though he intended to land an army. The deceptive ruse worked, and de Ruyter came out. On 11th August, 1673, the last battle of the Dutch Wars was fought off the Texel. *Warspite* was in Prince Rupert's own Red Squadron in the centre, and against it de Ruyter again, as at Solebay, massed his strength. While Sir Edward Spragge with the Blue Squadron in the rear fought an isolated battle with Cornelis Tromp (the son of the great Marten), Rupert was pressed very hard by his famous adversary; for once again the French squadron in the van took little part. Though Rupert extricated his force and joined Spragge, the greatest share of success undoubtedly lay with de Ruyter; for he had once again challenged a greatly superior fleet, and had handled it very severely. Few details of *Warspite*'s part in the battle have come down to us, but a pamphlet printed soon afterwards records that " About 5 o'clock de Ruyter with all his Flags and fleet came side by side with the Prince (Rupert); so there began a very sharp engagement; his Highness had none besides the Vice-Admiral and Rear-Admiral of the Blue to second him, but Sir John Harman, Captain Davis in the *Triumph*, Captain Stout in the *Warspite* and his Highness's own division."[16] It is therefore plain that *Warspite* was in the thick of this severe battle.

The general peace, for which war-torn Europe longed, was not signed until 1678, by which time the frustration of Louis XIV's ambitions had been accomplished—in no small measure thanks to Dutch resistance. Once more the Navy fell into decay. Pepys had been driven out of office in 1679 as a result of unscrupulous perjury by witnesses against him during the " Popish Plot " agitation, and did not return until four years later. By that time many ships were rotting at their moorings, those which were in commission were being misused as cargo-carriers, drunkenness and debauchery were rife in the fleet, and efficiency in seamanship and fighting had almost disappeared. There can be little doubt that the *Warspite* bore her share of the all-prevailing neglect, for no mention of her can be found until 1688, when she was in service on the Downs Station in the eastern Channel.

The accession of James II in 1685 at once transformed the prospects of the Navy. Until the Test Act debarred him from office on religious ground he had served with devotion as Lord High Admiral. The death of his brother brought him his real chance, and as soon as he ascended the throne he busied himself with the affairs of the Service to which he had already devoted his life. With Pepys as secretary of the Admiralty, reform and rejuvenation came fast, and the fleet soon regained much of the pride and efficiency which it had possessed at the start of the Dutch Wars. Whatever may have been James's failings as Monarch, and however greatly his tactless stupidity and religious intolerance may have brought his fate on him, the interests of the Navy lay close to his heart. Yet it was an English admiral, Herbert, who when the inevitable revolution came, led William of Orange on the " Protestant wind " to Torbay. There is high tragedy in the fact that the fleet which James himself had done so much to revive, struck no blow for its master. The fate of the last of the Stuarts was thereby sealed, William III mounted the throne and in 1689 the War of the English Succession broke out. On 15th September of that year *Warspite* was commissioned under Captain Sir William Jennens (or Jennings). This officer adhered to the Church of Rome and remained loyal to James II, who had given him his first command. When the crisis of 1688 was brewing, and the King " was alarmed to the utmost at the prospect of an invasion which threatened," Jennens was regarded " as one of the chosen few fit to be entrusted with command."[17] How far it was due to the prevalent conflict of religious and political loyalties, and how far to Jennens's own apparently violent temper it is hard to say ; but it is plain that, in the language of this century, *Warspite* was an unhappy ship at that time. We know that so distinguished a seaman as Captain George Rooke, who was soon to perform great feats in the Mediterranean, refused command of her because she was " ill-manned and likely to be paid off."[18]   Jennens's dismissal actually came about through a quarrel with the Earl of Dartmouth, and his career ended in melancholy fashion.[19] He complained to Pepys over his treatment, but got small satisfaction from that wise administrator.[20]   Then, after the revolution, he joined his former patron in France, and " condescended to become third Captain to a French Admiral."[21]

The exiled James's hopes of restoration rested mainly on Ireland, where he landed with French support in the spring of 1689, and proceeded to lay siege to Protestant Londonderry. William's fleet, under Herbert, was sent to attack the communications between France and Ireland, and fought an indecisive battle with the French off Bantry Bay, for which William made Herbert Earl of Torrington. Meanwhile Londonderry, the key to Ireland, was suffering the extremities of siege until relieved by Commodore Rooke from the sea—a success to William which the greatly superior sea-power of France should never have permitted. On 1st April, 1690, Captain Stafford Fairborne assumed command of *Warspite* for service in the Channel. Louis XIV had meanwhile assembled great strength by bringing his Mediterranean fleet to Brest, and with the seventy ships thus concentrated under Tourville he plainly intended to make a serious bid to command the Channel.

In the last week of June, 1690, Tourville appeared off the Isle of Wight. Torrington, with only fifty-five ships, was cruising to the east to guard the Straits of Dover, and playing a waiting game. He considered that as long as his fleet remained intact the French would not dare to risk landing their army, and he therefore refused to engage. It was he who at this time coined the phrase "a fleet in being," which has passed into the history of all maritime nations. In London, however, his strategy was not understood. William was still in Ireland, and his consort, abetted by Torrington's rival Admiral Russell, sent instructions prohibiting further withdrawal, and urging him to give battle. On the 30th June off Beachy Head he therefore made the best of a difficult situation. His intention was that Evertzen's Dutch squadron in the van should hold off from battle whilst containing a substantial part of Tourville's strength. Torrington would meanwhile concentrate the rest of his fleet against the French rear.

The admiral's tactical plan was sound; but it was ruined by the impetuosity or misunderstanding of his Dutch subordinate Evertzen, who hotly engaged the French van instead of merely containing it. He thus gave Tourville the chance to double on his adversaries' line, and so to turn the tables on Torrington, who was saved from utter destruction only by the turn of the tide carrying the French fleet out of range. He then destroyed his crippled ships, and withdrew to the Thames. *Warspite* was fifth in the line in Torrington's own Red Squadron, and as it is recorded that "musket shot lodged in the hammocks with which her nettings were stuffed," it seems that she was one of the few English ships to engage closely on that unhappy day.[22]

As soon as he reached the Thames the storm broke over Torrington's head. He was thrown into the Tower, and then tried by court martial. When his brother officers acquitted him, William, who had crushed James's army decisively at the Battle of the Boyne on the day after

Beachy Head, cancelled the court's findings and dismissed the admiral from the service. To his King and to the public it appeared that not only had he failed to defend the narrow seas, but that whereas the Dutch had fought hard he had not. Here, they considered, was sure evidence of incompetence or of disloyalty—or of both. One shrewd contemporary observer summed it all up thus. " Both the Admirals (Tourville and Torrington) were equally blamed —ours for not fighting and the French for not pursuing."[23] It is in fact quite certain that Torrington was guilty of no disloyalty to William; nor was he capable of the sort of intrigues in which his rival and successor, Admiral Russell, commonly engaged. His strategy has been judged sound by history, while his tactics were skilful, but were ruined by a subordinate who came from a different country and spoke a different language.[24]

None the less it is undeniable that with the fleet withdrawn to the Thames, there was nothing to prevent James's French allies from landing in southern England— had they been ready to do so. Rarely has this country been so open to invasion as in the early days of 1690.

After Beachy Head *Warspite* took part in the siege of Cork, where the remnants of the Jacobite army were trapped in September, 1690. A naval brigade was landed from the fleet, and Captain Fairborne went as a volunteer with the detachment, " under Brigadier Churchill [later Duke of Marlborough] and Lord Colchester which was ordered to assault the breach."[25]

Warspite next served in the Grand Fleet under Admiral Russell, who had replaced Torrington after the latter's dismissal. It has been mentioned that the new commander-in-chief was an ambitious and none too scrupulous man. Though it is doubtful whether the purpose of his correspondence was actually treasonable, he certainly kept in touch with James during the latter's exile.[26] By the 7th May, 1691, Russell had a powerful squadron, which included *Warspite*, ready for sea, and from June to September he cruised off Brest and in the western approaches to the Channel in defence of English trade against Tourville's marauding fleet. But the latter was altogether too skilful for his British adversary.[27]

Though the crisis of 1690 stimulated England to great endeavours, particularly in the matter of fitting out the fleet, discontent over William's politics was rife at home. It was probably this that caused Russell, who was certainly no Jacobite, to give James the hope that the fleet would support a new attempt at invasion. On hearing this promise Louis assembled a great army in Normandy, and a fleet of transports at La Hogue. At the same time he renewed the land campaign in the Netherlands. Russell now changed his tune, and with William gone abroad again to defend Holland, he assured Mary of his loyalty. This cut the ground from under James's feet, and when Tourville came up-Channel with forty sail he found himself opposed by more than double that strength. On 19th May, 1692, Tourville fought a skilful action with Russell off Barfleur. *Warspite*, now commanded by Captain Caleb Grantham, was stationed in the Blue Squadron of Admiral Sir John Ashby, but in the prevailing fog and light winds she saw little fighting. She had her boats out for much of the day, towing the ship after Russell's Red Squadron, which was more hotly engaged. Skilful doubling manœuvres by Sir Clowdisley Shovell from ahead of Russell, and by Admiral Carter from the extreme rear of the English line, put Tourville between two fires. As evening fell and the fog closed in, his fleet disengaged and escaped the trap into which it had fallen. No prizes were taken, but this did not greatly matter, because a few days later many of Tourville's ships were destroyed in Cherbourg and off La Hogue. On 23rd and 24th May, under the very eyes of James and the French Army, Admiral Rooke used his ship's boats to assault, capture and burn no less than twelve French battleships lying under the forts of La Hogue. It was one of the most complete victories of all time, and secured William on the English throne.

For generations of Royal Navy men yet unborn Barfleur and La Hogue brought one very happy result, for the royal palace of Greenwich was given by William and Mary as a hospital for seamen disabled in those battles. That great building, the birthplace of Henry VIII and of the first Elizabeth, embellished by the genius of Sir Christopher Wren, remains to this day the finest and best-loved home of the Royal Navy. As *Warspite* fought at Barfleur and La Hogue she may justly claim a share in the bestowal on her service of this magnificent gift. It is hardly surprising that, after this gruelling campaign, she was in need of refitting. Towards the end of the year she was put out of commission for a time.[28]

Although the sea battles of 1692 virtually settled the War of the English Succession, it dragged on for another five years, with little to mark it at sea except privateering.

Warspite, still commanded by Captain Grantham, served firstly in the Grand Fleet, and then in 1694 we find her in the Mediterranean, the sea with which her name was to be so gloriously connected 250 years later. English trade to and from the Levant had increased enormously, and the presence of a fleet was necessary to protect the convoys against French forays from Toulon. From July, 1694, until the autumn of the following year *Warspite* was with the combined English and Dutch fleet under Russell in the Mediterranean. Though no great battle was fought, he not only commanded the sea well enough to protect our trade, but his dominating presence undoubtedly checked the progress of French arms in Spain.[29] His accomplishment was all the more remarkable because he lacked any base nearer than Lisbon, and even there the resources were quite inadequate to maintain his fleet properly. His long cruise was commemorated by a ballad entitled " The Frighted French, or Russell Scouring the Seas," which reflected English feelings over Tourville's refusal to be enticed out of Toulon.[30]

By 1697 Louis XIV, who was increasingly beset by economic and religious troubles at home, was ready to make peace, and the Treaty of Ryswick was signed in September of that year. He surrendered all that he had gained in Europe since the Treaty of Nymwegen, and acknowledged William as King of England. In the same year *Warspite* was paid off. But the treaty was soon to prove but a truce, for in 1702 war was renewed over the Spanish Succession. On his death in 1700 Charles II of Spain bequeathed his vast empire to Louis XIV's grandson, who was proclaimed Philip V. This development, if allowed to mature, would have given France not only an alliance with Spain, but a firm grip on the Rhine delta, including the great port of Antwerp. This would have been intolerable to the English and Dutch, who therefore supported the claim to the Spanish throne of an Austrian prince, whom they styled King Charles III.

During the brief peace *Warspite* was rebuilt at Rotherhithe. She was completed as a larger and more heavily armed ship (952 tons with 70 guns) in the year 1702, just before war broke out, and commissioned at Chatham on 4th March under Captain Edmund Loades. There is a close parallel between the reconstruction of the second *Warspite* in 1701-2 and that of the seventh ship of the name at Portsmouth in 1934-37.* Both were carried out as a period of uneasy truce between two major wars was obviously coming to a close; and in both cases the ship emerged larger and more heavily armed.

The rebuilt second *Warspite* soon joined Sir Clowdisley Shovell's squadron, and in the summer of 1702 she sailed under him for the Mediterranean. It has been mentioned that the prime need of England was for a base in those waters, in which its ships could refit and replenish; and that until such a base was secured her sea power could never be effectively exercised. To meet the need an expedition was sent out under Sir George Rooke and the Duke of Ormonde ·to capture Cadiz. It was foredoomed to failure; for south-west Spain was wholly loyal to Philip V, and Rooke was stringently enjoined not to alienate the Spaniards. In its divided aims and in the restrictive orders issued to the expedition's commanders, the attempt on Cadiz may be compared with the fiasco at Dakar in 1940.[31] The results achieved were identical.

Luckily for Rooke's reputation he gained intelligence that a treasure fleet had arrived, and had ensconced itself behind the powerful defences of Vigo Bay. On 12th October his Vice-Admiral, Thomas Hopsonn, charged and broke the boom. Treasure to the value of over two million pounds was captured and the entire guardian fleet of forty-one ships was destroyed.[32] But the need for a base had not been resolved.

In November, 1703, Captain Loades fought his first action with *Warspite*. Rooke's fleet was returning home when she and two others intercepted and captured the French fifty-two-gun ship *Hasard*. It was a small compensation for having missed the forcing of Vigo Bay. In

* See pp. 161-165.

the following year Rooke sailed again from home, with orders to appear off Toulon, which base—not for the last time—an optimistic British Government hoped to seize. In May, 1704, the French Brest fleet came into the Mediterranean, and joined the ships in Toulon. Rooke, now heavily outnumbered, fell back to the Straits to meet Sir Clowdisley Shovell, whose squadron included *Warspite*. His " Line of Battle " dated on board the *Barfleur* at sea on 12th May, 1704, and another dated 8th June at Lisbon, both include " *Warspight* (Captain Loades, 440 men, 70 guns)."[33] Near Lagos Shovell and Rooke joined forces, and on the 23rd July the latter, with only his ships' guns and his landing parties of marines, assaulted and captured Gibraltar. Here, then, was the sorely needed base ; but it was one thing to seize it and, as Rooke and many others were to find over the centuries, another matter to hold it. In the first instance the reaction of the French Toulon fleet was prompt. The Count of Toulouse had fifty-one ships of the line, and a score of great galleys. He slipped past Rooke, and interposed himself between him and the Rock. Off Malaga on 13th August, 1704, was fought the first of the many battles on which the fate of Gibraltar has depended. It lasted two whole days, The first was marked by fierce fighting, with heavy casualties on both sides ; but at the end of it the English ships were almost out of ammunition. The second day consisted really of a bluff by Rooke that he was able and willing to renew the fight, and at the end of it his adversary put before the wind. The French claimed a great victory, but if the battle was really a drawn fight Rooke unquestionably saved Gibraltar. *Warspite* was the rear ship of Sir Clowdisley Shovell's White Squadron.[34] She was in the thick of the fighting, was heavily hit in hull, and suffered about sixty casualties. But her conduct earned the admiral's warm commendation.

Captain Loades's journal for 13th August, 1704, reads as follows:

"At noone—Malaga Point northward Distant 9 or 10 Leagues. Easey Gales, sometimes calm and fair weather. At 3 yester afternoone saw a fleet of ships to the Westward. Wee stood to them all night with easey saile, and maid all clear in the morn. At brack of Day sawe the fleet againe. Wee maid them to be frenchmen. They bore West Distant 5 miles, laying all in a Line of Battle with their heads to the Southward and their Larbord tacks onboard, consisisting (*sic*) about 54 saile in the Line with 30 sail of galleys, besides fireships etc. Wee bore Downe upon them before the wind. At 10 Sir George Rooke hoisted a Rad Flagg at foretopmast head to engage them; which began verry hott . . ."

On the following day he continued his account of the fight in this manner:

"The Ingagement continuing very hott till ½ past 3 yesterday afternoone. The Shipp that ware in Sir Clowdely Shovell Squadron with Likewise the Vann of there fleet bore away from us out of the Line, having as wee supposed received Grate Damage. But Sir George and the Rear of the fleet ware Ingaged telle near 7 a'Clock at night [was] coming on [when] the french fleet bore away and the Ingagement ceased. Wee lay by all night in Line of Battle. At 3 thim morning the wind came about to the Westward, so that the french got the weather gage of us. At 6 they were about 7 miles from us to Windard. Wee continued Lying by in the Line expecting there coming downe to us, but finding they kept there wind wee spent the Day in Fixing our Rigging, being verry much shott. Wee had about 17 men killed Out Right and 40 woun-ded."[35]

On the 17th *Warspite* lost sight of the French fleet, but " wee maid sail after them to the Westward, soposing they had gon that way." So ended a battle which had been most gallantly fought in very difficult circumstances. The result should have brought much credit to Rooke and Shovell, for they handled the enemy severely and saved Gibraltar. Yet in history the Battle of Malaga is hardly remembered.

After the battle it was decided to bring home the greater part of the fleet, leaving only those ships which were fit for winter service in the Mediterranean. *Warspite* was among those ordered back to England, probably on account of the damage she had sustained in the fight. She reached Spithead on 27th September.[36] Rooke next handed over his command to Admiral Sir John Leake, one of his ablest disciples, and left him with a small squadron, mostly of the smaller ships, to defend Gibraltar.[37] Though forced to work mainly from Lisbon, Leake kept a watchful eye on the safety of the newly acquired base.

By the beginning of 1705 it was again very seriously threatened. A large French and Spanish army was besieging it from the land, while a French fleet under Baron de Pointis blockaded the Bay. Luckily at the end of February Leake was reinforced by five ships from home, including *Warspite*, and on 6th March he sailed from the Tagus with his whole force of twenty-three English, eight Portuguese and four Dutch ships to relieve Gibraltar. Four days later five battleships were sighted standing out from the Bay, and Leake gave chase. *Warspite* and others engaged the

Lys (88 guns) and drove her ashore; and all the four other French ships were captured or destroyed off Marbella. They were actually a detachment from de Pointis's fleet, which had recently been forced by a gale to leave Gibraltar Bay for the greater shelter of Malaga roads. After suffering this defeat, and losing their admiral, the rest of the French ships retired from Malaga to Toulon.[38] Gibraltar and its small but heroic garrison of marines were once more saved, and in the nick of time; and *Warspite* had again played a part in preventing the loss of that invaluable base.

With Gibraltar secure and Lisbon now slightly less inadequate as a base, the fleet could at last work effectively inside the Straits. Thus began, for *Warspite*, a period of two years of service on that station. In August, 1705, a combined operation was staged against Barcelona, where it was hoped that " King Charles III " would land. By an astonishing feat of improvisation and endurance Shovell's men got their guns ashore to act as substitute for the siege train which the army lacked, and mounted them on the heights overlooking the town. Barcelona thereupon surrendered. But the foul weather of the following winter, lack of supplies, and disease combined together to cripple the fleet. Though Leake, by superhuman efforts, relieved Barcelona once, things moved from bad to worse, and the tales of suffering among the crews of his ships make shocking reading. *Warspite*, it seems, had gone home again temporarily, perhaps to repair the damage she received off Marbella. On 31st December, 1706, she reappears as one of a number of ships " coming from England " under the command of Sir George Byng.[39] Then, early in 1707, Shovell himself was sent out again to try and restore an increasingly critical situation. On 13th March at Lisbon he ordered Byng with a squadron which included *Warspite*, to enter the Mediterranean " with money, clothing, recruits and provisions . . . for the confederate army in Valencia."[40] But it was too late. The English and Portuguese army was decisively beaten on land, and when most of the exhausted fleet was brought home again at the worst time of the year, storms took a tragically heavy toll.

Perhaps the saddest part of this gruelling campaign in the Mediterranean was that, because of his Tory politics, Rooke, its chief architect, was never employed again ; and his great colleague, Shovell, and 2,000 of his men were lost when, on 22nd October, 1707, the flagship *Association* and three others ran on the rocks off the Scilly Islands.[41]

Captain Loades left the *Warspite* soon after the Battle of Malaga, to become " First Captain and Captain of the Fleet " to Shovell, and from 1706-1708 she was commanded by Captain Thomas Butler. Mention must be made of one more minor action in which she took part. In February, 1707, she and the *Swiftsure* were escorting a convoy of fourteen merchantmen bound for Lisbon when they were attacked by a squadron of French cruisers sailing from Brest to the West Indies, and several of the merchantmen were lost.[42] Captain Butler wrote in his journal that " our two men of war the *Swiftsure* and *Warspite* narrowly escaped some considerable ships of the enemy forereaching upon us. We were obliged to throw our Long boat and some of our Beer overboard to lighten."[43] Apart from the evident regret with which the beer was jettisoned, there is a singularly modern ring about the account of this fight ; for it bears close resemblance to many actions in the recent war, when convoys sailing between Britain and Gibraltar were defended against surface or submarine raiders working from ports in western France. The association between *Warspite* and *Swiftsure*, though doubtless fortuitous, is also interesting ; for the next ships to bear both names were to become famous comrades-in-arms half a century later in the great sea battles of 1759, as will be told in the next chapter.

Soon after the convoy action, while at anchor in Gibraltar Bay on 3rd April, 1707, *Warspite* was evidently struck by lightning. Her captain's journal graphically records what must have been an alarming experience : " At 1 yesterday," he wrote, " a severe clap of thunder came and carried away our Main top mast, Main topgallant mast and yard in splinters into the sea. It sprung our Main Mast in 5 several places, and made it wholly useless . . . The greatness of the rain keeping our people off Decke proved their preservation, and so much water on it. The tarpaulins laid saved her from Burning. Yet notwithstanding the ship was like a flame of fire between Decks and on the Orlope, and did great mischief in several places."[44] There is a striking similarity between the damage done to the second *Warspite* by this electric discharge and that suffered by the last ship of her name from man-made aerial missiles off Salerno nearly two and a half centuries later.* When the latter ship was heavily struck by wireless-controlled bombs they also " did great mischief in severall places " ; the smoke, flame and noise were terrific " between decks and on the Orlope " ; and just as the eighteenth-century captain had his main mast "sprung " and " made wholly useless," so did his twentieth-century successor remark that it seemed as though " the whole mast was coming down as it rocked, bent and whipped."

The turn of the tide in the War of the Spanish Succession came in 1708, when Queen Anne's government was at last convinced of what so plainly needed to be done. Leake was sent out again to the Mediterranean with ample force, and wide authority to take whatever base he fancied. It

* See pp. 267-270.

thus came to pass that the fine harbour of Port Mahon, Minorca, passed to the British crown; but two more years were needed to fit it out properly.

Warspite continued to serve under Leake in the Mediterranean, and in June, 1708, she and the *Lancaster* "rendered most valuable service to the cause of King Charles of Spain" by raising the siege of Denia on the Mediterranean coast of that country. Supporters of "Philip V" would have captured the town had not the two British battleships landed four hundred men, guns and supplies. The "Philipists" thereupon raised the siege.*

In 1709 *Warspite*, now commanded by Captain Josiah Crowe, came back from the Mediterranean and served for about two years in the Channel Fleet under Sir John Norris. On 13th December, 1710, she and the *Breda* sighted and chased the 60-gun French ship *Maure*. The *Breda* came up with the enemy first, but her captain was killed. The *Warspite* then closed and prepared to board, "whereupon the *Maure* at once struck."[45] The prize was added to the Navy as the *Moor*.

In May, 1711, a considerable fleet, thirty-five battleships in all, was assembled in the Channel "to secure the narrow seas and protect trade," and on the 8th Sir John Leake, now Admiral and Commander-in-Chief of Her Majesty's fleet, hoisted his flag temporarily in *Warspite* at Deal.[46] It was her last service with the admiral under whose flag she had so often fought in the Mediterranean approaches. Next, in 1712, she was on the Newfoundland station, but

*Although Laird Clowes (Vol. II, p. 516) says that Captain Butler was still in command of *Warspite* at the siege of Denia, there seems no doubt that this is incorrect. The Admiralty's records give Captain Gaspar (or Jaspar) Hicks (or Hickes) as her captain at that time, and this receives confirmation from the Life of Sir John Leake (Vol. II, p. 203) and from Charnock's Naval Biography (Vol. II, p. 259). Both these authorities also mention that in March, 1707, Hicks was sent with *Warspite* and other ships to "convoy the West India and Newfoundland trade one hundred leagues," and thereafter to "await the Brazil fleet" in the Azores.

the war was then drawing to a close. Although peace was not signed until the following year, on 31st August, 1712, she was paid off at Woolwich. She remained there until 1715, when she was renamed *Edinburgh*, and so passes out of our story.

To the student of maritime affairs the most interesting fact about the War of the Spanish Succession is that through it England gained a hold on the western Mediterranean. Although Gibraltar and Minorca were won and held at the cost of appalling suffering in the fleet, and our control of the sea unquestionably frustrated French ambitions in Spain, the immense benefits which were brought to this country by Rooke, Shovell and Leake received little appreciation at the time, and have been given scant attention in many histories. This is in some measure due to Marlborough's brilliant land campaigns, which were fought much nearer home and in which vastly greater numbers were involved, having obscured the significance of what happened in the south. Yet the events of the Seven Years' War, of the long struggle against Napoleon and of the recent wars of our own time, all make it plain that the foundation of our strength in the Mediterranean was laid between 1704 and 1709 by the small squadrons in which the second *Warspite* served for so much of the later part of her life.

CHAPTER TWO

The Next Four 'Warspites'

1758-1904

> " The winds obsequious at his word
> Sprang strongly up t'obey their lord,
> And saw two fleets a-weigh :
> The one victorious Hawke, was thine ;
> The other Conflan's wretched line
> In terror and dismay."
>
> *Ballad " Neptune's Resignation "**

IT HAS been told how the second *Warspite* did not long survive the Peace of Utrecht, signed in 1713. That by itself would not have mattered greatly to the country, for she was then nearly fifty years old ; but unhappily the whole Royal Navy entered another period of culpable neglect. It is true that the eclipse of the service between 1715 and 1740 was not as devastatingly complete as that which marked the end of Elizabeth's wars with Spain in 1604, or the short peace between the end of the Third Dutch War in 1674 and the outbreak of the War of the English Succession fifteen years later. But the events of the early decades of the eighteenth century none the less merit brief study of the consequences begotten by forgetfulness out of prosperity.

---

* Written to commemorate the Battle of Quiberon Bay, 20th November, 1759. (From " Naval Songs and Ballads," Navy Records Society, Vol. XXXVII, pp. 217-18.)

English trade had then spread all over the world, and was constantly in need of protection against privateers, if not against more organised enemies. England held the key to the Mediterranean at Gibraltar, and a potentially excellent base within the confines of that sea at Port Mahon, Minorca. Yet she managed to inflict on herself an almost fatal handicap by losing the one; and she nearly lost the other too.

Perhaps in the twenty-first century a historian will study the policies of British governments between the first and second World Wars of the twentieth century, and will compare them with those of England's rulers between 1713 and 1740. Should such a work be undertaken it would provide much food for thought, for it would inevitably include a comparison between the state of Port Mahon in 1740 and that of Malta two centuries later; while the consequences of the decline in naval strength during the reigns of the first two Georges could usefully be compared with those which derived from the small strength and high proportion of over-age ships with which Britain started the second World War.[1] The more the historian studied the more he would find to suggest that similar policies produce identical results. But it would, perhaps, be in the realm of internal policy and conditions that the deepest lessons could be learnt. In the early 1700's England was, thanks to her seaborne trade, enjoying a period of unparalleled prosperity. "London became the world's greatest exchange, and the United Kingdom grew fat, prosperous and comfortable. Money became the accepted standard alike in politics, in fashion and in the principles of conduct. Quick roads to wealth and fortune were indicated and followed with blind eagerness. Bribery and corruption raised their hateful heads, and the one unpardonable sin was to be poor."[2] In other words it was an earlier time when England enjoyed the butter and forgot the guns.

Then in 1740 the death of the ruler of Austria started a cycle of events not unlike those which followed on the assassination at Sarajevo in 1914; and the War of the Austrian Succession very soon spread over all Europe. England had already been at war with Spain for a year, but now found herself almost alone as the supporter of the Empress Maria Theresa against the rapacity of Frederick II (the Great) of Prussia, and of the might of France as well. Between 1742 and 1744 the Mediterranean fleet was reinforced until in the latter year Admiral Mathews commanded a strength which in line-of-battle ships was equal to the combined fleets of France and Spain in Toulon ; but, as so often before and since, he was desperately short of frigates. This deficiency contributed greatly to the failures which now took place. An indecisive battle off Toulon on 11th February, 1744, led to an unsavoury toll of courts martial, and to the disgrace of Mathews. Though ships had been collected and sent out, the morale of the fleet must have been very low.

Then came the landing of Prince Charles Edward in Scotland, and the southward advance of the Pretender's army. The rebellion of 1745, until repressed by the savagery which followed Culloden, paralysed English action overseas.

Fortunately for England, a new generation of great seamen was now coming forward. On 15th June, 1744, a few months after the Battle of Toulon, Anson returned from his four years' journey round the world. He brought with him a number of splendid officers, trained in his own rigorous school, and fired by his genius. Their services were available to England just when she most needed them, and she very soon gathered the first harvest of their efforts. Off Cape Finisterre on 3rd May, 1747, Anson, with fourteen ships, engaged a French squadron which was escorting a convoy, and captured all six of the enemy battleships. It was the most complete victory since La Hogue. After the battle Anson returned to the Admiralty, where he served in all for no less than seventeen years (1744-62). While the men he had trained were establishing a complete ascendancy at sea, he revolutionised the organisation of the fleet and its tactical handling in battle ; and he also vastly improved the design and construction of the Navy's ships. The weapon which Anson forged, and his experience and knowledge of the sea affair, were thus available to the genius of Pitt when the time came for him to use them.

Five months after the First Battle of Finisterre, on 14th October, 1747, Hawke won almost as complete a success as Anson's in the second battle of the same name. It confirmed the new spirit of the Navy, it enabled a reasonably satisfactory peace to be concluded at Aix-la-Chapelle in the following year, in spite of French successes on the Continent, and it added another stone to the wall of England's naval supremacy. From 1748 to 1756 England and France were in a state which this century would describe as " cold war." There were plenty of clashes, especially in North America, which could at any moment have brought a declaration of war, but in fact this did not happen until 1756. By that time Prussia had thrown in her lot with England, who was thus able to reduce her continental commitments, and so turn her full attention to resolving her recurrent quarrels with France for supremacy in the New World.

To keep his adversary occupied nearer home, Louis XV, although still nominally at peace, adopted the common strategy of preparing to invade these islands, and also assembled a fleet to threaten Minorca. This latter was read as a bluff in London, and the government sent out only small reinforcements to Admiral Byng. The main strength of the fleet was kept in the Channel. But the French move against Minorca was not a bluff. In May, 1756, Byng learnt at Gibraltar that the enemy had landed on the island, and had laid siege to Port Mahon in greatly superior strength. He sailed north from Gibraltar, and on 20th May fought an indecisive battle, after which he withdrew. The result was the loss of Minorca. The story of the subsequent trial of the admiral by court martial, and of his execution by firing squad is well known.

A worse beginning to the Seven Years' War could hardly have been devised. England had not only lost her one base within the Mediterranean, but the confidence of the country in the Navy was badly shaken. It was the leadership of Pitt, the presiding genius of Anson at the Admiralty and the fighting spirit of Hawke, Boscawen and Saunders which, in the short space of three years, transformed the course of the war and altered the map of the world.

Such, then, was the state of affairs while the third *Warspite* was building. She was a 74-gun ship of 1,580 tons, and had been laid down in November, 1755; but she took much longer to complete than her predecessors. Admiralty records show that her total cost was £9,440 12s. 11d. On 8th April, 1758, she was launched at Deptford, and on the 27th July she sailed from her building berth. She was not commissioned by Captain John Bentley until the following October.

The third *Warspite* was one of a comparatively new type of line-of-battle ship which owed much to Anson's re-organisation of the classes of warships, and to the improvements in building and rigging achieved by his administration. Early in that century our ships had been scathingly described by one admiral as "manufactured by the mile and cut off in chunks when required."[3] Now the "seventy-four" became the backbone of the British battle fleet, the tool ready-made to await the hand of many seamen of genius, and finally of Nelson himself.* The choice of the new *Warspite's* first captain augured well for her fighting career, for he was an ardent and devoted disciple of Anson, had served as his Flag Captain at the First Battle of Finisterre, and had commanded the *Defiance* under Hawke at the second battle. He had recently been a member of the court martial which had tried the unfortunate Byng, and had lost his last ship the *Invincible* when, through no fault of her captain, she grounded off the Isle of Wight.

After the loss of Minorca the government hurried Hawke out to Gibraltar in a tardy endeavour to restore British prestige, and he did much good work. Unhappily the government's next venture, a combined operation against Rochefort in 1757, ended as badly as the expedition to the same coast in which the first *Warspite* took part in 1627.† It was the only failure of Hawke's career. On the continent of Europe and in India things did not go badly for England in that year; for Frederick of Prussia crushed the French at Rossbach, and Clive avenged the Black Hole of Calcutta at Plassey. The following year, 1758, opened with still better prospects. Boscawen was sent out with one force to attack the main French base at Louisburg on Cape Breton Island and captured it, Hawke avenged 1757 by sweeping into Rochefort Bay and scattering Louis's intended reinforcements for Canada; successful raids were made on

---

* At Trafalgar of the 27 ships of the line under Nelson and Collingwood no less than 16 were "seventy-fours."

† See pp. 33-34.

St. Malo and Cherbourg, while Admiral Saunders kept effective hold on the Straits of Gibraltar and scored a notable success against Duquesne off Carthagena. But these were but a prelude to the mighty events of 1759—and in them the third *Warspite* played a great part.

While Saunders carried Wolfe's army to the St. Lawrence, and destroyed French North American ambitions by the capture of Quebec, Boscawen was sent out with reinforcements to blockade the Toulon fleet, and to prevent it coming to Brest or reinforcing Canada. Early in May he was off Toulon with fifteen ships of the line, including the recently commissioned *Warspite*. The loss of Minorca made it inevitable that the fleet should suffer severe privations, as in the days of Rooke, Shovell and Leake earlier in the same century. A close blockade of Toulon simply could not be maintained so far from any base, and in July Boscawen was forced back to Gibraltar to replenish and repair his ships; but he kept a constant patrol in the Straits. On 16th August the *Gibraltar* signalled the approach of de la Clue's Toulon fleet, and in three hours Boscawen had shaken his ships clear of the dockyard and led them out to sea. The twelve French ships meanwhile passed westward through the Straits in darkness. Five of them put into Cadiz in the night, and dawn on the 17th revealed the leading ships of Boscawen's scattered fleet in close pursuit of the remaining Frenchmen. First they picked up a slow French sailer, and then the *Warspite*, *Swiftsure* and Boscawen's own *Namur* forged ahead to overtake and engage the main enemy force. The British flagship was soon disabled up aloft by de la Clue's *Océan*, and Boscawen transferred by launch to the leader of his rear division, which was now coming up to the fight.

All that night the pursuit continued, and two of de la

Clue's remaining ships abandoned their admiral and fled. The last four took shelter in the neutral Portuguese waters of Lagos Bay; but Boscawen was not to be baulked of his prey, and on the 18th he followed in. The French flagship ran aground, and was burnt, as was the *Redoutable*; but the *Modeste* and *Téméraire* were captured, and the latter was carried out in triumph by Captain Bentley. The *Warspite* thus not only added a fine ship to the Royal Navy, but brought to her Service a fighting name which was to become as famous as her own. The Battle of Lagos cost her only eleven men killed and forty wounded, and Captains Bentley and Stanhope of the *Swiftsure* were both knighted when they returned briefly home in the following September.*

Meanwhile away to the north Hawke was trying to blockade the Brest fleet, much as Boscawen had tried to contain that of Toulon. For six months he never relaxed his grip, but, as always, the strain of such a blockade took toll of the ships. As winter approached, the storms periodically forced him off station to seek shelter in Torbay. Louis XV's invasion threat was plain to see, for the transports were assembled in the harbours of Brittany, and troops were massed for embarkation. In England feeling was tense, and agitation against Hawke rose from the mobs of London whenever it was known that he had been forced by the winter gales to seek shelter. It is curious how unwilling the people of Britain have been to learn that, try as he will, no continental enemy has found a short cut

* The fact that in the eighteenth century the " nautical day " started at noon has caused confusion regarding the date of many events, including the Battle of Lagos. Boscawen's report (London Gazette of Friday, 7th September, 1759) uses nautical time throughout, and states that the enemy was first sighted on the afternoon of the 17th, that the chasing action took place on the 18th and the final attack on Lagos Bay on the 19th. In " civil time," which a historian should undoubtedly use, all these dates need to be put back one day. Unhappily both Laird Clowes and Schomberg adhered to " nautical times " in their accounts of Lagos, and this has perpetuated the confusion.

to enable him to launch his invasion armies against these islands without having first won command of the sea by defeating our maritime forces. Philip II of Spain, Louis XIV and Louis XV of France, Napoleon, and in our own days Hitler, have all of them massed their armies, assembled their boats and barges, and concentrated their warships. They have then waited, and waiting has taught them that unless they could control the sea the fate of their expeditions was settled in advance. Rather than accept such risks, they have then marched their armies elsewhere. But such repeated lessons from history have not always protected those responsible for controlling the narrow waters from the criticisms of their own government, or from the angry recriminations of the mob.

In October and November, 1759, Hawke was several times forced back to Torbay. Anxiety grew, and so did the recriminations against him, especially when it became known that the French West Indian fleet had slipped into Brest while he was sheltering in the Channel. On 14th November Conflans at last left harbour with twenty-one battleships, and turned south to pick up the transports at Vannes. On that same day the British fleet got back again to its blockading station, in the nick of time to save the frigates which Hawke had left to watch the invasion fleet. Conflans, in whose ship Breton pilots had been embarked, sailed into Quiberon Bay confident that no foreigners would dare to follow in those reef-studded waters. In a storm of wind and rain, and with nothing but the splendid seamanship of his crews to save his fleet from utter disaster, Hawke never hesitated. It must have been an awe-inspiring sight to the scattered French ships who had so recently believed themselves safe; for the British battleships set every sail and plunged through the breaking seas in hot pursuit under a storm-blackened afternoon sky. Howe was leading in the *Magnanime*, then came the *Centurion* and third in the chase was Bentley's *Warspite*. Then came the *Dorsetshire*, the *Defiance*, Captain Stanhope's *Swiftsure* (*Warspite*'s comrade of Lagos Bay), and Keppel's *Torbay*. Hawke himself in the great *Royal George* was flying the signal for " Chase " and " Line ahead " combined, to allow his fastest sailers full rein. At two o'clock in the afternoon, right inside the Bay, between the rocky Cardinals and the Four Bank, the battle began.

The *Formidable* was the first French ship to feel the impact of this headlong pursuit. She fought well, but surrendered finally to the *Resolution*. Howe and others engaged and crippled the *Thésée*. She opened her lowest gun ports, but the seas came in and she sank like a stone, with all her crew. Then the *Héros* surrendered. The *Royal George* came tearing past to seek Conflan's flagship, the *Soleil Royal*, in the inner waters of the Bay. On his way he sank the *Superbe* with a single broadside. Then with darkness falling on a scene of elemental and man-made fury which can rarely have been paralleled, the surviving enemies fled into the innermost recesses of the harbour, and Hawke made the signal to anchor.

Next day Hawke started to collect the cripples, but two of his ships sent to finish off the *Héros* grounded on the Four Bank and had to be destroyed. Only one prize, the *Formidable*, was taken ; but the *Thésée* and *Superbe* were sunk, the *Héros* and the *Soleil Royal* were burnt, while seven other French ships lightened themselves and escaped over the bar of the River Vilaine. There they grounded. The last nine of Conflan's fleet fled to the south, and eight of them reached Rochefort safely. The British casualties numbered under 300, but the French lost between four and five thousand seamen.

Thus was the last French fleet shattered and scattered,

and the threat of invasion dissipated. Rarely can so much have been accomplished by so few ships, for less than half Hawke's ships had entered Quiberon Bay. It was the unhesitating ardour of the pursuit, and the splendid seamanship of the crews which made the victory possible. But quite apart from defeating Louis's invasion plans, this victory and Lagos together brought very far-reaching results for Britain. The recent capture of Quebec by Saunders and Wolfe, which gave Britain control of North America, was thereby confirmed; for there was no French fleet left capable of challenging it. And the nascent British Empire, with all that it meant by way of world-wide trade and influence, was saved. It is appropriate that the third *Warspite* should have had as big a share in these great events as her predecessor had in first establishing British influence in the Mediterranean.

Sir John Bentley served in *Warspite* a short time longer, and took part in the blockade of Brest with Hawke's Grand Fleet. But the victories of 1759 had been so complete that there was little more fighting at sea. On 5th May, 1763, the year when peace was signed, the *Warspite* was paid off at Plymouth.

After the splendid accomplishments of the third *Warspite*'s youth, the end of her story is an anti-climax. On the outbreak of the War of American Independence she was converted into a hospital ship, and she served in that inactive capacity from 1778 to 1783. Then she became a "receiving ship"—the equivalent to a modern naval barracks. Finally in 1800 she was renamed *Arundel* and so passes out of our story.

One cannot but regret that she was not renamed when the Admiralty first decided to use her for non-combatant purposes. Her name is indeed so inappropriate to a hospital ship that it seems surprising this was not done. But quite apart from the misuse of her name, she was kept on inactive service for so long that it brought a very unhappy result in breaking the long tradition established by her and her predecessors. Obviously a new *Warspite* could not be built while the former one was still in commission and bearing that name. Consequently there was no fighting *Warspite* in the fleet right through the War of American Independence and, worse still, during the greater part of the Napoleonic Wars. One would give a lot to have her name among the ships of similar records and tradition—*Vanguard*, *Bellerophon*, *Minotaur*, *Dreadnought* and many others—which fought at the Nile or Trafalgar. Her comrade of Lagos and Quiberon Bay, the *Swiftsure*, was luckier; for a new ship of that name fought in both those battles. Finally, as if to add irony to the sadness of her temporary eclipse, the *Téméraire*, which *Warspite* had captured at Lagos, was represented in Nelson's fleet, while her captor could only chafe at a hulk's buoys in harbour. Not until 1807, by which time the days of England's greatest glory in the Napoleonic Wars had passed, was the name revived.

The fourth *Warspite* was, like the third of her line, a 74-gun ship; but she was a good deal larger and displaced 1,890 tons compared with the 1,580 of her predecessor. She was launched at Chatham on 16th November, 1807, and her total cost is recorded in the Admiralty as having been £59,725—about six times the cost of the third of her name. Her first captain was the Hon. Henry Blackwood. In him we can at least pick up a link with Nelson, for he had been Captain of the *Euryalus* when she brought home the news of Villeneuve's escape from Ferrol in 1805, and he was with Nelson on board the *Victory* while she closed the French and Spanish fleets on the morning of 21st October, 1805. He was a man for whom Nelson had the deepest affection; whom he called his "favourite frigate captain," and whose account of his last minutes on board the *Victory* has passed into history.[4] His last command had been the *Ajax* which was destroyed by fire while with Duckworth's squadron bound for the Dardanelles in February, 1807. Blackwood was picked up after surviving for more than an hour in a "cold, dark sea of a stormy night." When he was dragged into the boat his first words were, "I am quite cool and collected, sir; I am quite cool and collected." The midshipman of the boat, who had not recognised him, replied, "I don't know whether you are collected or not, but I should think you are pretty cool."[5]

Far from easing the strain on Britain and on her fleet, the year following Trafalgar brought another and perhaps the greatest crisis of the whole long struggle. By 1807 the war was going very badly. Prussia had been overthrown at Jena, and the third coalition against Napoleon fell finally to pieces with his victory over the Russians at Friedland. There then took place the meeting of the Russian and German Emperors on a raft in the River Niemen, and the signature of the Treaty of Tilsit in July. By gaining Russia's acceptance of his "Continental System," Napoleon hoped to close all ports from the Gulf of Finland to the Dardanelles against British ships, thus strangling her export trade and reducing her to bankruptcy. The British Government reacted promptly in the direction whence an immediate threat was evident, and in September Admiral Gambier seized the Danish fleet in Copenhagen. Britain also instituted what was virtually a blockade of all the ports which refused to trade with her. But cracks soon became evident in the solid wall which Napoleon believed he had built around Europe, and the most important of them grew out of the revolt of Spain and Portugal. Once again the Navy found itself carrying the British armies overseas, supporting them after they had landed, and securing their line of retreat should evacuation become necessary, as happened at Coruña in 1809. Then, when the time came for Wellington to make his great march across Spain it was, as he put it, " our maritime superiority [that] gives me the power of maintaining my army, while the enemy are unable to do so."[6] Meanwhile things had not gone well in the north, and the Walcheren expedition of Lord Chatham and Sir Richard Strachan, undertaken to help Austria, was a fiasco which is remembered chiefly by the derisive doggerel of the pamphleteers.* By 1811 British industry was suffering severely, and bankruptcy was approaching. Then the United States, unnecessarily and against her own real interests, declared war. Not until 1812, when Russia revolted against a system which was bringing her starvation, did relief come to Britain.

Such was the state of the war during the new *Warspite*'s first commission. Though she narrowly missed Gambier's action against Copenhagen, she first served in the Baltic, the Channel and in support of the Army in Spain. Then early in 1810 Blackwood took her out to the Mediterranean, and one can imagine the memories which must have crowded through his mind as he rounded Cape St. Vincent in *Warspite*, passed Lagos Bay and Trafalgar, and sighted Gibraltar ahead. Since Nelson's death Collingwood had commanded the Mediterranean Fleet. After Trafalgar it was still a very active station, for there was a powerful French fleet in Toulon, Russia was for a time an enemy and was sending reinforcements to the French, the Dardanelles had to be watched and Turkey cajoled ; and

---

* " Brave Chatham with his sabre drawn
Stood waiting for Sir Richard Strachan.
Sir Richard, longing to be at 'em,
Stood waiting for the Earl of Chatham."

until Spain threw off Napoleon's yoke Cadiz also demanded the fleet's attention.

It was shortly after Collingwood's death in 1810 that *Warspite*'s name was heard once more inside the Straits. As so often before, the main strength of the fleet was employed in blockading Toulon, where the French had rebuilt their strength to thirteen battleships, three of them with 120 guns or more. Admiral Cotton's blockading force had about the same strength as the enemy's, but he was beset by shortage of frigates; like his predecessors, he had to contend with the severe gales which sweep the Gulf of Lyons. Blackwood with *Warspite* and two other battleships commanded the Inshore Squadron.* On 20th July, 1810, his ships had a brush with a superior French force, which had sallied out of Toulon to protect a convoy which Blackwood had forced to take shelter in a nearby harbour. The fighting was at long range and achieved nothing, but despatches from Admiral Cotton to the Admiralty and from Blackwood to his commander-in-chief were published in London, and the latter's claim to have " driven back into their port " a force of six French battleships and four frigates which had declined engagement certainly seems to have been exaggerated. It aroused some very caustic comments in the French press.[7]

In 1812 *Warspite*, still commanded by Blackwood, was transferred to the Channel Fleet under Lord Keith. A " List of Foreign Seamen and Marines Serving on Board H.M.S. *Warspite* at Spithead, 28th October, 1812," which has come down to us, throws an interesting light on the way in which the fleet was manned at that time.[8] Out of fifty foreign seamen from at least a dozen countries ranging from Java to Newfoundland, only twenty were volunteers.

* This title was revived in the 1939-45 war and given to the small ships which supplied and supported the Army during the African Campaigns. See Roskill, *The War at Sea*, Vols. I and II.

All the rest were "Impressed" or "Prisoners," and some of the pressed men had been twenty years in the service. In addition to the foreign seamen, thirty others are euphemistically described as "Volunteers from Prison Ships" at Chatham, Portsmouth or in Scotland. These were men who had been offered a life in the Navy instead of continuing to serve their prison sentences, and had accepted it as the better alternative in what was doubtless a "Hobson's Choice." In the Marines the standard of the men was plainly higher, for of fourteen foreigners named, mostly Russians or Germans, all were enlisted men. But the record shows how, after more than twenty years of war, the fleet still included many of the dregs of human society. It is not surprising to find Lord Keith protesting to the Admiralty over "the number and extent of punishments that occur in the squadron under my orders," and urging that since "almost every crime . . . originates in drunkenness . . . no more essential service could be rendered to the nation than to reduce the quantity of spirits now used in the Navy."[9] However, British seamen have always been, and still are, very sensitive to any attempts to curtail their rum ration, and the commander-in-chief admitted that "the present may not be the moment for reforming so great an evil." He hoped, however, that reform might be possible after the war. Many senior officers have thought likewise since.

On the Channel Station the *Warspite* was employed on protecting British trade in the south-west approaches against American privateers, and to intercept ships carrying cargoes between America and France. The London Gazette records that on 26th February, 1813, she captured an American brig carrying cotton and tobacco to Bordeaux, and in the following month a schooner outward bound "with brandy, wine, silks, etc.," for Philadelphia.[10] Other captures of American ships, both privateers and trading vessels, are reported by Blackwood in letters to Lord Keith at this time. It may therefore be presumed that he collected satisfactory prize money on his new station.[11]

Captain Blackwood left *Warspite* soon after she gained these successes, and under her new Captain, Lord James O'Bryen (or O'Brien), she next served on the other side of the Atlantic. In June, 1814, she embarked troops in western France for service in North America. It is likely that this was a detachment of soldiers from Wellington's Army of the Peninsula, which had recently carried its remarkable campaign across the Pyrenees into France. The *Warspite* and *Asia* took their convoy up the St. Lawrence, and anchored off Quebec. It was the first time that a battleship of her class had sailed so high up that great river.[12] On her return from this combined operation, which was a typical example of the way in which British maritime power enabled, and still enables, her land forces to be rapidly switched from one theatre to another, the *Warspite* was paid off.

After the battle of Waterloo and the exile of Napoleon peace at last descended on Europe. It was the beginning of the long period on which we now look back with nostalgia—the period of " Pax Britannica." For the best part of a century the Royal Navy's ships patrolled the world, England's trade flourished exceedingly, and the Industrial Revolution brought an undreamt of expansion of exports, and so of the country's wealth. It was not a period of unbroken peace, though to look back at it from the anxiety-ridden years of the mid-twentieth century makes it almost appear so. Wherever trouble might be brewing the Navy was sure to turn up, and many incidents which might have become serious dissolved before its silent, overwhelming force.

Warspite re-commissioned in 1817 with a new armament of 76 guns. For the next fifteen years she served all over the world—in the East Indies, South America and the Mediterranean. Her long foreign commissions were typical of the unspectacular, but immensely influential, work undertaken by the fleet throughout the nineteenth century. Little of note happened during these foreign commissions, but we find a mention that under Captain the Hon. Richard Dundas *Warspite* circumnavigated the globe in 1826-27; and that she was the first line-of-battle ship ever to do so.[13] In April, 1831, now under Captain Charles Talbot, she was at Rio de Janeiro when an insurrection broke out against the rule of the Portuguese. The Emperor of Brazil, Dom Pedro VI, was the son of King John VI of Portugal, whom we had persuaded to leave for South America in 1807, when British control of his country was essential to the prosecution of the war against Napoleon. After his father had returned to Portugal Pedro proclaimed Brazil's independence in 1822, and was crowned Emperor. With the help of Admiral Lord Cochrane, who had entered Brazilian service, the Portuguese garrisons were gradually forced out, and in 1825 the independence of Brazil was recognised. Unhappily for his dynasty Pedro then engaged in a costly and disastrous war with Buenos Aires, and lost the province now called Uruguay. In the face of rising discontent he abdicated in April, 1831, and it was *Warspite*'s crew which rescued " Their Imperial Majesties and their suite," and carried them to the safe haven of a British battleship.[14] There is a certain irony in the rescue of a foreign Royal family by a British warship shortly after a British admiral had contributed greatly to the expulsion of that same Royal family's countrymen.

In 1833 the *Warspite* was paid off again, at Portsmouth,

to reappear seven years later cut down to a 50-gun frigate. Once more she went abroad, this time to the Mediterranean, and she was present when the French Navy attacked and destroyed the Barbary pirates' nests at Tangier and Mogador in 1844. The Royal Navy lent the support of its presence to the operations, but took no active part itself. In the following year she fulfilled a similar watchful role off the coast of Syria, where civil war had broken out. In 1846 she came home and was paid off again. This time it marked the end of her active career, though not the end of her life of useful service.

On 27th May, 1862, the Admiralty lent her to the Marine Society to serve as a training ship for boys destined for the sea. Thus there began for the *Warspites* a long period of dual existence; for while one ship of the name was training boys under the Society's auspices another was generally flying the White Ensign at sea. The Marine Society had been founded by a public-spirited merchant of the City of London in 1756, when great difficulty was being experienced in manning the fleet for the Seven Years' War. Originally its purpose was to provide seamen's outfits to volunteers for service in the Navy.[15] These "Landmen," as the volunteers were called, were intended to supplement the inadequate number of men available from the seafaring population proper. They were an eighteenth-century form of Royal Naval Volunteer Reserve. Very soon after its foundation the Society extended its bounties to poor boys from distressed families, whom it equipped and sent to the King's ships. The Society's records show that over 10,000 men and boys were helped in this way before the end of the Seven Years' War, so that it plainly fulfilled a very important naval recruiting function. It is pleasant to conjecture on the probability that boys helped by the Society served in the third *Warspite* at Lagos and Quiberon Bay.

The Marine Society's splendid work in helping boys from poor families to serve in the Royal and Merchant Navies continued right up to the outbreak of the Second World War. But ill-fortune dogged its training ships. The fourth *Warspite*, while serving in that capacity, was destroyed by fire at Woolwich in 1876. The Admiralty promptly replaced her by re-naming the *Conqueror*, a second-rate of 2,845 tons, and lending her to the Society. She thus became the fifth *Warspite*. She was the first ship of her name to have steam engines (developing 500 horse-power); but her main means of propulsion was still by sail, and her armament of smooth-bore, muzzle-loading guns differed but little from the weapons used at Trafalgar. The full tide of the revolution in propulsion and armament was not to be felt until the sixth *Warspite* was launched in 1884. The career of the fifth ship with the Marine Society spanned, however, the whole of the active life of the sixth and part of that of the seventh *Warspite*; for she survived until 1918, when she suffered a fate similar to that of her predecessor and was destroyed by fire.

Once more the connection between *Warspite* and the Marine Society was preserved. In 1922 the Society acquired the ex-light cruiser *Hermione* (4,360 tons) and renamed her. As this ship did not obtain her new name from the Admiralty, she has not been included in the long line of naval *Warspites*. She was moored firstly off Greenhithe and later off Grays (Essex), and served as a training ship until September, 1939. About 140 boys passed through her every year, and most of them went into the Royal and Merchant Navies. Then the outbreak of World War II broke a tradition which had lasted for 183 years; for the Society's work could not continue in its original form, and the "Training Ship *Warspite*" ceased to exist.[16]

The sixth *Warspite* was launched at Chatham on 29th January, 1884. She was an armoured cruiser of 8,400 tons and was originally designed as a full-rigged sailing ship. Later the design was altered to give her only one "military" (as opposed to sailing) mast. Her engines could develop 8,000 horse-power giving her a speed of seventeen knots, and she was one of the first warships to be lit by electricity. Her main armament was four 9.2-inch breech-loading guns in single barbettes. One gun was mounted ahead, one astern and one on each beam. Her secondary armament consisted of ten 6-inch guns, mounted on the broadside. She was built with a ten-inch armour belt, and also had two to four inches of armour on her main deck. At the time when she was laid down warship design was in a state of flux, because of the revolution in guns, shells, armour and propulsion then in progress. She really marks the final stage of the transition from the nineteenth century warship to that of the twentieth, and her design was not repeated in later classes of armoured cruisers.

In the summer months of 1888 and '89 she took part in naval manœuvres at home. Then she served three years (1890-93) as flagship of the Pacific Station, which stretched from Alaska to Cape Horn. One of her midshipmen, later to become Admiral of the Fleet Lord Chatfield, states that " we steamed up and down the station continually, spending the summer in each hemisphere and occasionally visiting the Pacific Islands."[17] The same biography records that she had an exciting and varied commission, including a revolution in Chile during which there was considerable fighting between the rival warships. But the event which left the clearest mark on that observant midshipman's

memory evidently was the occasion when the ship's pet
llama arrived on the quarter-deck while church was being
held. Although "the Master-at-Arms tried to shoo him
away reverently," the animal got behind the admiral, who
was in full dress. Approaching gently, the llama finally
"took a huge bite out of the Admiral's left epaulette."
We are told that dignity was only preserved with difficulty,
and that "the Parson speedily pronounced the blessing."
It is obvious that the church service that day was
thoroughly enjoyed by the gun-room.

After returning from the Pacific the sixth *Warspite*
served for three years as flagship at Queenstown. Then,
from 1899 to 1902, she was again on the Pacific Station.
In 1904 her name appeared on the sales list. From that
date until 26th November, 1913, when the seventh *Warspite*
was launched at Devonport, the name was kept alive only
by the Marine Society's training ship already mentioned.

CHAPTER THREE

The Evolution of the 7th 'Warspite'

"A ship is . . . a large hollow building, made to pass over the sea with sails."

From Mr. Derrick's Appendix (1546)

HAVING BRIEFLY surveyed the service of the *Warspite's* six historical ancestors from 1596 to 1904, we may turn to a different, but equally important, succession from which the seventh ship of the name was descended. She had in fact a large number of distinguished twentieth-century antecedents in design, though not in name or in history. Though they were far more closely spaced in time than her historic ancestors, covering little more than a decade instead of three centuries, they played a great part in the evolution of the last *Warspite*, and of the weapons which she mounted.

The development of her main armament of eight 15-inch guns in twin turrets will be considered first. The revolving turret dates to Captain Cowper Coles's ingenuity and enthusiasm, and the first example was fitted in the wooden battleship *Royal Sovereign* in 1864; but the next development had a tragic ending. Coles was given free rein in the design of the *Captain*, a ship of over 6,000 tons. To obtain great sail power he accepted a freeboard of only six feet, and many seamen considered her dangerously "over-masted." Their worst fears were fulfilled when, on 6th September, 1870, she capsized off Cape Finisterre in a heavy squall. Five hundred officers and men, among them Captain · Coles, lost their lives. Meanwhile the *Monarch* had been built to a more conventional design with a freeboard of 14 feet. She was completed in 1869 and had a pair of armoured turrets, each mounting two twenty-five-ton muzzle-loading guns, on the centre-line of the ship. She displaced 8,320 tons, and was the first proper turret ship. The *Devastation* and *Thunderer* followed in 1871 and '72 and were the first ships to have " all-big-gun " armaments. They displaced 9,300 tons, and mounted twin turrets on the centre-line, each with two thirty-five-ton muzzle-loading guns. These were the first " mastless turret ships," and their highly successful design sealed the direction of future developments.

The next step came in 1881 with the design of the *Inflexible*, which was a " rigged turret ship," and still carried the masts and yards of the sailing era. She displaced 11,400 tons and mounted two turrets on the beam " en échelon "—that is to say both turrets could fire on either broadside. Her four guns, still muzzle-loaders, weighed no less than eighty tons each. This ship is of special interest not only for the new arrangement of the main armament, but because Captain J. A. Fisher (later Lord Fisher of Kilverstone) and Mr. Philip Watts (later Sir Philip Watts) collaborated over the design, and Fisher actually commanded her at the bombardment of Alexandria in 1882. These two men were to exercise great influence over battleship design for the next twenty years. Watts, who was Director of Naval Construction from 1902 to 1912, later described Fisher as " the Naval officer who for forty years had more than any man to do with the design and construction of our warships."[1] In fact, it was the technical ability of Watts, combined with the imaginative genius and fiery energy of Fisher, which produced not only a new type of battleship, which rendered all her prede-cessors obsolete, but transformed the whole face of the fleet.

The next step after the *Inflexible* was an attempt to combine the special features of her design and that of the *Devastation*, by fitting both centre-line and " *échelon* " turrets ; but this increased the size of the ship so greatly that it was considered unacceptable. Then came the intro-duction of breech-loading for large guns, and of rapid-firing smaller weapons. It was now possible to give battleships secondary as well as main armaments, and because the latter no longer had to be loaded through the muzzle from outside the turret, they could be made much longer, with great gain in ballistic accuracy. In 1887 the *Collingwood* of 9,500 tons was completed with four 12-inch, 43-ton breech-loading guns in two turrets on the centre-line, and six 6-inch guns on each broadside in between the turrets. Six of this " Admiral " class of battleship were completed, and because of their greatly increased fire-power and excellent sea-keeping qualities they remained on the active list of the Navy for more than twenty years.

Early in the twentieth century design of an " all-big-gun " ship like the *Inflexible* was again discussed, and was strongly favoured by Fisher, then Commander-in-Chief, Portsmouth. But he was still much ahead of his time, and his ideas were rejected in favour of ships with a twin 12-inch turret at each end and three twin 9.2-inch on each broadside.* These were the *Lord Nelson* class, of which only two were built. They displaced 16,500 tons and had a speed of 18½ knots.

In October, 1904, Fisher became First Sea Lord. He had brought back with him from the Mediterranean the design of a 21-knot " all-big-gun " ship, with six pairs of

---

* The twelve 9.2-inch guns were reduced to ten before the ships were completed.

12-inch guns, all on the centre-line of the ship. The turrets were to be placed in steps, so that the upper ones could fire over the lower. Once again the visionary nature of Fisher's ideas is to be remarked, for this design marked the genesis of the super-imposed turret. In due time it was to become a normal feature of many classes and types of warship, and remains so to this day. But, like so many of his proposals, it was not at once adopted.

In 1904 Lord Selborne, then First Lord, appointed a " Commission on Design " to assist the Board of Admiralty in considering the various alternative possibilities in battleship development. Fisher's twelve-gun ship was much discussed by the Commission, but turned out to be far bigger and more costly than its protagonists had expected. Finally the turrets were reduced from six to five, and all of them were brought down to the upper-deck level. Three were placed on the centre-line and two on the broadside opposite each other amidships. Eight guns could fire on either beam, six ahead and a like number astern. She also mounted twenty-four 12-pounder guns, and had five submerged torpedo tubes. Parsons turbines, developing 13,000 horse-power, were fitted for the first time in a big ship. She finally displaced 17,900 tons and was capable of 21 knots. Such, in brief outline, was the *Dreadnought* of the programme year 1905-6. She was the only ship of her class to be completed, but was the proto-type of every battleship which followed.[2]

There now followed a succession of " Dreadnought " type battleships in each year's naval programme from 1906 to 1909. We cannot here follow the changes made in the *Bellerophon, St. Vincent, Neptune* and *Colossus* classes in detail, but they are shown in Appendix A. Then, in the 1909-1910 programme, the *Orion* class, the first to have 13.5-inch instead of 12-inch guns, the design which Fisher had put forward in 1904 was at last realised.[3] The four ships of the class had two twin turrets at each end, with the upper ones super-imposed above the lower, and a fifth turret amidships. All ten guns were thus in the ship's centre-line; but displacement had gone up to 22,500 tons.

The *King George V* and *Iron Duke* classes which followed varied but little from the *Orions*. Then, in the 1912-13 naval programme came the next big step. Design of a 15-inch gun and turret had already been proceeding for some time, though to preserve secrecy it was long called the " 14-inch experimental " gun. In the 1912-13 programme, ships were ordered to mount the new armament, and these ships were the five " Queen Elizabeths "—the *Warspite, Barham, Valiant, Malaya* (the gift of the Federated Malay States) and the *Queen Elizabeth* herself.

In 1912 Sir Eustace Tennyson d'Eyncourt succeeded Sir Philip Watts as Director of Naval Construction, a post he was to hold until 1924. Responsibility for the design of the *Queen Elizabeths* was therefore mainly his. They were revolutionary ships in other respects than the calibre of their main armaments, for they were wholly oil-fired and their maximum speed was 25 knots; but to make them four knots faster than the *Iron Dukes*, the horse-power developed by their engines had to be more than doubled. We will look at the broad features of their design a little more closely.

The *Queen Elizabeths* were exactly 600 feet long, and just over 90 feet in the beam. Their original displacement was 27,500 tons, but this increased steadily as their life progressed and additions were made to their armaments and armour. *Warspite* finally displaced about 32,500 tons. They carried in their fuel tanks, 3,400 tons of oil, and twenty-four Yarrow " large tube " boilers originally supplied the steam for the Parsons turbines which drove the four propeller shafts to develop between them 75,000 horse-power. Their main side armour belt was thirteen inches thick at the water-line, and seven to eleven inches of armour was fitted to their turrets, barbettes and vital control positions. The deck armour, nowhere more than three inches, was comparatively light, but it was increased after Jutland, where it was shown that our ships were not well enough protected against plunging fire.* Later still the bomb threat caused an even greater thickness of deck armour to be added.

The main armament was reduced from the five turrets of the *Iron Dukes* to four, to compensate for the much heavier weight of the 15-inch turret. The secondary armament originally consisted of eight 6-inch guns on each broadside. These were soon reduced to six, and later to four each side; and in the final reconstruction of the *Valiant* and *Queen Elizabeth* they were wholly replaced by dual-purpose (i.e. anti-aircraft as well as low angle) weapons. Down below were four submerged 21-inch torpedo tubes, but they too were to disappear with the passage of time and the great changes in maritime strategy and tactics which came to pass during the 1930's. As an indication that these changes were on the way, though in 1912 the cloud was no bigger than a man's hand, the *Queen Elizabeths* were originally each given two 3-inch anti-aircraft guns.

From the foregoing brief account of naval developments between 1905 and 1912, and a study of Appendix A, the reader will see that a remarkable series of twenty-seven battleships was ordered by the Admiralty, and that each new class developed logically from its predecessor. Together they formed an exceptionally homogeneous fleet, such as the world has not seen again; and that quality brought immense tactical benefits to our fleet and squadron

* See pp. 110 and 111-116.

commanders. Jointly these ships formed the Grand Fleet in which *Warspite* served her first commission, and which held the German Navy firmly in its grip throughout the first World War.

In passing it may be mentioned that the loss of homogeneity in the Royal Navy between the wars can confidently be attributed to the naval limitation treaties of the 1920's. By imposing a maximum displacement and a maximum size of gun for each class of ship, the treaties forced all naval powers to build right up to the limits, and to mount the heaviest permissible guns. Britain thus abandoned all the experience accumulated by two decades of ship and gun design and, to keep pace with other powers, built 35,000-ton battleships and 10,000-ton cruisers with 16-inch and 8-inch turrets of completely new design. Not only were they not very successful ships, but the Royal Navy thereby started the second World War with such a mixed collection of pre- and post-treaty ships, with armaments of widely differing performance, that problems of supply, repair and replacement became excessively complicated, and tactical handling in battle presented captains and flag officers with ever-recurrent and scarcely soluble difficulties. Looking back to-day one cannot but conclude that of all the ideas hopefully devised by man to reduce the likelihood of war, and of all measures of alleged economy forced by politicians on the fighting services, the naval limitation treaties will stand for all time not only as the most ineffective, but also the most dangerous to those nations which loyally tried to abide by their restrictive terms.*

To return to the *Queen Elizabeths*, it can confidently be stated that in them the arts of the big ship and big gun

---

* After about 1935 neither Germany nor Japan paid the slightest attention to the treaties, and all their major warships greatly exceeded their published displacements. See Roskill, *The War at Sea*, Vol. I, pp. 57-58.

designer reached their peak of success. Nor can it be doubted that their success was to a great extent made possible by the steady continuity of the yearly building programmes authorised between 1906 and 1912. Warship design is such a specialised task that it cannot be undertaken in fits and starts, building one class of ship suddenly to meet a government's anxious realisation of the country's weakness, and a short while later, when the international horizon appears temporarily to be set fair, leaving the building slips and the gun-mounting shops empty and idle, and their skilled men to seek employment elsewhere. Continuity of construction, even if only on a small scale, is one of the most important factors in preserving the nation's maritime security; and it was achieved to a remarkable degree in the decade prior to the launching of the *Queen Elizabeths*. Lest it be claimed that their cost (for *Warspite* £2,524,148) was high, and to-day would be vastly higher, let it be remembered that because they were such successful ships they remained in service for over thirty years; and their record in the second World War must surely suggest that rarely can such great benefits have been derived from so small an initial expenditure.

Having thus given due praise to the success of the broad design of these five ships, it is right to mention where certain weaknesses lay. Firstly their turrets suffered from one grave fault in that, as originally designed, an explosion in the gunhouse could ignite a chain of cordite charges reaching right down to the magazines, and so blow the ship up. It is also true that the outstanding success of British gun designers was vitiated by the fact that the anti-ship shells which they fired did not penetrate enemy armour satisfactorily, and in a fit state to explode behind it. The first of these weaknesses was to cost us several fine ships, and many hundreds of seamen's lives, before it was rectified; and the second one contributed to the German Navy escaping from its rare encounters with our heavy ships between 1914 and 1918, without receiving the damage which our shell hits should have caused. Further reference to these matters will be made when we come to consider *Warspite*'s part in the Battle of Jutland.*

One more class of battleship, the five *Royal Sovereigns*, must be mentioned because they were the last of the long line here described. They were ordered in the next programme after the *Queen Elizabeths*, and mounted the same armament. But because supplies of oil fuel were considered dangerously uncertain in war, they were originally designed for coal-firing, and their much lower horse-power gave them considerably less speed than their predecessors. They were not such a successful class.

The five *Queen Elizabeths* were, considering their size and complexity, built remarkably fast. None took much more than two years to complete. The *Queen Elizabeth*, *Barham* and *Warspite* were finished between January and October, 1915, and the *Malaya* and *Valiant* followed them into service in February, 1916. Whereas the complement of the *Dreadnought* had originally been 773 officers and men, and that of the *King George V* class had remained about the same, the *Queen Elizabeths* at first needed nearly 950 men to man them, and *Warspite* herself had her complement increased to no less than 1,284 at the outbreak of the second World War.[4] This was, of course, a measure of the ever-increasing complexity of the weapons and equipment fitted in her.

Because the story of *Warspite* is so very much the story of the eight big guns she mounted, it may be worth explaining briefly how those weapons were loaded and fired. A 15-inch twin turret weighed about 700 tons, and the guns themselves each weighed 100 tons. The guns were over 54 feet long and consisted essentially of a rifled tube round which some 185 miles of flat-section wire were wound. Over the wire were shrunk the outer jackets. The making of such guns took between two and three years, and each one cost about £17,500. It was a very specialised process, and demanded not only a high degree of human skill and experience, but also special machinery such as the enormous lathes in which the barrels were turned, and the special tool to cut the rifling with great accuracy. Very few firms engaged in this type of work. *Warspite*'s four turrets were built in the heavy gun-mounting shop of Sir W. G. Armstrong-Whitworth at Elswick, near Newcastle-on-Tyne. Four of her first outfit of eight 15-inch guns were made by William Beardmore at Parkhead, Glasgow, and the other four were made in Vickers' River Don Works at Sheffield. The life of a 15-inch gun was about 335 full charges, and after firing that number of rounds it would have to be re-lined. *Warspite* had a new set fitted in 1929, and they were in turn replaced between 1941 and 1944 as she wore them out on war service.

When a new battleship was approaching completion the normal practice was for the partially assembled turrets, and also the guns themselves, to be sent round by sea to the yard where the ship herself was building. The transporting ship would be berthed alongside the battleship, and first the turret, then the guns and finally the turret's armoured roof would be hoisted out by crane and lowered into place. The working of the giant crane to place such loads with precision needed a steady nerve and great care. With the turrets and guns in place, the installation of all the complicated machinery necessary to work the armament could go ahead. The power used to work all the machinery in the 15-inch turret was hydraulic, and the pressure was generated by four steam engines deep in the bowels of the ship.

It was no simple matter to raise a shell weighing nearly a ton (1,940 lb.) and four quarter-charges of cordite, each of 108 lb., from the fixed structure at the bottom of the ship into the revolving structure of the turret, and then to load them all into the guns. Yet the whole cycle could be performed once a minute by a well-trained crew. The shell-room was right at the bottom of the ship, with the great projectiles lying in tiers like so many jeroboams of champagne. Above the shell-room was the magazine which, after our experiences at Jutland, was totally sealed off from the turret. The cycle of loading the gun is shown in the accompanying diagram. The shell was first lifted from its bin by a hydraulic grab, and traversed to a bogey which revolved round, and could be clamped to the turret trunk. Inside the trunk were the main hoisting cages, into which the shell was traversed. Meanwhile on the deck above four quarter-charges had been passed out of the magazine through a flash-tight scuttle, and placed in the upper part of the hoist cage.

When the cages were loaded a signal went to the operator in the "working chamber", which lay inside the revolving turret just beneath the guns. He raised the cages up to his own level, rammed the shell and charges out of the main hoist cages and into the gun-loading cage, and at once sent down the former for the next round. Meanwhile another operator in the gun-house would raise the gun-loading cage right up to the gun, ram the shell into the gun and then follow it with the charges, one half at a time. The gun-loading cage was then sent down again to the working chamber, the breech closed with a mighty slam, the gunlayer laid his gun on the target either by eye

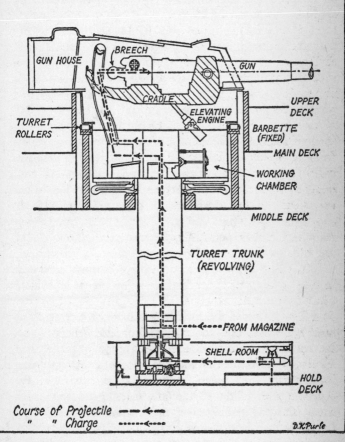

DIAGRAM OF 15" TURRET AS FITTED IN H.M.S. WARSPITE

GUN HOUSE

BREECH

GUN

CRADLE

UPPER DECK

TURRET ROLLERS

ELEVATING ENGINE

BARBETTE (FIXED)

MAIN DECK

WORKING CHAMBER

MIDDLE DECK

TURRET TRUNK (REVOLVING)

FROM MAGAZINE

SHELL ROOM

HOLD DECK

Course of Projectile ◄ ─ ─ ─ ─
  "   " Charge ◄ ┄┄┄┄┄

D.K.Purle

Map 1

or by following electric pointers from a remote " director."
As soon as the gunlayer and turret trainer were " On,"
the electrical firing circuits were closed. The gun could
now be fired either by the director layer up on the mast,
or locally by its own gunlayer. "Director firing" was
new when *Warspite* commissioned, but was soon to be
fitted throughout the fleet.

The normal British practice in day action was to fire
four gun salvos, from the right guns of all turrets, followed
a few seconds later by another similar salvo from all the
left guns. Later, when we developed battleship night
action to a fine art, eight gun broadsides were always fired
at night. To a stranger the incessant and overwhelming
noise of the fast-moving machinery in the turrets, with
every one of the seventy men in the crew carrying out his
part with split-second precision, would be only less unnerving than the blinding flash and the stunning con-
cussion of the salvo or broadside being fired. But to the
men who controlled and worked the great guns, it all
became almost second nature. Much drill and practice was
needed to attain perfection, but the men always prided
themselves on having the smartest turret, with the best
shooting record ; and in a good ship no turret's crew ever
went through its daily drill and maintenance routine
unwillingly.

To carry out a firing with an armament such as *Warspite*'s, to speak the few quietly telephoned orders needed
to set in motion the whole intricate cycle of loading and
firing the eight guns, gave a sensation of controlling vast
power with one's finger-tips which can hardly ever have
been equalled. Though the Gunnery Officers of that era
were always the subject of much good-humoured chaff
from their shipmates, neither party really had any doubt
as to what was the most important duty in the ship.

The future *Warspite*'s keel plate was laid at Devonport by Mrs. Stokes, the wife of the Admiral Superintendent of the Dockyard, on 31st October, 1912.* While the hull rose gradually above the building slip the gun-mountings were being erected at Elswick, the main propelling machinery was being built by Messrs. Hawthorn Leslie at Newcastle-on-Tyne, and the heavy guns were slowly taking shape in the big-gun makers' shops in Sheffield and Glasgow. By the time she was ready for launching on 26th of November, 1913, 12,000 tons of material had been built into the hull. The launching ceremony aroused unusual interest, for not only was she a representative of a new class, far more powerful than her predecessors, but she was the first wholly oil-fired ship to be built at Devonport. The crowd which thronged both sides of the building slip on the day of her launching was estimated at 30,000 people. Mr. A. E. Richards, the Constructive Manager of the dockyard, was responsible for the launch, and the naming ceremony was performed by Mrs. Austen Chamberlain. The First Lord, Mr. Winston Churchill, was present on the launching platform. The bands of the Royal Naval Barracks and of the Royal Marine Light Infantry were there, but the singing at the religious service was, we are told, led by the rather unusual combination of a harmonium and a cornet.[5] The launch appears to have gone without a hitch, in spite of " the enormous weight of the vessel " necessitating more than the usual number of blocks being left under her. She took the water, dropped anchors in the Hamoaze to bring her up, and was then towed to the North Yard, where her construction was to continue.

A letter from Lord Fisher to Admiral Beatty, written in

* The destruction by enemy action of the records of H.M. Dockyard, Devonport, has deprived us of all but the barest particulars of the building of the *Warspite*. I am indebted to the Editor of the *Western Morning News* for such information as is here included.

February, 1915, shows that the new First Sea Lord had directed his fiery energy to the question of making the *Warspite* and her sisters able to steam even faster. "I am busy," wrote Fisher, "dragging masses of weights and luxuries out of the *Warspite* to make her go faster, 27 knots, I hope, and be a fit companion to *Indefatigable, New Zealand* and *Australia*."[6] But it needed more even than the dynamic efforts of the old admiral to turn battleships into battle cruisers, and in fact *Warspite* was never capable of more than her designed speed of about 25 knots.

The ship was first commissioned on 8th March, 1915, under Captain E. M. Philpotts. He was a gunnery specialist himself, and as a young officer had held some of the most coveted appointments. Unhappily the wayward habits which the ship developed, and the chain of misfortunes from which she suffered, soon proved her a capricious mistress. Her executive officer was Commander H. T. Walwyn,* who later achieved high rank in the service, and after his retirement was Governor of Newfoundland from 1936 to 1946. One of the best-loved characters in her wardroom was the padre, Walter Carey, who later became an outstanding missionary bishop.[7]

The dockyard records of her first steaming and gun trials have not survived, but it is known that she carried them out from Devonport, and brief entries in her Ship's Book indicate that all went well with them. Her crew embarked on 5th April, 1915, and on the 11th she went to sea for the "acceptance trials," which are always carried out by a new ship before her officers take her over from the building and machinery contractors on behalf of the Admiralty. Off the west coast of Ireland she steamed for one and a half hours at full power for the first time. Her engines then developed their designed horse-power, and

* Now Vice-Admiral Sir Humphrey Walwyn, K.C.S.I., K.C.M.G., C.B., D.S.O.

her speed was recorded as about 24½ knots. It is likely that Captain Philpott's officers took over the ship from the contractors after these trials, for her log shows that on the 13th April *Warspite* arrived at Scapa to join Admiral Jellicoe's Grand Fleet, and was at first attached to the 2nd Battle Squadron. Her career had begun in earnest.

CHAPTER FOUR

First Commissioning to Jutland
1915-1916

"The two leading ships, the *Barham* and *Valiant*, were engaged with the enemy's battle-cruisers; the rear ships, the *Warspite* and the *Malaya*, fought the whole of the finest squadron in the German Fleet."

W. S. Churchill. "The World Crisis"

THE NEW *Warspite* having now joined the Grand Fleet it may be helpful to the reader's understanding of what follows if the meaning and purpose of a maritime strategy is first briefly discussed. A maritime nation is, of course, one in whose life the sea is a vital factor, and to whom seaborne trade is essential to survival. Throughout her three or four centuries as a world power there has never been any doubt that England (and later Britain) came within this definition; for her history contains innumerable examples not only of the wealth and benefits which she drew, and still draws, from overseas, but of the dire consequences which have befallen her when the influence of the sea on her prosperity has been forgotten, and her navy has been neglected. Several examples of this were quoted in telling the story of the earlier *Warspites*.* In order to protect the merchantmen which bring in her imports of food and raw materials, and carry overseas her exports of manufactured goods, a fleet of fighting ships

* See pp. 33-34 and 59-60.

was found very early on to be essential. If Britain lacked such a fleet her merchant shipping fell an easy prey to the next envious or rapacious enemy who came along—and there have been many of them. The enemies, or potential enemies, of this country have always realised that their best hope of imposing their will on her lay in building a fleet themselves, and in challenging British sea-power with it. From the sixteenth century to the two world wars of recent times, the pattern of such challenges has altered only in the nature of the weapons deployed at sea against us— not in their purpose. In order to frustrate that purpose one solution, and one only, has been proved completely effective—namely the defeat of the enemy's main fleet. The first object of a maritime strategy can therefore be described as being to gain or retain command of the sea by destroying the enemy's main forces. But if the enemy declines to engage in battle at sea, and keeps his fleet in harbour (as has in fact very often happened), we are unable to achieve our purpose immediately, and must therefore adopt the arduous and exacting alternative of watching and blockading his ships where they lie, thus denying them egress on to the trade routes. If the blockade is effective we shall still hold command of the sea, and our trade will continue to flow; but the enemy's threat will remain, and any relaxation of vigilance on our part might have serious consequences. This was precisely the state of affairs which prevailed in 1915. The enemy's overseas raiding ships and squadrons had virtually all been eliminated, but the High Seas Fleet at its North Sea bases was still a constant and serious threat to our command of the sea; the Germans continued to deny us the opportunity of decisive action, and their fleet had therefore to be blockaded. In this case the blockade was a distant one, maintained by the Grand Fleet from Scapa Flow with light reconnaissance forces in

the south, and not a close blockade such as had been kept
off enemy ports in many earlier wars. If the enemy fleet
could be enticed out and defeated the threat to our command of the sea would be removed for good and all, and
victory would then be in sight; but it was equally certain
that if the enemy defeated and destroyed the Grand Fleet
we should lose the war. As Mr. Churchill put it later,
" the standpoint of the Commander-in-Chief of the British
Grand Fleet was unique. His responsibilities were on a
different scale from all others. It might fall to him as to
no other man . . . to issue orders which in the space of
two or three hours might nakedly decide who won the war.
The destruction of the British Battle Fleet was final."[1]
The chain of events which would have followed hard on
the heels of such a defeat can easily be imagined. The
Germans would then have been able to send out not single
raiders to sneak around the oceans, sometimes in disguise,
to snatch up a defenceless merchantman here and there, or
submarines to lurk in ambush beneath the surface of the
sea, but whole squadrons of warships and their attendant
supply vessels. Overseas bases could have been seized,
and our trade would quickly have been brought
to a standstill. If that did not bring the country to its
knees through starvation and bankruptcy, invasion would
have become a perfectly practical proposition; for there
would have been no adequate forces left to contest the
passage. To quote again from Mr. Churchill, " Ruin utter
and final would have overwhelmed the Allied cause."[2]

We have indeed quite recently experienced the dire
consequences of defeat at sea; but because it occurred in
a theatre far from Britain's shores they seem never to have
been brought fully home to our people. When in December, 1941, at one single, treacherous blow Japan destroyed
the greater part of the American Pacific Fleet, and three

days later eliminated the embryo British Eastern Fleet, Allied maritime strategy over a vast area was laid in ruins.[3] Not only was British trade at once swept from the eastern seas, but vast and wealthy territories were placed at the mercy of the enemy's invasion armies, untold suffering was inflicted on countless millions of innocent people, and British influence received a blow from which it has not yet recovered. The causes of that defeat unquestionably lay in the peacetime failure to keep our maritime forces at a strength adequate to meet their responsibilities in all parts of the world. It will be told later how, during the latter part of her career, *Warspite* played a part in restoring British maritime power in eastern waters.*

To implement a maritime strategy demands therefore firstly *strength* in the form of a properly balanced and up-to-date fleet. Serious lack of any of the components of maritime strength, be they big ships or smaller ones, submarines or aircraft, is bound to be fatal. In the East in 1941 the fatal deficiency was of maritime aircraft. After strength comes the need for *security* of the fleet's bases ; for without properly defended bases the fleet cannot maintain itself, nor replenish with fuel, stores, ammunition and all its other multifarious needs. To quote another example from the last war, the failure to defend Malta in time of peace very nearly caused us to lose our grip on the Mediterranean in 1942, and so on the whole Middle East theatre.[4] The third element of a maritime strategy comprises the Merchant Navy, which not only brings in our imports and takes our exports overseas, but carries the Navy's fuel and stores all over the world, and transports our soldiers to the theatres where the Government may require to have them landed. And since in the final stages of a war the enemy's armies must be defeated by our own, it is in executing this

* See pp. 252-255 below.

last purpose that a maritime strategy can be crowned with final victory.

In 1915 Britain possessed a barely adequate margin of naval superiority, and it was in capital ships—which were the matrix of the fleet and the hub of the wheel around which our whole maritime strategy revolved—that the margin was narrowest. We had only to lose or have disabled a small number of that class of ship to find ourselves faced with an equal or even a superior High Seas Fleet; and it was obvious that the Germans were endeavouring all the time to reduce our superiority by mine and submarine warfare.* Furthermore, because our fleet was constantly at sea we were all too likely to suffer losses and damage, while the enemy avoided such misadventures by remaining safely in harbour.

It is sometimes suggested that a maritime strategy is a defensive method of waging war, but this is certainly not the case. Though modern experience seems to show that a democratically governed nation will always be at a disadvantage at the beginning of a war, because of its inevitable unpreparedness, and will therefore have to act defensively during the early phases, this does not in any way alter the basically offensive purpose of a maritime strategy—which, as has been said, is to defeat the enemy's main fleet and then to carry our armies overseas to enable them to gain the final victory. Again and again in her history have Britain's strategists and naval commanders accomplished these very purposes; and in 1915 they were still the main objects of our strategy. Because, however, our margin of superiority in capital ships was so slender the reinforcement of the Grand Fleet was a matter of the

---

* The battleship *Audacious* was sunk by a mine off north-west Ireland on 27th October, 1914. So narrow was our margin of superiority at the time that the loss of the ship was not officially admitted until after the war. (See Corbett, Naval Operations, Vol. I (1939 Edition), pp. 239-242.)

first importance. Hence arose the need to complete the *Queen Elizabeths* as fast as possible, and herein lay the significance of the *Warspite*'s arrival to join the fleet.

The new *Warspite* spent the remainder of April and the whole of May, 1915, at Scapa, working up efficiency and carrying out exercises both inside and outside the Flow. Between 11th and 14th of June she was at sea cruising for the first time with the Grand Fleet, so it may be presumed that by that date she had passed through the inevitable period of adolescence and had emerged as a fully-fledged fighting unit. Her first summer passed very busily with sweeps and exercises in the North Sea, and all the usual fleet activities in harbour. In September there occurred the first of the chain of misfortunes which punctuated the whole of her long career, and which might well have given her the reputation of being an unlucky ship. To so superstitious a race as British seamen that might have proved a far greater handicap than landsmen may realise ; for once it becomes firmly established that a ship is unlucky, she is unlikely to be happy or successful. Yet *Warspite* never gained such an ill-favoured reputation. Thirty years after she was commissioned the first sub-lieutenant of her gun-room, who was to command her in a later war, wrote : " We had a very happy ship indeed, but also our bits of trouble. . . . Still they seemed to make no difference."* And so it continued throughout her life.

On 16th September she sailed from Scapa for Rosyth in the Firth of Forth. At about 5.30 a.m. next morning in rather misty weather she sighted land on an unexpected bearing, and shortly afterwards grounded off Dunbar. Her speed at the time was fourteen knots, and Captain Philpotts had not reduced earlier because he was in submarine-

* Admiral Sir Herbert Packer to the author 29th June, 1955. Admiral Packer served three commissions in *Warspite*. As sub-lieutenant 1915-17, as her gunnery officer in 1926 and as her captain 1943-44.

infested waters, and the destroyer escort which he had expected had not joined. The board of inquiry supported the use of high speed during the approach, but considered that it should have been reduced earlier and more drastically. The Admiralty acquitted the ship's officers of any negligence but considered the " temporary disablement of this important vessel was due to a grave error of judgment," and reprimanded the captain and the navigator. The accident was indeed typical of the serious hazards which always have to be accepted in war, when high speed has to be used regardless of the weather, and large numbers of ships, totally darkened by night, are often steaming in close order. On 22nd September *Warspite* sailed for the Tyne, and entered the floating dock of Smith's Docks at South Shields the same day for repairs to her outer bottom. She did not undock until 20th November. Two days later she sailed again for Rosyth, and thence onwards to Scapa.

Meanwhile on 2nd November the new 5th Battle Squadron had been formed under Rear-Admiral Hugh Evan-Thomas at Scapa. It consisted at first of the *Queen Elizabeth*, *Barham* and, as soon as she rejoined the fleet, the *Warspite*. The latter, unhappily, was soon in trouble again, for on the forenoon of 3rd December, while at sea with the Grand Fleet, she collided with her sister ship *Barham* during fleet manœuvres. A signal for eight knots was misread as eighteen. When *Warspite* increased to that speed she overtook the flagship, and her port bow struck the *Barham*'s starboard quarter. Blame was attributed to several officers in both ships, but luckily there was no serious damage to either of them. On 9th December *Warspite* sailed to her home port of Devonport, to effect repairs and give leave. But if her crew entertained hopes of spending Christmas in their homes, they must have been quickly disillusioned ; for at that stage of the war Admiral

Jellicoe could not afford to have one of his 15-inch battle-ships out of action for a day longer than was essential. On Christmas Eve *Warspite* arrived back at Scapa and rejoined the fleet.

The year 1916 opened with a period of much the same fleet routine. Exercises took place inside the Flow, where there was room to carry out practices such as sub-calibre firings and torpedo-running; tactical manœuvres were carried out with the other ships of the 5th Battle Squadron or with larger sections of the fleet off the Orkneys; and operational cruises were made with the Grand Fleet in the North Sea. On 18th February the *Malaya* arrived, and on 3rd March the *Valiant*. The 5th Battle Squadron was now complete, and was a redoubtable force of five fast battle-ships, mounting between them forty 15-inch guns.

Meanwhile British plans and intentions were being reviewed in London. Two considerations were involved. Firstly there was a strong desire to create an opportunity for offensive action by the fleet. Admiral Fisher's project for a Baltic operation, remarkably similar to that which Mr. Churchill pressed as First Lord in 1939 (Operation " Catherine "[5]), was much discussed, as were landings in the Frisian Islands; but close scrutiny of both projects proved that neither was practicable. The second factor was heavy public and parliamentary pressure on the Admiralty to move a proportion of the Grand Fleet south to Rosyth and the Humber in order to make it easier to defend our east coast towns against bombardment by fast raiding warships. Ever since the enemy had shelled Scarborough, Hartlepool and Whitby in December, 1914, and had escaped home without loss, loud if not very well informed opinions had been expressed to the effect that the Navy should be able to prevent such attacks. It is indeed notoriously difficult to convince British public opinion that however effective our command of the sea may be, and however skilfully and devotedly it may be applied, brief forays into our home waters can never be wholly prevented. Although on 24th January, 1915, Admiral Beatty's Battle Cruiser Fleet had gained a success against an enemy raiding force in the Battle of the Dogger Bank, a decisive victory had eluded him, and the fight did nothing to mitigate the public outcry. To divide our forces in an endeavour to protect every point of a long coastline simultaneously could only assist the enemy by weakening our maritime control, and might at any moment result in small squadrons being overwhelmed. Yet the pressure to disperse our forces in this unwise manner continued and, as will be seen shortly, such a policy was in some degree adopted. The only result was to deprive the main fleet of ships which might have been invaluable in the major clash now pending.

And so we come to the month of April, 1916, pregnant with anxieties and with a sense of impending crisis. On the 23rd (Easter Sunday) the German-supported rebellion broke out in Ireland, and it was expected that the High Seas Fleet would come out. Next day the German battle cruisers were believed to be moving, so the Grand Fleet from Scapa and the Battle Cruiser Fleet from Rosyth both put to sea. Jellicoe, who had the 5th Battle Squadron with him, cruised south-east of the Orkneys until the 26th and then returned to harbour.

Meanwhile the whole east coast had been warned that another raid appeared imminent, while the commands responsible for the safety of our Channel communications were told to guard against surprise and to hold all their forces immediately ready. Submarines and light surface ships were sent to patrol the enemy's likely approach routes.

The Admiralty's intelligence on which all these precautionary moves were based was accurate; for we were reading many German cyphered messages at that time. Scheer, who had recently relieved Admiral von Pohl in command of the High Seas Fleet, and had promised to introduce a more forceful naval policy, had actually intended to send four battle cruisers to bombard Yarmouth and Lowestoft, and to support them with his main strength. But the mining of the battle cruiser *Seydlitz* delayed his plan.

Then very early on the 25th Commodore Tyrwhitt's Harwich Force sighted the enemy battle cruisers and light cruisers as they approached Lowestoft. By skilful tactics Tyrwhitt saved Yarmouth from bombardment, but the fact that shells were fired into Lowestoft, though they actually caused very few casualties, added fuel to the flames of public exasperation in Britain. The immediate result was further discussion on the need to move a substantial part of Admiral Jellicoe's strength to the Humber and the Thames, and to base the Grand Fleet on Rosyth rather than Scapa. In fact the 3rd Battle Squadron and one cruiser squadron were detached to the Thames early in May, and when Beatty sent the three *Invincibles* of the 3rd Battle Cruiser Squadron from Rosyth to Scapa for exercises he asked Jellicoe to replace them temporarily with the four ships of the 5th Battle Squadron.[6] It thus came to pass that Admiral Evan-Thomas's ships fought initially under Beatty on 31st May. Though the official historian holds that the commander-in-chief was thereby unluckily deprived of his most modern and powerful squadron, the support which the *Queen Elizabeths* gave to Beatty at the crisis of the battle cruiser action was of great value.[7]

On the enemy's side the most important result of the

Lowestoft raid was that the High Seas Fleet was considered thereby to have justified itself. In consequence the German Government decided that it was unnecessary to proceed with the unrestricted submarine campaign, which had recently aroused strong American protests. The Germans therefore accepted all the demands made by the United States Government.

Political influences were also making themselves felt in Germany with regard to the future employment of the High Seas Fleet. Our blockade was making civilian life more and more rigorous, and the very heavy losses suffered before Verdun had depressed public morale. The German Government looked to its fleet to restore the balance. Moreover, the postponement of the unrestricted submarine campaign had placed a large number of U-boats at Scheer's disposal.

The new German commander-in-chief accordingly decided to send Admiral Hipper's battle cruisers to bombard Sunderland, to station many submarines off our bases, and to bring out the High Seas Fleet in support of the bombarding force. When, however, the weather prevented airship reconnaissance he cancelled the bombardment, and substituted a raid by Hipper against our shipping and forces in the Skagerrak. He himself would follow with the High Seas Fleet.

At about noon on 30th May the Admiralty warned Jellicoe that something unusual was afoot, and that evening our wireless interception service reported that Scheer's fleet was on the move. The Grand and Battle Cruiser Fleets were ordered to sea, and to concentrate east of the " Long Forties " (about 100 miles east of Aberdeen), but the Harwich and Nore forces were held back until enemy intentions were clearer; for the Admiralty was apprehensive about the safety of the east coast towns and of our

Channel shipping. The *Warspite*'s log shows that she sailed from Rosyth at 10.20 p.m. that evening. A short while later all Grand Fleet forces were at sea, and heading for a rendezvous 90 miles west of the Naze.* Beatty, with Evan-Thomas under him, was to be 69 miles S.S.E. of his commander-in-chief by 2 p.m. on the 31st.

Although history can produce examples of sea battles in which as many fighting ships were engaged, never before or since Jutland has comparable power been flung into a fight. It is perhaps this, combined with the fact that the issue of a world-wide struggle hung in the balance during those few hours of a summer day and night, that gives to the battle such deep and permanent interest. It may be helpful to the reader's understanding of what follows if the organisation of the two opposing forces on sailing from their bases on the 30th and 31st May is first given. Admiral Jellicoe's consisted of the 1st, 2nd and 4th Battle Squadrons from Scapa and Invergordon, in all 25 battleships, and the 3rd Battle Cruiser Squadron of three ships. Eight cruisers were with him, and his light forces consisted of twelve smaller cruisers and fifty-one destroyers, organised in three flotillas. Admiral Beatty's Battle Cruiser Fleet consisted of the six ships of the 1st and 2nd Battle Cruiser Squadrons and the four new 15-inch battleships of the 5th Battle Squadron. Three light cruiser squadrons totalling twelve ships, twenty-seven destroyers in three flotillas led by two more light cruisers, and the seaplane carrier *Engadine* completed his array.

On the German side Scheer's High Seas Fleet comprised 22 battleships organised in three squadrons, while the fast forces under Admiral Hipper were the 1st Scouting Group of five battle cruisers, and the 2nd and 4th Scouting Groups of four and five light cruisers respectively. Two

* The headland in southern Norway, also called Lindesnes.

more light cruisers led six and a half flotillas of destroyers, each of eleven boats.

From the foregoing summary of the strength of the two great fleets now approaching each other across the North Sea it will be seen that Jellicoe was superior in all classes, but especially in capital ships, of which he commanded 38 against Scheer's 27. The British ships were, moreover, the more heavily armed. In such circumstances it was not to be expected that the Germans would stand and fight a fleet action, unless circumstances arose to offset the British superiority. Scheer was in fact likely to try to inflict damage and losses whilst himself avoiding close engagement.

Early intelligence of the enemy's presence, strength and intentions is always vitally important in sea warfare, but never more so than when it is desired to force action on an unwilling enemy. Jellicoe was, however, deprived of any such advantage by the call-sign of Scheer's flagship being transferred to a shore wireless station when he sailed from Wilhelmshaven at 2.30 a.m. on 31st May.*

Early in the afternoon the Admiralty told Jellicoe that although the enemy had made all preparations to sail there was no definite news that he had done so; directional wireless, they said, placed the German flagship in the Jade at 11.10 a.m. that morning. The result of this incorrect deduction was that the day was far advanced before Jellicoe received any intimation that the enemy's main fleet was moving in his direction.

In the North Sea the 31st May, 1916, was a fine and calm day, but the horizon was misty, and visibility was never extreme—especially to the eastward. As the day

* In Scheer's report on Jutland the times used are two hours ahead of the time kept by the British fleet, which was British Summer Time (G.M.T. plus one hour). In this account of Jutland both sides' times have been adjusted to G.M.T.

drew on the setting sun cleared the western horizon some-what, and a pronounced advantage fell to whichever side's ships lay to the east. Visibility thus played an important part from the start of the fighting. Not only was the light variable and deceptive, but the whole battlefield soon became obscured by smoke, which the light winds did little to disperse. Not only were some 200 warships, most of them coal-burning, manœuvring at high speed in a comparatively confined area, but to their funnel smoke were very soon added the smoke of many guns and the columns sent up by burning and sinking ships. The inevitable fog of battle was thus made denser, and at times became almost impenetrable. To a generation which has grown accustomed to air reconnaissance and radar, the fact that at Jutland there was absolutely no means of penetrating the all-pervading obscurity, except by the human eye, may well be difficult to understand. Yet it exerted a great influence on the day's events, and probably handicapped the British commanders in their aim of forcing an action as much as it aided their enemies in extricating themselves from difficult situations.

During the forenoon of 31st May Beatty's battle cruisers were steering about east towards the Jutland Bank. His light forces were spread ahead on a line which ran from about N.E. to S.W., while the four ships of the 5th Battle Squadron (*Barham*, *Valiant*, *Warspite* and *Malaya*) were stationed five miles on the port quarter of the battle cruiser flagship. This formation has been criticised by one well informed, if not unbiased, student of the battle on the grounds that it was too far away for the battle squadron to give early and effective support to Beatty's faster but less well protected battle cruisers.[8] Because these dispositions greatly influenced the part played by

Warspite and her squadron it is desirable to examine the various factors which may have contributed to their adoption.

The first point to be borne in mind is that owing to the shift ashore of the call-sign of the High Seas Fleet flagship, already mentioned, the Admiralty and both British admirals had no idea that Scheer's ships were at sea until visual contact was made the following afternoon. Though it seems unlikely that Beatty's battle tactics would have varied very greatly had he known of Scheer's presence, it is at least possible that he would then have kept the Fifth Battle Squadron in closer support of his own ships. Secondly, until two of his fleet blew up Beatty had no means of knowing that his ships were so defective in magazine protection that fatal disaster might fall on them at any moment. Furthermore, it was not until after our ships were back in harbour and the detailed results of the battle were becoming known, that suspicion was aroused that all was not as it should have been with the performance of British heavy armour-piercing shell. The consequences of these two failures was that Beatty not only fought under the severe handicap of equipment which was defective both in defence and offence, but that he started the battle in complete ignorance that this was so.

By 2 p.m. Hipper's 1st Scouting Group had, unknown to any of our forces, reached a position well up the coast of Denmark. The High Seas Fleet was about fifty miles astern, and about the same distance to the west of Hipper were Beatty's battle cruisers, which at this time turned to the north to make their rendezvous with Jellicoe. The impression in Beatty's fleet now was that the operation on which they were engaged would turn out merely to be another of their many abortive sweeps and searches of the North Sea. One of Beatty's staff remembers that, when the fleet turned north he " settled down in the sun to read a book."[9]

Thus was the stage set for the only fleet action of the 1914-18 war.

So far the situation was developing wholly in the British favour; for Scheer had received no intelligence to suggest that his opponents had left harbour, and he was completely unaware that he was steering straight into the arms of a greatly superior concentration. Then, just after Beatty had started his turn to the north, the right wing ship of his cruiser screen and the left wing ship of Hipper's screen both went to investigate a merchantman. The two cruisers sighted each other, and this chance encounter led directly to the battle cruiser action; for both admirals turned inwards to support their light forces.

The *Warspite*'s Executive Officer (Commander H. T. W. Walwyn), who was in general charge of the ship's fire and repair parties, kept a diary of events as he saw them from inside the ship. At 2.40 p.m. he received a message from the captain " to get the hands up at once," and from the sighting cruiser's signal he realised " that there was something serious doing."[10] " I passed the word round to everybody that we were in for the real thing," the diary continues, " and went round all mess-decks, wetted the decks . . . and lit all Action candles, etc. Saw all doors and everything closed, and went up on deck; they were just finishing washing down the weather decks. I sent all hands away to their stations and went up [to the bridge] to report everything ready. There was nothing in sight, except our own ships, but we were steaming hard. Hoisted Battle Ensigns and Union Jack at after struts and masthead. Went to my Action Station, B turret . . . It was now about 4 o'clock . . . Got orders to ' load and train on Red 20° ' [i.e. 20° on port bow]. Could not see anything at all, hazy and a lot of smoke about. . . . I made out five columns of smoke in the mist and that was all I could see —no masts or anything else."

As Beatty steered S.S.E. at full speed to cut off the enemy, the 5th Battle Squadron dropped as much as ten miles behind, and although Evan-Thomas did his best to decrease the distance by cutting corners, by 3 p.m. he had only reduced the gap between him and Beatty to about five miles. The battle squadron was thus still outside the range at which the *Lion*'s flag signals could be distinguished. At 3.32 Beatty, closing at 25 knots, sighted the German battle cruisers. He formed his ships on a line of bearing north-west to south-east, steering E.S.E., and both sides opened fire nearly simultaneously at about 16,000 yards.* The Germans were relieved not to come under fire earlier, when the heavier British armaments might have told against them. The reason why Beatty held his fire was that in the deceptive light of that misty afternoon his ships' range-finders were over-reading.

Beatty thus went into action with six ships against Hipper's five—a reasonable though hardly a decisive superiority. His biographer categorises it as " unthinkable " that the speed of the battle cruisers should have been reduced by the two and a half or three knots necessary to enable Admiral Evan-Thomas's battle ships to keep close station on him[11]; and one must agree that in the earliest stages of forcing an action on a probably reluctant enemy this would have little to commend it. The biographer also defends the stationing of the 5th Battle Squadron five miles from Beatty's flagship on the grounds that " this was designed to assist Evan-Thomas in taking up his appointed station in the van of the battle fleet after the junction between the two fleets had been effected."[12] He further

* See Map 2.

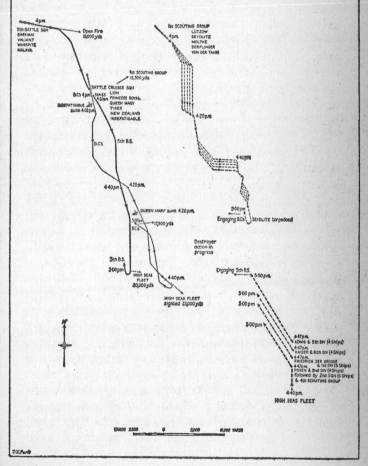

THE BATTLE OF JUTLAND
31st MAY 1916

The Battle Cruisers' & 5th Battle Squadron's Action
4·00 p.m. to 5·00 p.m.

British Ships & Tracks —○— Battleships · · · Battle Cruisers

German · · · · —·—·—· ·····

4 pm

5th BATTLE SQN
BARHAM
VALIANT
WARSPITE
MALAYA

Open Fire 19,000 yds

1st SCOUTING GROUP
LÜTZOW
SEYDLITZ
MOLTKE
DERFLINGER
VON DER TANN
4 pm

1st SCOUTING GROUP 15,500 yds

BATTLE CRUISER SQN
B.C's 4 pm   5th B.S
4·20 pm
LION
PRINCESS ROYAL
QUEEN MARY
TIGER
NEW ZEALAND
INDEFATIGABLE

INDEFATIGABLE
sunk 4·03 pm

4·20 pm

4·40 pm

B.C's   5th B.S.

4·40 pm   4·20 pm

5·00 pm
Engaging B.C's   SEYDLITZ torpedoed

QUEEN MARY sunk 4·26 pm

5·00 pm
B.C's   17,300 yds

Destroyer action in progress

5th B.S.

5·00 pm

HIGH SEAS FLEET 20,000 yds

4·40 pm

Engaging 5th B.S.   5·00 pm

HIGH SEAS FLEET signted 23,000 yds

5·00 pm

5·00 pm

5·00 pm

4·47 pm
KÖNIG & 5th DIV (4 Ships)
4·47 pm
KAISER & 6th DIV (4 Ships)
4·47 pm
FRIEDRICH DER GROSSE
& 1st DIV (5 Ships)
4·47 pm
POSEN & 2nd DIV (4 Ships)
Followed by 2nd SQN (6 Ships)
& 4th SCOUTING GROUP

4·40 pm
HIGH SEAS FLEET

YARDS 5,000   0   5,000   10,000 YARDS

D.X.Purt

Map 2

considers that had the battleships been in closer support
"Hipper, on finding himself confronted with such a
superior force, would certainly have refused action."[13]
These latter arguments seem harder to accept; for it
must surely be admitted that had Admiral Hood's 3rd
Battle Cruiser Squadron been with Beatty, in place of the
four *Queen Elizabeths*, he would have gone into battle with
nine ships, manœuvring in one integrated force, instead of
six. Finally we may note that in the same ably argued
analysis it is admitted that " It was not fully realised at
the time what a valuable replacement they [i.e. the 5th
Battle Squadron] were"[14] and, accept that statement as at
least one reason why the part played by *Warspite*'s squadron,
though very important at two critical junctures, was not
sufficiently prolonged to be decisive—as it well might have
been had what Mr. Churchill aptly called " their unique
combination of speed and power" been more fully
exploited.[15]

A running fight now took place with both sides
steering to the south-east. The light was in the Germans'
favour, and they gained a further advantage from an error
made in the distribution of the fire of Beatty's six ships
against their five adversaries. The second ship in Hipper's
line, the *Derfflinger*, was thus left unfired at for about ten
minutes. The range closed rapidly, and the German
gunnery was excellent. Hits were being scored rapidly on
our ships. Just after 4 p.m. Beatty's rear ship, the
Indefatigable, was heavily struck and blew up. Almost at
the same moment his flagship, the *Lion*, very nearly suffered
a like fate. A shell hit her centre turret, and the magazines
were flooded only just in time, on the orders of the
mortally wounded turret officer. It was at this critical
moment that the 5th Battle Squadron, struggling south
behind Beatty, first came into action at about 18,000

yards' range; and their tremendous volume of fire at once told.

Warspite first fired a few salvos at a light cruiser, which turned away. Then, in the words of Commander Walwyn, who was watching the start of the fight from B turret, " we were turning fast to starboard . . . and as we came round eight points [90 degrees] I saw five enemy battle cruisers on the port bow. They were steaming the same way as we were and going very hard . . . I could only see their masts and the tops of their funnels above the horizon. . . . We opened fire on Number 5 . . . range, I think, 23,000 yards. . . . I distinctly saw one salvo hit. She turned away in a cloud of black and white smoke, and we turned our attention to Number 4."[16] *Warspite*'s first target was the rear ship in Hipper's line, the *Von der Tann*, which had actually just sunk the *Indefatigable*. It is certain that she was heavily hit before *Warspite* shifted to the next ship ahead, the *Moltke*. The German account leaves no room for doubt regarding the dramatic effect of the battle squadron's arrival. Admiral Scheer himself remarks that " superiority in firing and tactical advantages of position were decidedly on our side until 4.19 p.m., when a new unit of four or five ships of the *Queen Elizabeth* type, with a considerable surplus of speed, drew up from a north-westerly direction and . . . joined in the fighting. It was the English 5th Battle Squadron. This made the situation critical for our battle cruisers. The new enemy fired with extraordinary rapidity and accuracy. . . ."[17] There could be no clearer tribute to the effect of the British battle squadron's gunfire. Hipper's comment on this phase of the battle was that " only the poor quality of the British bursting charges saved us from disaster," and Beatty noted in his despatch that " the enemy's fire now appeared to slacken "; but his troubles were not at an end. At 4.26

the *Queen Mary*, third ship in his line, was struck by a salvo of shells and blew up almost instantaneously. Beatty's remark to his Flag Captain, "There seems to be something wrong with our bloody ships to-day," shows how completely unaware he was of their defective magazine protection. The 5th Battle Squadron had, however, by then come to close grips with Hipper, and a destroyer attack by one of our flotillas was developing from ahead. For all that they had gained a substantial success, the German 1st Scouting Group's position was unenviable.

Then, at 4.33, the battle was suddenly and dramatically transformed by Commodore Goodenough's *Southampton* reporting "battleships in sight to the south-east." "What he had seen," states the official historian, "was a sight no British ship had enjoyed since the war began." It was the High Seas Fleet, of twenty-two battleships, "deployed in battle order, line ahead."[18] Both British admirals had, up to this moment, presumed that Scheer's ships were still in the Jade. Beatty now signalled to his force to turn sixteen points (180°), but Evan-Thomas, who was still coming down from the north, could not read the *Lion's* flag signal. The battle squadron and the battle cruisers were thus approaching each other at a relative speed of about fifty knots, all ships firing as fast as possible and under heavy fire. *Warspite's* Commander noted in his diary : "I suddenly saw our battle cruisers coming close by about half a mile off [steaming] in the opposite direction [to ourselves], and I realised they had turned back. I noticed that *Queen Mary* and *Indefatigable* were adrift, but never for a moment realised they had sunk."[19]

One of Beatty's staff now asked the admiral on which side of the battle cruisers the rapidly approaching battle squadron was to pass.[20] He was told that the battleships were to keep on the disengaged side of the battle cruisers, and the two squadrons thus passed each other at a distance of about one and a half miles shortly before 5 p.m. Beatty's biographer commends this decision on the grounds that, had the alternative been adopted, the 5th Battle Squadron's fire " might have caused Hipper to turn away and place himself out of range "[21]; and it is true that to allow the battleships to pass on his engaged side Beatty would have had to make a fairly large turn away from the enemy—tactics which were doubtless entirely unattractive to him. None the less it now seems that heavier damage might well have been done to Hipper's ships, and some of the weight taken off our own battered battle cruisers had Beatty given Evan-Thomas's ships the opportunity for closer engagement with all their 15-inch guns. Be that as it may Beatty's flag signal to the *Barham* to turn and follow him to the north was not at first seen. After the two squadrons had passed it was repeated in the *Lion*, and Evan-Thomas then altered right round in the wake of the battle cruisers.* " Very soon after the turn," continues Commander Walwyn's diary, " I suddenly saw on the starboard quarter the whole of the High Seas Fleet ; at least I saw masts, funnels, and an endless ripple of orange flashes all down the line . . . the noise of their shells [falling] over and short was deafening . . . crack, crack, crack going on the whole time. I felt one or two very heavy shakes, but . . . it never occurred to me that we were being hit."[22]

The Germans, as was natural, had seized the chance to concentrate on the battle squadron's turning point. The visibility was still much in the enemy's favour, with our ships silhouetted against the western sky, while his were only dimly discernible against a dark and misty background. The *Valiant* and *Warspite* turned in safety, but the *Barham* received several hits. The *Malaya*, last in the

* See Map 2.

line, came under a storm of fire and was constantly straddled. But the enemy battle cruisers and his leading battleships all suffered heavily at this time, and *Warspite*'s first adversary, the *Von der Tann*, by now had all her turrets out of action. "At 4.55 p.m.," wrote Captain Philpotts, "the [leading] enemy battle squadron was sighted and as their battle cruisers were very bad targets . . . the leading ship of the enemy's battle fleet was engaged; range 17,000 yards." This was almost certainly the battleship *König*. An officer who had an excellent front-row view from the cruiser *Southampton* wrote: "The 5th Battle Squadron were a brave sight. They were receiving the concentrated fire of some twelve German heavy ships but it did not seem to be worrying them, and though I saw several shells hit the *Warspite*, just ahead of us, the German shooting did not impress me very favourably."[23] It is indeed certain that Evan-Thomas's squadron gave a very good account of itself during these hectic minutes; Commander Walwyn noted: "I distinctly saw two of our salvos hit the leading German battleship. Sheets of yellow flame went right over her mastheads, and she looked red fore and aft like a burning haystack. I know we hit her hard . . . [B turret] machinery working like a clockwork mouse, no hang-up of any sort whatever."[24] But the *Warspite* herself at this time received five or six heavy hits. One shell entered the mess-decks through the side armour, and burst "in a terrific sheet of golden flame, stink and impenetrable dust."[25] It started a souvenir hunt by the ship's fire brigade. "Another hit blew in the side aft and began to flood the steering compartment. Yet another burst in the captain's lobby, reducing it to a state of indescribable wreckage. Farther forward, X Turret was hit, and water was flooding through a hole in the side, and going down the engine-room [air] supply trunk. Another took away the engineer's office."[26] Yet she suffered remarkably few casualties.

From 5 p.m. till about 6.30 *Warspite*'s commander and her fire and repair parties never had a dull moment, what with fires to tackle, holes in the ship's side to plug, damaged bulkheads to be strengthened and shored up, and —most important of all—the ship's own fighting efficiency to be maintained. Yet Walwyn found time to note and remember many examples of the sailors' imperturbability, and their humour in moments of stress. He had to stop two men who were trying to chip the fuse out of an unexploded German shell. When a 12-inch one " came into the galley and blew down through the deck," a stoker remarked, " There goes my bloody dinner " ; and he found the Marines of the 6-inch ammunition supply party (whose guns were not in action) cheerfully playing cards on the deck in the middle of the battle.[27]

Shortly before 5 p.m. Hipper conformed to Beatty's turn to the north so that he, Beatty's battle cruisers and the High Seas Fleet were all steaming towards Jellicoe ; but whereas the British commander-in-chief now knew that Scheer's full strength was out, the latter was still completely unaware of the Grand Fleet's proximity. Once more the tables had been turned in the British favour.

The Grand Fleet was meanwhile steering south-east in the normal cruising formation of six columns disposed abeam. Each column consisted of four ships, and Jellicoe's *Iron Duke* was leading the fourth column from the right of the formation. The fleet could not, however, fight effectively in this formation, because the gunfire of the centre columns would be masked by the neighbouring ships. To enable the heaviest possible weight of fire to be brought to bear on the enemy the formation had to be changed to line ahead, and this movement, or " deployment," as it was called, took a considerable time to carry out.* The normal method was to send one or other of the wing columns ahead, whilst the other columns first of of all turned 90 degrees towards the leader and then another 90 degrees in succession to follow in her wake. To deploy to the best advantage, and with the minimum loss of time accurate information of the enemy's position and course. was essential; and it was one of the functions of the battle cruisers to provide this information. At 4.45 Beatty had signalled: "Have sighted enemy's battle fleet bearing S.E.," and gave his position; but as the *Lion's* wireless aerials had been shot away the message had to be passed through the *Princess Royal*. By the time the report reached Jellicoe it had become so mutilated as to be positively misleading; for it gave the enemy's *course* as south-east, instead of his *bearing*. This, combined with the errors in dead reckoning, made it very hard to visualise the true situation in the fleet flagship. The *Southampton's* enemy reports and German signals intercepted and passed on by the Admiralty did, however, make it plain that Scheer was coming north. Jellicoe accordingly now made the historic signal that "Fleet action was imminent."

Meanwhile Beatty and Evan-Thomas continued their "run to the north," leading the High Seas Fleet straight into the arms of the Grand Fleet. Shortly before 5.30 Beatty turned towards the enemy, and the fight was renewed. *Warspite* and *Malaya* again engaged the van of the High Seas Fleet, while the battle cruisers and Evan-Thomas's other two ships were firing at Hipper. The situation in which the latter now found himself was most precarious—more so in fact than he could have realised at the time. For though he knew that Beatty and Evan-Thomas were to the west of him, he did not yet know

that Admiral Hood with his three untouched ships of the
3rd Battle Cruiser Squadron was hastening down from
the north, nor that Jellicoe's main strength was not
far behind Hood. All Hipper's ships had by this time
been severely damaged, and Beatty's relentless pressure
from the west was forcing him farther and farther to the
east.

Next, at 5.55 p.m., Hood and his three *Invincibles* came
into action from the north-east—almost at the moment
when Beatty sighted the leading ships of the Grand Fleet.
The much desired contact had been made, but it had
been made at such close range that not a moment was to
be lost in deploying the Grand Fleet into line of battle.
Jellicoe, however, was still completely in the dark regarding
Scheer's position—which knowledge he urgently needed to
enable him to prepare his deployment. Just after 6 p.m.
he signalled to Beatty: "Where is the enemy's battle
fleet?" Five minutes later Beatty replied that the German
battle cruisers bore south-east from him, but gave no
course. This did not clarify the situation to the commander-in-chief, who thereupon repeated his question.
By that time Beatty had no enemy in sight; for Hipper
had retired towards Scheer. Rarely can a flag officer have
been faced with a more difficult decision than that which
Jellicoe now had to take, and take quickly. For the purposes of this narrative it must suffice to say that, although
still uncertain of the bearing on which the enemy would
be sighted, he started to make arrangements to deploy to
the eastward—that is to say with his port wing column
leading.

At 6.14 Beatty re-sighted the enemy battle fleet and
reported it. It was now suddenly clear to Jellicoe that
Scheer was not ahead of the *centre* of the Grand Fleet as
he had hoped, but well to *starboard* of it. There was not a

moment to lose. "Never," writes the official historian, "had there been a situation which demanded higher qualities of leadership, ripe judgment and quick decision."[28] One minute after receiving Beatty's report the commander-in-chief signalled that Admiral Jerram, with his powerful 2nd Battle Squadron of eight modern ships on the port wing, was to lead the deployment.*

Meanwhile Beatty was pressing on to the east to take up his appointed station ahead of the Grand Fleet's mighty array. This, though tactically impeccable, had the effect of masking Jellicoe's vision and his fire at a critical juncture, and also forced the leading battleships to reduce speed drastically to allow the battle cruisers to get clear. Time was thus lost in completing the deployment. Evan-Thomas realised that he could not possibly reach a similar position to that for which Beatty was steering, and therefore ordered his squadron to take up its alternative station astern of the last ships of the Grand Fleet. These misfortunes were the consequence of contact between the battle fleets having been made at such close range.

Before deployment by the battleships was completed the British fleet suffered two more serious setbacks. Firstly Admiral Arbuthnot's 1st Cruiser Squadron pressed ahead of the Grand Fleet to engage the German cruisers, and came under overwhelming fire from Hipper. His flagship the *Defence* blew up, and the *Warrior* very nearly suffered the same fate. "Labouring away with damaged engines

* For the reasons why Jellicoe decided to make his deployment to the east with Admiral Jerram's 2nd Battle Squadron leading, rather than to the west with Admiral Burney's weaker 1st Battle Squadron in the van the reader must be referred to the commander-in-chief's own account of the battle (*The Grand Fleet*, Cassell, 1919, pp. 348-350). Sir Julian Corbett (*Naval Operations*, Vol. III, pp. 361-2) wholly supports Jellicoe's decision, but Mr. Churchill condemns it (*The World Crisis*, Vol. III, pp. 139-142 and 147-150), and considers that he should have deployed on his centre division. In the circumstances prevailing at the time this would, however, have involved much signalling, and it may be doubted whether so complicated a manœuvre could have been carried out without causing fatal confusion.

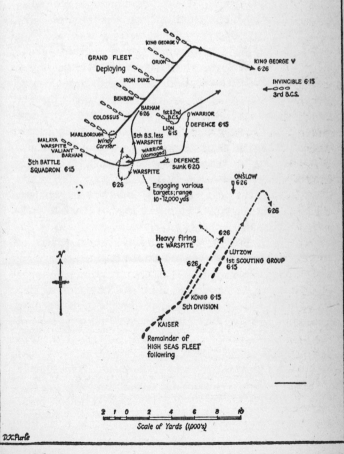

THE BATTLE OF JUTLAND
31st May 1916 6·15 p.m. – 6·26 p.m.
H.M.S. Warspite at 'Windy Corner'

British ○○ Battleships ━━▶ ● ● Battle Cruisers ━━▶

German ● ● ● ● Battleships ━ ▶ ● ● Battle Cruisers ━ ▶

KING GEORGE V

ORION

GRAND FLEET
Deploying

IRON DUKE

KING GEORGE V
6·26

BENBOW

INVINCIBLE 6·15
3rd B.C.S.

COLOSSUS

BARHAM
6·26

1st & 2nd
B.C.S.

WARRIOR

MARLBOROUGH

LION
6·15

DEFENCE 6·15

MALAYA
WARSPITE
VALIANT
BARHAM

Windy
Corner

5th B.S. less
WARSPITE

WARRIOR
(damaged)

DEFENCE
sunk 6·20

5th BATTLE
SQUADRON 6·15

WARSPITE

6·26

ONSLOW
6·26

Engaging various
targets; range
10-12,000 yds

6·25

Heavy firing
at WARSPITE

6·26

LÜTZOW
1st SCOUTING GROUP
6·15

N

6·26

KÖNIG 6·15
5th DIVISION

KAISER

Remainder of
HIGH SEAS FLEET
following

Scale of Yards (1,000's)

2 1 0   2   4   6   8   10

D.K.Pearle

Map 3

she was," says Sir Julian Corbett, "only saved by the *Warspite*."[29]

What happened was that as Evan-Thomas manœuvred his four ships to form astern of the Grand Fleet—not at all a simple matter at high speed and in the circumstances then prevailing—the *Warspite*'s helm jammed. Captain Philpott's account of this mishap, and of its dramatic consequences, must be quoted verbatim: "At 6.18 p.m.," he wrote in his report, "course was altered to the northward, following the motions of *Barham* and *Valiant*; but as we were apparently closing *Malaya* I ordered 'Port 20°,' and then the steering engine started to give trouble.* I have been unable to ascertain the exact cause of the trouble as subsequent events followed rapidly in succession, and *Warspite* closed the enemy's battle flect so fast that she came under a very heavy fire." (Here follows a technical explanation of the possible cause of the steering engine trouble. Damage from a shell hit and putting the wheel over too fast when steaming at twenty-five knots probably combined to produce the jammed rudder.) "*Warspite* shaved close under *Valiant*'s stern, and every attempt was made by helm and engines to bring her head back to port, with the dire result that she only closed the head of the enemy's battle fleet at decreasing speed. I then decided to go full speed ahead, and continued the turn to starboard.† I am unable to give further details, except that I managed to get away to the northward after practically turning two circles under the concentrated fire of several of the enemy's battleships. During this time centralised [gunnery] control was impossible, but fire was kept up in local control. Closest range was estimated to be about 12,000 yards, and the ship was badly damaged by shellfire but not completely

* At this time the helm orders in use in the Royal Navy referred to a ship's tiller, i.e. Port helm turned a ship to starboard and vice versa.
† See Map 3.

disabled." She actually received thirteen heavy shell hits on this day, about half of them during this unpremeditated manœuvre.

Warspite's sub-lieutenant was officer of A Turret at the time, and he has remembered his share of these exciting minutes vividly. " In the end," he writes, " my turret was the only one left in action. The director had gone, the transmitting station had gone, and I fired about twelve rounds at the Huns in local control. I was mentioned in despatches and specially promoted to Lieutenant—but *not* for hitting the target ! "[30]

One of *Warspite*'s midshipmen, who had an excellent view from the after torpedo control, has also left an account of the incident. " Suddenly," he wrote, " we found ourselves hauling out of the line and rushing towards the German fleet. . . . All that we knew was that we were in a hail of fire ; in fact, so much so that the salvos falling short and over made such splashes that a lot of water came into the tower, and we got quite wet. . . . Once or twice we got a good view of the Germans, the range being only about 8,000 yards, and they looked enormous at this distance.* We thought that our own 6-inch guns were firing, but discovered later that it was the enemy's shells bursting on our armour belt. This had not been going on for long when the end of the world seemed to come. The deck below me seemed to open up, and I had the sensation of falling—falling . . ."[31]

Seen from outside the ship, the *Warspite*'s actions appeared gallant to the point of folly ; for when, as Sir Julian Corbett puts it, Philpotts decided to " make virtue of necessity " and continued the unintended turn to starboard at full speed, he circled completely round the disabled

---

* This was a substantial under-estimate. The closest *Warspite* approached to the High Seas Fleet was about 12,000 yards.

Warrior and enabled her to escape. The destroyer *Onslow*, commanded by Lieutenant-Commander Tovey,* who was to command the whole Home Fleet in a later war, was limping off the battlefield severely damaged after taking part in a torpedo attack. She saw "*Warspite*, apparently stopped in a forest of water spouts, doomed as it seemed to destruction, but replying to the enemy's fire with all her guns—an inspiring sight for the lonely destroyer."[32] Down below Commander Walwyn and the fire and repair parties had a hectic half-hour. "The men," so he noted, "were simply splendid everywhere, and all so cheery"— in spite of the deafening noise, and the repeated hits which the ship was receiving. A cordite fire broke out in the starboard 6-inch battery and many men were burnt. There "Father Pollen, the Roman Catholic Chaplain, did very well with the wounded, although badly burned himself."

Meanwhile the three remaining ships of the 5th Battle Squadron had slipped into the Grand Fleet's battle line, and were trying to shield their comrade with their fire. Captain Philpotts was struggling to take station astern of the *Malaya*, but found that his ship was still unmanageable. He therefore drew off to the north to shift over to an alternative steering position. Because the damage received by *Warspite* might have flooded the engine-rooms if high speed was used, her captain reported that he could steam only sixteen knots, and also asked for the position of the battle fleet, which he plainly still hoped to rejoin. Admiral Evan-Thomas, however, considered that a severely damaged ship with unreliable steering gear might well prove more of a danger than an asset, and he therefore ordered *Warspite* to return to Rosyth. Captain Philpotts continues in his report: "I shaped course accordingly at 8.30 p.m., steam-

---

* Now Admiral of the Fleet Lord Tovey of Langton Matravers, G.C.B., K.B.E., D.S.O.

ing sixteen knots, and every endeavour was made to plug holes and shore bulkheads." We will tell her subsequent adventures later, for it is time to return to the battlefield.

It was 6.33 before Beatty's battle cruisers had got clear of the van of the battle fleet, and Jellicoe was able to increase speed again. The latter's promising opening had certainly been somewhat marred, for precious minutes had been lost before even the centre ships of his line, let alone those in the rear, could come into action. Hood's three ships were meanwhile in station ahead of Beatty, and on them fell the concentrated fire of all Hipper's squadron. The range closed rapidly to as little as 9,000 yards, the British ships were giving as much punishment as they were receiving, the admiral had just congratulated his gunnery officer on his good shooting, when suddenly the *Invincible*, " the mother of all battle cruisers and a victor of the Falkland Islands," blew up.[33] There were only six survivors. It was a devastating start to what all on the British side hoped and believed would be the decisive phase.

We can here only follow the rest of the battle in brief outline, for our *Warspite* was now disabled and preparing to withdraw. In spite of the sudden loss of a third British battle cruiser, Scheer's predicament was now acute; for he had come under the concentrated fire of an immense line of battleships spread over an arc of at least 90° ahead of him. " It was," wrote Scheer in his report to the Kaiser, " mainly [Hipper's] 1st Scouting Group and the leading squadron of the High Seas Fleet that had to ward off the attack. The German battle cruisers were forced to turn away so sharply that at 6.35 I found it necessary to turn the battle fleet [away] sixteen points, ships turning together to starboard until they headed due west." This difficult even dangerous, manœuvre was called "the battle turn away altogether." It had been thoroughly rehearsed by the German fleet, for use in precisely such circumstances as had now arisen. In British circles it had not been believed that such a movement could be successfully executed in battle, and no counter-measure had therefore been devised.[34] Had Jellicoe at once turned in pursuit, Scheer's peril would have been extreme. The German admiral therefore launched his destroyers against the British fleet, and covered his retirement with smoke; and in face of the torpedo threat Jellicoe turned away. Contact between the main fleets was thus lost, and Jellicoe decided to place himself across Scheer's probable return course to the Heligoland Bight. At 6.44 the Grand Fleet turned from E.S.E. to south-east, and eleven minutes later to a southerly course. These gradual alterations towards the enemy were, however, insufficient to regain the initiative.

After slipping out of the clutches of the Grand Fleet by his turn away, Scheer held on to the west for nearly half an hour. Then he reversed course again, all his ships turning together once more—directly in Jellicoe's direction. It is worth while quoting the reasons which Scheer himself gave the Kaiser for making this apparently suicidal manœuvre. "It was still too early to assume the course for the night," he wrote. "The enemy would still have had time before dark to bring us to action as he willed, to wrest the initiative from us, and even to cut off our return to the Heligoland Bight. The only means of preventing this was to deliver a second blow in the form of another all-out attack. . . . The manœuvre had to take the enemy by surprise, upset his plans for the remainder of the day and . . . facilitate our disengagement for the night. . . . Accordingly at 6.55 the line was once more brought round to starboard on to course east."[35] It was a bold, even desperate plan; but it failed of all its purposes. Scheer found his escape route to the east barred by the same ships which had threatened him so seriously half an hour earlier. From 7.12 to 7.25 p.m., with visibility now in the British favour, first Hipper's sorely tried and badly damaged ships and then the leading squadron of the High Seas Fleet, were " enveloped in a flaming arc of gunflashes."[36] Scheer could not afford to hesitate for a minute. He ordered the battle cruisers and destroyers to attack, while he himself repeated the " battle turn away." All that he said in his report regarding this hasty retreat was : " The attack by the torpedo-boat flotillas had achieved its purpose. Consequently at 7.17 the line was reversed by simultaneous turn. . . . This was done to counter the encircling movement by the enemy . . . and to hold open our way of retreat." By 7.20 Scheer's second turn away had been safely accomplished, Hipper's battle cruisers and also the attacking destroyers were recalled, and the firing died away. Jellicoe, knowing that the enemy destroyers had attacked, meanwhile acted as he had always intended to do in such circumstances ; nor had the Admiralty disagreed with his intention.[37] He turned away 45° in two stages for about fourteen minutes, and then turned back in the direction in which Scheer's ships had disappeared. It is perhaps in making this and the earlier turn away from the enemy, after having initially placed his fleet in a position of overwhelming advantage, that Jellicoe's tactics can most justly be criticised. The threat from the German destroyers' torpedoes does not now appear to have been sufficiently dangerous to justify movements which were bound to increase the distance between himself and the retiring High Seas Fleet.

At 7.45 Scheer's ships were sighted again by Beatty, who signalled to his commander-in-chief suggesting pursuit ; but by that time the van of the battle fleet, though still far behind, was pressing on to the south-west in Beatty's wake, and little more could be done.

Scheer actually held on to the south-west till well out of range, and then turned south. His plan was to make for the Horn Reef by the shortest route, covering his retreat by destroyer attacks.

At 8.15 Beatty was again in action with Hipper's squadron and the rear German battleships. Jellicoe now steered towards the sound of this renewed fighting, and once again the advantage passed to the British; for the enemy was not only suffering further punishment, but was being forced to the west—the opposite direction to that in which Scheer wanted to steer. The sun had set soon after eight o'clock, but Beatty clung on tenaciously in the gathering darkness until about nine, when he made the last of his many enemy reports. At 9.17 Jellicoe took up his night cruising formation on a southerly course, to await renewal of the action at daylight. Both he and Beatty rejected night action as too hazardous, but expected to gain the final, crushing victory in the early hours of 1st June.

To a generation of naval men who grew up between the wars and fought in the second of them, the decision to decline night action must seem surprising; for the Royal Navy started the second war specially equipped and highly trained for that very purpose, and taking all theatres of that war together, more night than day battles were fought between 1939 and 1945. But while the accepted policy was for the heavy ships not to seek engagement in darkness, and bearing in mind that Scheer and Hipper were both well to the west of our fleet at sunset, the decision to await daylight while covering the Germans' most probable return routes is easily to be understood. All that was needed was to prevent the enemy slipping past to the eastward during the short hours of darkness.

There were, as Jellicoe well knew, three routes by which the enemy might try to reach his home bases. The first was by passing to the west of Heligoland through the minefields, and the second was to make for the Frisian coast and thence steer along the coastal swept channel to the Jade estuary. These were both well covered by the Grand Fleet. The third possibility, however, was to steer south-east directly towards the Horn Reef and thence south along the Danish coast; and this route was less well covered. Jellicoe sent submarines and a minelayer to obstruct this last route, and as a further precaution massed his light forces astern of the Grand Fleet to prevent the enemy slipping across his wake undetected. We had, however, suffered considerable losses and damage to destroyers in the day's fighting, and the Harwich Force, which would have been an invaluable reinforcement at this juncture, was still held in harbour by the Admiralty.

At 9.30 Scheer's van led round in a south-easterly direction, thus converging with the British fleet. First the opposing cruisers, and then the High Seas Fleet's destroyer screen came into action with Jellicoe's rearguard. Though there was a great deal of fierce, close-range fighting and losses were suffered by both sides, no report reached Jellicoe to suggest that enemy heavy ships were involved. Believing that all the fighting was between the light forces, and that Scheer himself was still far to the west of him, Jellicoe held to his southerly course. Now that the positions of both sides' forces can be accurately plotted it is plain that some of our ships, notably the *Malaya* of the 5th Battle Squadron, did sight units of Scheer's fleet; and it must be classed as a grievous error that not one of these sightings was reported to the commander-in-chief.

Confusion is always likely in night encounters, and there was plenty of it on this occasion; but Scheer and his captains knew that their only salvation lay in breaking through to the east. They therefore held stubbornly to their purpose, while their light forces fought well, and held off attacks by our own.

At 10.41 p.m. the Admiralty told Jellicoe that the enemy was returning home on a south-easterly course, but the commander-in-chief did not accept the intelligence. He had already been badly misled once regarding the High Seas Fleet's movements, and he did not know that this information was based on a deciphered enemy signal.[38] A message sent by Scheer asking for air reconnaissance at dawn off the Horn Reef—a plain indication of his intentions —which the Admiralty also took in, was not passed to Jellicoe at all.[39] The failure to pass on all the intelligence which was in the Admiralty's hands, and to indicate that the source from which it was derived made it virtually infallible, certainly contributed to the escape of the High Seas Fleet.

The final chance came at about 1.45 a.m. when enemy battleships were sighted and recognised by the last British destroyer flotilla barring their way. They attacked the rear of the High Seas Fleet and sank one old battleship; but the wireless report of the contact was never received in Jellicoe's flagship. At about the same time, away to the north-east, the Germans were abandoning the hard-hit *Lützow*—the only one of Hipper's battered squadron not to reach harbour.

At 2.30 a.m. Jellicoe turned north again, but by that time Scheer had nearly reached safety. Half an hour later the Admiralty released the Harwich Force, and Commodore Tyrwhitt hurried east with five light cruisers and eighteen destroyers. They were too late to play any part. Finally at

4.15 the Admiralty signalled that at 2.30 Scheer had been only sixteen miles from the Horn Reef, steering in that direction. But the time when use could have been made of this intelligence had long since passed.

Scheer actually stopped off the Horn Reef Light Vessel at dawn, and counted his wounds. "The 1st Scouting Group," he wrote later, "could no longer fight a serious action"; the leading ships of his battle fleet were in little better state, and he had few cruisers left. He therefore "abandoned any further operations"—a remark which sounds, and must have been intended to sound, as though for the previous hours he had been seeking battle, and not merely trying to save himself from what must have seemed certain destruction. At 3.54 a.m. he ordered all his ships to return to harbour.

At daylight Beatty swept across and around the scene of the previous day's fighting, but sighted nothing. The Grand Fleet re-formed into cruising order and remained on the battlefield for eight hours after Scheer reached the Horn Reef. Having concentrated again with Beatty, collected his destroyers, rescued survivors and succoured the cripples, at 11 a.m. Jellicoe set course for Scapa.

Meanwhile *Warspite* was approaching Rosyth, gradually working up speed as her injuries were temporarily patched. At 6 a.m., knowing that he had to pass through one of the U-boat traps originally set to catch our ships as they came out, Captain Philpotts warned all his officers that submarine attack was almost certain, and that every precaution must be taken. His officers and men, exhausted though they were after the previous day's fighting and a night spent in plugging holes and shoring strained or damaged bulkheads, braced themselves to deal with the new menace. "At 9.35 a.m.," states the captain's report, "two torpedoes passed close to the ship, one on either side." Then, just as the escort vessels sent out from Rosyth were joining, " a periscope was sighted close under the bows." The port 6-inch guns opened fire and the captain tried to ram; but the ship was still being steered from the engine-room and it was difficult to manœuvre her. The submarine " was missed by a few yards."

The narrow escape from the U-boats was the last of her adventures. One officer wrote: " I am bound to say I heaved a sigh of relief as we passed under the Forth Bridge, and the cheers from the troops made one feel quite gulpy."⁴⁰ At 3.15 p.m. *Warspite* reached Rosyth and went straight into dock. She was drawing 35½ feet aft at the time, instead of her normal 31 feet. Considering the damage she had sustained, her casualties were remarkably light. Only one officer and thirteen men were killed, and four officers and thirteen men wounded. There could be no finer tribute to the sturdiness and effective protection of her class. Admiral Evan-Thomas signalled to her captain:

" I am much grieved at the sad losses *Warspite* has sustained. I warmly congratulate you on the way she was handled both during the action and afterwards, under most difficult circumstances—with the result that she arrived safely in port. It is hoped that it will not be long before she is able again to take her part in the same gallant manner she did on Wednesday."⁴¹

She stayed in dock until 4th July, and her ship's company were given a brief spell of well-earned leave. On the 22nd she sailed again for Scapa, and rejoined the Grand Fleet next day. But it was a long time before the damage she received at Jutland was permanently made good. When, in 1935, she was under reconstruction at Portsmouth and her hull was stripped right down, it was found that many of her wounds had merely been plated over. Permanent repairs to her plates and frames were thus undertaken nearly twenty years after the battle. Even so, some of the scars she received on 31st May, 1916, remained with her to the end of her days. Though men who in subsequent commissions passed through the after compartments on her main deck may not have realised it, the distortions and unevenness in the deck were caused at Jutland; and the tendency of her steering to give trouble recurred again and again—to the constant anxiety of her later captains.

In conclusion it should be recorded that whereas in England, and especially in the Fleet, the first reports on the Battle of Jutland caused acute disappointment, in the enemy's camp there was great jubilation. The Kaiser endorsed Scheer's report with the remark " Excellent," and the latter claimed, not unreasonably, to have achieved a success. Many months were to elapse before either side was in a position to re-assess the results, especially with regard to the influence of the battle on the war as a whole. It then gradually became clear that in the long view Jutland did much to destroy German hopes of victory. The Kaiser and Scheer himself both seem to have realised this, for the latter ended his report with a warning that although most of the High Seas Fleet would " be ready by the middle of August for further strikes against the enemy . . . nevertheless there can be no doubt that even the most successful outcome of a fleet action in this war will not force England to make peace "; and the Kaiser's marginal comment was the one word " Correct." " A victorious end to the war within a reasonable time," concluded Scheer, " can only be achieved through the defeat of British economic life—that is by using the U-boats against British trade. . . .

I feel it my duty again to advise your Majesty against the adoption of any half-measures." Such, then, became German strategy in 1917; and such was it to become once again in 1939.

The decisive sea battles of history have not left behind them any trail of controversy or of recrimination. But where a clear decision was obtained by neither side there has always been a tendency to criticise the commanders, to analyse their actions and to express opinions regarding what they should have done differently. Several battles in which earlier *Warspites* fought provide good examples of this. After Beachy Head (1690) Torrington and Tourville were both severely criticised, and the former was persecuted to the point of imprisonment, court martial and dismissal.* After the Battle of Malaga (1704), in which Rooke and all with him knew that they had achieved remarkable success, even if the results fell short of a great victory, the admiral was treated little less badly than Torrington; nor was he ever employed again.†

In spite of the forty years which have elapsed since the Battle of Jutland was fought it is still difficult for a historian to analyse impartially the various causes which contributed to the indecisive outcome of the encounter. For one thing the complete records of the battle, and of the aftermath of controversy which followed it, have not yet been made available for study; and until that day arrives certain important aspects of the battle will remain obscure. There are, for example, serious doubts whether the track of Beatty's flagship, the *Lion*, is correctly shown in the narrative which the Admiralty published in 1924. It is known that Admiral J. E. T. Harper, who compiled the official record of the events of 31st May, 1916, believed the reproduced plans of the *Lion*'s movements to be incorrect in certain instances. A second factor is that the strong partisanship aroused by the Jutland controversy of the 1920's produced a great mass of books and articles, very few of which can be classed as completely objective. It is certain that Sir Julian Corbett laboured under severe difficulties and disabilities in his endeavours to write a balanced account in the Official History; for the Admiralty specifically repudiated his work in a more strongly worded disclaimer than is generally inserted in such books. An attempt was made, perhaps too soon after the event, to write an impartial analysis in the form of a confidential "Naval Staff Appreciation"; but it was never issued to the Service. It seems probable, however, that Mr. Churchill's account of the battle owed a good deal to that document; and he, as has already been mentioned, was highly critical of certain of Admiral Jellicoe's actions. To this writer, however, there seem to be few, if any, grounds for criticising Jellicoe's deployment on the port wing column of his fleet; and it is sheer conjecture to suggest, as does Mr. Churchill, that deployment on the centre column would have brought decisive results. Such a hypothesis falls down not only because of its conjectural nature, but because the deployment actually carried out unquestionably placed the British fleet in a position of such great advantage that the enemy at once took drastic action to extricate himself. It seems to this historian that no commander could accomplish more than that in his preliminary movements. It is, however, harder to accept the slowness of Jellicoe's pursuit of the retreating enemy, and the timidity of his two turns away in face of torpedo attacks. To pursue a retreating enemy relentlessly, and to accept great risks while doing so, has always been a cardinal need in maritime war; and victories such as Hawke's at Quiberon Bay or Boscawen's at Lagos, which have already appeared briefly in these pages, could never have been won had those two commanders pursued their enemies less vigorously. The main reason why Jellicoe did not drive home the advantage he had gained seems to have been the rigidity of the tactical principles on which his fleet had been trained. It is, of course, true that well-disciplined movements are essential to successful handling of fleets and squadrons, and to the avoidance of confusion in battle; but to maintain such rigidity at a crisis when a temporary advantage might be turned into a decisive victory seems the negation of effective battle tactics, and the denial of centuries of British tradition. At Jutland the result was to lose a fleeting opportunity which, as so often happens in war, did not recur.

On Beatty's side, the handling of the Battle Cruiser Fleet undoubtedly showed the vigour, and the calculated acceptance of risks, lack of which lost the Grand Fleet its only chance of forcing a decision. But Beatty had ready to hand the strength wherewith to overwhelm Hipper's First Scouting Group. Apart from the defective British shells and the tendency of his ships to blow up, the reason why he did not accomplish that purpose now seems to have been the failure to bring the 5th Battle Squadron into action with his own battle cruisers, and to keep Evan-Thomas's ships in close support throughout the first stages of the encounter. Had the battle cruisers and the four *Queen Elizabeths* been manœuvred in close co-ordination it is hard to see how, in spite of the loss of two of Beatty's ships, Hipper's force could have survived; and the elimination of the 1st Scouting Group would certainly have made Jellicoe's task far easier.

When darkness fell upon the field of battle two im-

portant weaknesses in British training seem to have had
important influence. These were inadequate enemy-
reporting and inefficient night fighting arrangements. In
the latter respect the German fleet was certainly the better
equipped and trained.

There is little doubt that the Admiralty itself contributed to Scheer's final escape by keeping the Harwich
Force in harbour long after the need to guard against a
raid on the east coast towns, or against our cross-Channel
communications, should have been superseded by the need
to concentrate every available ship at the only place where
a decision could be gained. It is likely that political pressure
to protect the coastal towns from bombardments by raiding
forces played a part in holding back Tyrwhitt's ships.
Finally there was the failure to pass on to Jellicoe the
vital intelligence regarding Scheer's movements which
was in the Admiralty's hands.

The post-war discussions on the battle led to no con-
clusions—nor could they very well have done so. But,
happily for Britain, officers such as Captains A. E. Chatfield
and W. W. Fisher,* who had commanded ships at Jutland
and later commanded our major fleets, studied the lessons
of the battle—such as the need for intensive training in
night fighting—to such good effect that they gave the
Royal Navy inestimable advantages in the second war;
while other officers who had fought in a subordinate
capacity on 31st May, 1916, had reached high command
by the time that Germany was ready to renew the challenge
for command at sea. The leadership of such admirals as
Cunningham, Tovey and Vian in the second World War
represented a return to an earlier tradition of less rigid
tactics than Jellicoe's, of the acceptance of heavy risks

* Later Admiral of the Fleet Lord Chatfield and Admiral Sir William Fisher,
Commanders-in-Chief, Mediterranean Fleet, from 27th May, 1930, to 31st October,
1932, and from 31st October, 1932, to 20th March, 1936, respectively.

whenever opportunities arose, for forcing action at close ranges, and for relentless vigour in pursuit. It may therefore be that the real fruits of Jutland did not come to harvest until a quarter of a century later, and were reaped at the River Plate battle, at Taranto and Matapan, in the second Battle of Sirte, in the chase of the *Bismarck* and the sinking of the *Scharnhorst*, and in a hundred lesser fights. But that runs ahead of the stage now reached in our story.

CHAPTER FIVE

From Jutland to the German Fleet's Surrender, 1916-1918

"You have given us their army, and we have given you their fleet."

Field Marshal Sir Henry Wilson to Admiral Beatty
21st November, 1918

THE MONTHS which followed the Battle of Jutland were difficult for the Grand Fleet. In the first place there was acute disappointment that, for all the losses we had suffered, a decisive victory had not been gained. Secondly, and more serious, were the revelations that not only were many of our ships inadequately protected against magazine explosions, but our heavy shells were defective and must be replaced. Thirdly was the fact that the submarine campaign, launched with full virulence after the Germans had come to accept that success could not be obtained by their surface fleet, was soon causing us immense losses of merchant shipping. On 27th November, 1916, Beatty took over command of the Grand Fleet from Jellicoe, who had been appointed First Sea Lord. Responsibility for facing the issues involved in the defective equipment of the fleet therefore lay to a great extent with Beatty. Taken together, the proved vulnerability of our ships and the unsatisfactory performance of our shells made it temporarily impossible for him to win a decisive victory, and doubtfully wise for him to seek battle until such time

as the defects had been remedied. As the new shells for
the big guns could not reach the fleet until the spring of
1918, the commander-in-chief was forced to accept a
defensive strategy which, to a man of his forceful character,
must have been intensely galling. Had the Germans offered
a challenge Beatty would, without doubt, have accepted it,
and would have fought with all his outstanding vigour and
determination; but in the circumstances prevailing for
many months after Jutland, it would hardly have been
wise to entice the enemy to battle.

Beatty chose the *Queen Elizabeth* as his fleet flagship,
but she was not ready for him until February, 1917. The
day when he first hoisted his flag in her marked the beginning of a long tradition, for she and *Warspite* were to share
the honour of flying the white flag with the St. George's
Cross of a full admiral and commander-in-chief, at home
or in the Mediterranean, in almost unbroken continuity
from 1917 until 1941. Beatty was delighted with his choice
of ship, and many later commanders-in-chief—Keyes,
Field, Chatfield, W. W. Fisher and Cunningham—may
have echoed his remark to his wife: " I like my *Queen
Elizabeth* . . . it is no trouble to her to travel at high
speed."[2]

The maritime side of the First World War thus underwent a change of emphasis after the middle of 1916.
Though the Grand Fleet had to be kept at the highest pitch
of efficiency, ready to deal with a renewed challenge for
command of the North Sea, the crisis of the war shifted
to the struggle against U-boats—mainly fought in the
Western Approaches; and after the convoy system had
been adopted in the Atlantic in the spring of 1917 more
and more destroyers had to be diverted to escort duties.
Beatty's broad policy was to maintain efficiency by continuing his predecessor's routine of constant practices and

exercises, to keep up the morale of officers and men by encouraging competitions, entertainments and innumerable educational and social activities; and to take the whole fleet to sea about once a month in order to consolidate the experience gained in the training programmes, and to convince the enemy that British command of the North Sea was as effective as it ever had been. But the truth about the state of his ships' main armament projectiles was carefully concealed from all except a very few highly-placed officers.

In the matter of providing entertainment for the fleet when in harbour, *Warspite* was one of the most outstanding ships. Serving in her was Lieutenant-Commander H. D. Simonds, who possessed quite exceptional gifts as songwriter, producer and stage-manager, and Commander Walwyn himself invariably painted the scenery for all her shows. One well-remembered turn in a variety entertainment was the appearance of the principal medical officer as a snake charmer, complete with a snake which reared up, waved about and hissed to the music of the charmer's pipe. It was actually worked by fine threads of cotton, operated by midshipmen stationed in the wings. One distinguished member of the audience signalled next day: "What a wonderful show! Do tell me how the snake was done." To which Commander Walwyn replied: "There was no snake"—a statement which it took the visitor a long time to live down.[3] Perhaps *Warspite*'s most famous entertainment was a complete light opera to the music of Edward German, called *The Pirates of Mevagissey*. How Simonds got the composer to agree to the use of his *Merrie England* music is not now remembered; nor, unfortunately, have copies of Simond's libretto survived. The setting was Elizabethan and an able seaman called Collins, who "looked the image of Drake in real life," was cast for the part of Drake. The fact that the ship had a large number of Welsh " hostilities only " ratings in her company explains why the singing is remembered to have been superb.⁴

On the 18th of August, 1917, about a month after *Warspite* had rejoined the fleet, she took part in a big operational sweep in the North Sea. In the very early hours of 20th, while steaming darkened and in formation, her helm jammed, and she had to haul out of the line. It was the first warning that the rudder trouble experienced at Jutland had not been reliably remedied. On this occasion she soon got back into station, but the experience was an uncomfortable one, for no one could tell when it would happen again. Then, a few days after the fleet arrived back in Scapa, she was in serious trouble. When returning to her berth in the Flow at night after carrying out firings, she collided with the *Valiant*, which was moving out for similar exercises ; and *Warspite* was extensively damaged. The Board of Inquiry blamed both ships equally and the Admiralty ordered the two captains to be tried by court martial on charges of hazarding their ships. Both were found guilty and sentenced to be reprimanded, and although for technical reasons the sentence on Captain Philpotts was annulled, it can hardly be doubted that this incident, taken with *Warspite's* earlier misadventures, ruined the career of one of the Navy's most able and promising officers. She sailed for Rosyth on the day following the collision, docked at once for repairs and did not rejoin the fleet until 29th September. The last three months of the year each saw another sweep by the Grand Fleet in full strength in the North Sea, but again they did not produce any action. On 19th December Captain Philpotts was relieved in command of *Warspite* by Captain

C. M. de Bartolomé*, and on that same day she went to
sea with the fleet to exercise off the Shetland Islands.

The year 1917 saw great events, which transformed the
whole face of the war. In April the United States at last
declared war, and although it was plain that many months
would elapse before her tremendous strength could be
deployed against the enemy, the long-awaited decision was
immensely encouraging to the Allied cause. But before
any benefits could accrue from that event revolution had
broken out in Russia, and by the end of the year the
Empire of the Tsars had collapsed, and its armed forces
had disintegrated. Germany was thus able to concentrate
most of her military might in the west, and hoped to win
a decisive victory before the American armies had arrived
in Europe in force. At sea the year saw the adoption of
ocean convoys, and then their ever-widening extension.
Tardy though this measure certainly was, it achieved the
defeat of the German submarine campaign. By the end of
1917 our losses of merchant shipping were steadily declin-
ing, and it was plain that the German belief that six months
of unrestricted U-boat warfare would bring Britain to her
knees had been proved false.

Warspite and her sisters of the 5th Battle Squadron
alternated between Scapa and Rosyth throughout the year.
She was at the northern base when at 11.30 p.m. on the
9th July, an internal explosion destroyed the battleship
Vanguard with heavy loss of life. In common with the
rest of the fleet, she sent boats to rescue survivors, but
only two of the 806 officers and men on board at the time
were picked up.[5] At the time it was believed that the
disaster might have been caused by sabotage, and *Warspite*'s
log shows that she thoroughly examined all her own
magazines as a precaution. In fact, it was discovered later

* A complete list of all Captains of the 7th *Warspite* is given in Appendix B.

that the destruction of the *Vanguard*, like that of the *Bulwark* and several other British ships, was almost certainly caused by deterioration of the cordite charges to the point at which they exploded spontaneously.

In the autumn the Germans made two successful attacks with light forces against our Scandinavian convoys.[6] It was exceedingly difficult constantly to protect this important trade against forays by the enemy; for the convoys sailed daily, the German bases lay on the flank of their route between the Shetlands and Bergen, and by making use of bad weather or deceptive ruses it was fairly easy for a fast force to reach the eastern end of the route undetected. After the second attack the western assembly point of the convoys was shifted from the Shetlands to the Firth of Forth, and a battle squadron was included in the covering forces. The real problem posed by these convoy attacks was, as Beatty forcefully pointed out to the Admiralty, that they showed how easily the enemy could surprise and overwhelm our detached forces in the eastern North Sea. What could be done by enemy destroyers and cruisers to one of our convoys and its escorts, could equally well be repeated by a more powerful force against our covering warships. The only security against surprise lay in the Admiralty gaining fore-knowledge of German intentions and movements. And that, for all the remarkably high standard of our naval intelligence throughout the 1914-18 war, the Admiralty could not guarantee. The problems posed by these Scandinavian convoys of 1917 were indeed rather similar to those which faced us in the Arctic in the 1939-45 war, when ships had to be fought through to Russia along a route with enemy bases close off its flank.[7] In November, 1917, in between the two attacks on the Scandinavian convoys, a rather unsatisfactory fight took place in the Heligoland Bight between our light forces, which were endeavouring to attack the German mine-sweepers, and the enemy's covering warships.[8] Although this difficult and depressing year thus had a sombre ending, and the Allied situation on land was far from encouraging, it did at least appear that we were mastering the U-boats; and we knew that in the summer serious disorders had broken out in the High Seas Fleet. Although it was intensely disappointing that the Germans continued to deny the Grand Fleet the opportunity for action, and the material weaknesses already mentioned were still the cause of much anxiety, Beatty was only awaiting the supply of the new shells to entice the enemy to battle once again. Meanwhile he could only watch and contain the High Seas Fleet, envying all the time the luckier ships of the Harwich and Dover forces, which were often at close grips with the enemy, or even the convoy escorts anxiously shepherding their flocks homeward and outward in the Atlantic. The first duties of the Navy were now to bring in the munitions and supplies for the Allied armies, and the food for the British people; and to guard the transports from America bearing the rising tide of the New World's youth ready to fill the terrible gaps torn by more than three years of war in the ranks of British and French manhood.

As Beatty had always expected, the enemy did not neglect the opportunity which our detached forces operating between the Shetlands and Norway offered him.[9] Moreover, he knew that in the important matter of destroyers his fleet was, because of detachments to southern waters or to escort duties, far below strength. Scheer laid his new plans skilfully. A sortie of the High Seas Fleet against our Scandinavian trade and its escorting and covering forces was timed to take place soon after the German armies, greatly reinforced from the eastern front, had launched their offensive of March, 1918, in the west,

and while the British armies in Flanders were reeling
under the impact. In March the Grand Fleet, including
Warspite and the 5th Battle Squadron, had been at Scapa;
but in April it moved once more to Rosyth. On the 22nd
of that month the High Seas Fleet assembled with the
utmost secrecy in the Heligoland Bight. It was entirely
by coincidence that this took place while Admiral Keyes
was launching his famous attack on Zeebrugge; but the
news of that operation had resulted in the Harwich Force
being at sea to cover Keyes' ships, and in the Admiralty
watching and listening most carefully for any sign of movement by the High Seas Fleet. Yet in spite of these pre-
cautions Scheer succeeded in concealing his assembly. His
intention was to attack our convoys and the detached forces
working with them on the 24th of April. In fact a convoy
of thirty-four ships, escorted by a cruiser and two destroyers
and covered by the 2nd Battle Cruiser Squadron and one
light cruiser squadron, sailed from a fiord near Bergen on
the afternoon of the 22nd. In spite of dense fog the convoy
reached the Forth safely on the morning of the 24th.[10] An
outward convoy sailed from Methil in the Firth of Forth
that same evening. Meanwhile Scheer had been delayed
by the same widespread fog, but on the evening of the 23rd
he slipped out into the North Sea undetected. A submarine
which sighted many of his ships mistook them for British
and made no report. None the less on the following morning the Admiralty began to suspect that something unusual
was afoot, and issued precautionary orders. A serious
accident in the engine-room of the German battle cruiser
Moltke, however, forced Hipper to break wireless silence;
and this gave the Admiralty the first firm intelligence that
the main enemy strength was approaching the south-west
coast of Norway. At 10.45 a.m. the Grand Fleet was
ordered to sea. Beatty decided not to recall the outward

convoy and its covering force, and in the early afternoon he sailed with his full strength of thirty-one battleships, including *Warspite*, four battle cruisers, twenty-six cruisers and light cruisers and eighty-four destroyers. Unhappily he was moving against an enemy whose purpose had already failed; for, on finding the convoy route empty at the intended intercepting position, the German forces retired south. When the Admiralty learnt that the High Seas Fleet was withdrawing, Beatty was authorised to return to harbour at his discretion. The only result of the foray was that a submarine hit the damaged *Moltke* with a torpedo; but she got into port. This, though no one could have known it at the time, was the last sortie by the High Seas Fleet as a fighting force. But at the time it seemed alarming that such great enemy strength should have been concentrated in secrecy, and moved successfully to one of our most vulnerable points. Had the enemy's plan been timed for a day earlier or a day later he would probably have succeeded in overwhelming a convoy and its covering force—exactly as Beatty had always warned might happen.

By May the gloom of the early months of the year was lightening. In France and Flanders the enemy had, for all his great advances, not broken through to Paris or the Channel ports; the attacks on Zeebrugge and Ostend had brought light in a dark hour; in the Atlantic not only were merchant shipping losses falling, but American troops were pouring across to Europe in an uninterrupted stream, now rapidly becoming a flood. At the end of May the Germans had broken through the French front on the Aisne, and were pressing on to the Marne—occupying cities which had not previously fallen to them; but by then a great concentration of U-boats against our convoys had failed to achieve substantial results, and there were

700,000 American soldiers under arms in France. The First Battle of the Atlantic had been won, and the spring tide of German success had passed.

The last summer of the war produced no events of striking interest for *Warspite* and her sisters of the Grand Fleet. As they had done throughout so many long and weary months of waiting, they exercised off Scapa or Rosyth, and carried out operational sweeps in the North Sea. But not an enemy was encountered. Meanwhile victory was succeeding victory in France and Flanders, and the end was plainly approaching. In October came the first German feelers for an armistice. On the 21st Scheer recalled all U-boats from the trade routes, and ordered Hipper to take the High Seas Fleet to sea to operate against the Thames. While the Allied leaders were discussing on what conditions an armistice might be granted, the Admiralty became increasingly convinced that the High Seas Fleet was coming out. On 27th of October the enemy's known dispositions and his wireless traffic indicated preparations remarkably like those which had preceded the Battle of Jutland. In fact, Scheer and Hipper intended to provoke a fleet action while armistice negotiations were proceeding. Their intentions may be compared with the Dutch attack on the Medway in June, 1667, which so greatly affected the terms on which the Second Dutch War was concluded.* But the German fleet never went to sea again as a disciplined body. When on 29th October orders were given to raise steam, the crews, divining their leaders' intentions, mutinied. Hipper thereupon dispersed the fleet to various bases. After about a month of discussion between the Allies regarding the proposed armistice —discussions much be-devilled by the sudden publication of President Wilson's famous "Fourteen Points," many

* See p. 39.

of which were quite unacceptable to the governments of Britain and France—the armistice terms were presented on 8th November, and were signed three days later in a railway coach near Compiègne. They included naval clauses ordering that ten German battleships, six battle cruisers, eight light cruisers and fifty modern destroyers should be disarmed and interned at Scapa Flow until disposed of finally at the peace conference. All other German warships were to be disarmed and placed under Allied supervision, and 160 submarines were to be surrendered complete with their armaments and equipment. On 13th November Hipper's representative, Admiral Meurer, arrived at Rosyth in a light cruiser. He was received by Beatty on the evening of the 15th, when one of the most memorable scenes in naval history was quietly enacted in the after cabin of the *Queen Elizabeth*. Next day Meurer returned to Germany bearing orders for the execution of the naval clauses of the armistice.

The German surface ships were to come initially to Rosyth, and the submarines to Harwich. By midnight on the 20th-21st November the High Seas Fleet was known to be 100 miles from the Firth of Forth. We will view the never-to-be-forgotten events that followed mainly from *Warspite*'s bridge. At 2.30 a.m. Captain Hubert Lynes, who had taken over command from Captain de Bartolomé in the previous June, sailed from Rosyth in company with the rest of the fleet. When clear of the defences the thirteen squadrons formed into two gigantic columns each comprising between thirty and forty capital ships and cruisers, and steered to the east. At nine o'clock the Grand Fleet went to " Action Stations." Beatty's orders for the operation had laid down that all ships were to be at " immediate readiness," with their guns trained outboard. The light cruiser *Cardiff* had been sent ahead to make contact with the High Seas Fleet, and soon after 9.30 the first German ships emerged from the mist and murk of a heavily overcast day. The *Cardiff* led the Germans between the two British lines " looking for all the world like a school of Leviathans led by a minnow."[11] When abreast of the Germans the Grand Fleet turned by squadrons through 180 degrees, thus wheeling back on its own track and retaining position on either side of the German line. Overhead flew a British naval airship. By about ten o'clock the whole vast concourse was steering slowly west. The German battle cruisers were in the lead. First came the *Seydlitz*, then the *Moltke, Hindenburg, Derfflinger* and *Von der Tann*—all of them except the new *Hindenburg* Beatty's rivals at Dogger Bank or Jutland. Then came nine battleships—five *Kaiser* class, the new *Bayern* and three of the *König* class. Astern of them the light cruiser *Castor* was leading fifty German destroyers, surrounded by three times that number of British destroyers.* By noon " the great captive fleet " was at anchor in the Firth of Forth and, so noted *The Times* correspondent, " on every side of them were their British warders." Then the main body of the Grand Fleet steamed to its berths. As Beatty's *Queen Elizabeth* passed to her moorings, " she was cheered again and again by the men of the rest of the fleet ". On board *Warspite* a short service of thanksgiving was held before the men dispersed to their midday meal, and from the flagship downwards all the rest of the fleet also offered their thanks to God before the day ended. At sunset the German flag was hauled down in all their ships, and Beatty ordered that it would not be hoisted again without permission. The inspection of the German ships, to ensure that they were properly disarmed, started next day, and they were then transferred to Scapa in batches. In all the long history of British sea-power there had been

---

* Appendix C contains a full list of the Germans ships surrendered.

no parallel to this surrender of an undamaged and virtually complete enemy navy. Only a few days earlier it could still have struck heavy blows—and indeed was expected to do so. Little did the men who dispersed from *Warspite's* decks that day, hearts full of thankfulness for peace regained and victory won, guess that twenty-five years later another company of British seamen would witness the surrender of another enemy fleet from those same decks.*

* See pp. 264-266.

CHAPTER SIX

Between the Wars, 1919-1939

"History shows no instance of sea supremacy once yielded being regained."

From Admiral Beatty's address as Lord Rector of Edinburgh University, 28th October, 1920

ON 7th April, 1919, Beatty's union flag was lowered from the *Queen Elizabeth*'s main mast-head for the last time, and the Grand Fleet ceased to exist.* Its ships were already being dispersed to the various foreign stations where in peace-time British influence was represented and British interests were guarded mainly by the Royal Navy. The two principal fleets were at home and in the Mediterranean, and it was in the former, now re-named the Atlantic Fleet, that the *Warspite* served from 1919 to 1926 and again from 1931 to 1933. Those years were, we now realise, of tremendous importance to the British Empire; for they saw the world-wide maritime control, which Britain had exercised virtually alone for more than a century, replaced by a system of joint responsibility based on the League of Nations; and the old diplomacy gave way to the new era of open conferences between the nations. Part and parcel with these changes were the attempts to combine security with economy through treaties limiting the number and size of the major warships which the great powers would retain, and the armaments which they would mount. At

---

* The union flag flown at the mainmast is the distinguishing flag of an Admiral of the Fleet.

the Washington Conference of 1921 Britain accepted parity with the United States in capital ships, but retained freedom to keep her cruiser strength high enough to meet her world-wide needs—subject only to the limitation of 10,000 tons displacement and 8-inch guns mentioned earlier.* The responsibility for handling these intricate negotiations for the Admiralty lay mainly with Beatty, who became First Sea Lord on 1st November, 1919, and held that office until 30th July, 1927. His general policy was that reductions in naval strength had to be accepted, but that this very fact made it essential to achieve the highest possible quality in the ships which were retained. He and his successors worked consistently along these lines until German rearmament and the plain approach of a new challenge on the seas at last caused the shackles of the naval limitation treaties to be loosened. That Britain was able to hold her own and more than her own at sea, almost unaided, from 1939 to 1941, owed much to the far-sightedness of the naval leaders who strove so hard to preserve what Lord Chatfield aptly called "the essentials of sea defence" throughout the two preceding decades, and to the commanders-in-chief at sea who worked unceasingly to improve the fleet's fighting efficiency.

Admiral Sir Charles Madden, who had commanded the 1st Battle Squadron at Jutland, was the Commander-in-Chief of the newly constituted Atlantic Fleet; and *Warspite* and her sister ships served at first under him in the 2nd Battle Squadron. Various alterations were made to her at this time. Before the end of the war she, in common with most other British battleships, had been fitted with platforms on their two super-imposed turrets from which a light aircraft such as the Sopwith "Strutter" could be launched. The first time *Warspite*'s aircraft were embarked

* See p. 86.

appears, from her log, to have been in November, 1918. To fly off the aircraft, the turrets were trained into the wind, and the aircraft ran down the short platforms to become airborne before they reached the gun muzzles. As it was impossible to land on the launching platforms, the pilots had to come down on shore. The aircraft were then brought back to the ship by lighter, and hoisted inboard by derrick. The intention was to use them for spotting ships' gunfire, and the primitive arrangements described were the forerunners of the hangar and catapult fitted amidships during her reconstruction in 1934-37.*

After serving in home waters throughout 1919, *Warspite* sailed for Gibraltar with the rest of the Atlantic Fleet in January, 1920, to take part in combined exercises with the Mediterranean Fleet. This annual meeting of the two fleets was the occasion for investigating many tactical and technical problems, and was one of the busiest periods of the year. In May our battleship was in home waters again and was ordered to Ireland, where the Sinn Fein troubles were serious. She moved slowly along the south and west coasts, ready to support the Army with her landing parties, should they be needed. Early in June she embarked a Royal Marine battalion at Plymouth, and landed them at Queenstown.

The next two years, 1921 and 1922, passed in very similar fashion, starting with the spring cruise out to the Mediterranean for the combined exercises and then service in home waters. When the long coal and railway strikes of 1921 broke out *Warspite* was sent to Clydeside. There, so one of her officers remembers, " we spent most of our time playing football with the strikers[1]," which was typical of the Navy's tactful conduct during industrial strife. The spring cruise of 1924 brought her first visit to the Mediter-

* See p. 163.

ranean fleet's base at Malta, with which she was to become so intimately acquainted during the next twenty years. On 26th July of that year, soon after the Atlantic Fleet ships had returned home, the first post-war Royal Review took place in Spithead. *Warspite* and most of her sister ships were present. Nearly 200 warships under Admiral Sir John de Robeck were anchored in ten long lines, with the *Queen Elizabeth* and *Barham* at the head of those comprising the big ships. *Warspite* lay two places astern of *Barham*. It was the second time that King George V had reviewed the Fleet, and it had changed greatly since the first occasion in 1911. *The Times* correspondent remarked that there were " craft strange to eyes inexpert, like aeroplane carriers, which seemed all deck and mighty little superstructure."* Little could it be foreseen that King George V's granddaughter would review the Fleet again nearly thirty years later, that all but one of the big ships present would then be the descendants of those same " craft strange to eyes inexpert," and that 300 naval aircraft would fly past in review on that occasion.

After acting as Guard Ship during the Cowes Week sailing regatta, *Warspite* was paid off at Portsmouth to undergo a major refit, and she did not return to service until April, 1926. During the refit she had " bulges " added to her hull. These were external water-tight compartments which ran throughout almost the whole of her length and stretched from some six feet above her waterline almost to the bottom of the ship. Their purpose was to provide additional protection against torpedoes by causing them to explode some distance away from the ship's true hull. All the older British major warships were modified in this manner between the wars. The fitting of

* *The Times* of 28th July, 1924. Two aircraft carriers, the *Hermes* and *Argus*, were present at the 1924 Review.

bulges did, however, reduce *Warspite*'s maximum speed by about 1½ knots. The next steaming trials carried out give her speed as 23½ knots, when developing the same horse-power as previously (75,000). During this refit her aircraft platforms were removed, and she was fitted with four 4-inch anti-aircraft guns and two 2-pounder pom-poms. In consequence of these and other changes her displace-ment had increased from 27,500 tons to 31,300, and she drew slightly more water.

On 6th April, 1926, *Warspite* recommissioned at Ports-mouth, with a complement of fifty-four officers and 871 men, this time for service in the Mediterranean Fleet under Admiral Sir Roger Keyes. All the five *Queen Elizabeths* were being transferred to that station to form the recon-stituted 1st Battle Squadron, in which famous force *Warspite* and her sisters were to fight during a great part of the 1939-45 war. She spent the rest of the month of April at home, carrying out trials and working up efficiency, and was about to leave for her new station when the General Strike broke out. She was ordered to Greenock on 3rd May, the day before the strike started, and at once sent her landing parties ashore to guard Prince's Dock. Other warships were doing the same all round the coasts of Britain. On 12th May the strike collapsed, *Warspite* at once recalled her landing parties and sailed for Malta. She arrived on 20th, and next day hoisted the flag of the Commander-in-Chief, Mediterranean, for the first time.

After eighteen months as fleet flagship *Warspite* was succeeded by *Queen Elizabeth*, and early in 1928 she became a " private ship " once more, under Captain J. F. Somer-ville.* From the fewer entries in her log it is plain that her humbler role had its compensations; for there were none

* Later Admiral of the Fleet Sir James Somerville, G.C.B., G.B.E., D.S.O., commander of the famous "Force H" at Gibraltar from 1940-42 and Commander-in-Chief, Eastern Fleet, from 1942-44.

of the official visits and ceremonial occasions which loomed so large in a fleet flagship's life. On 12th July, however, she suffered another misfortune when she struck an uncharted rock in the Ægean off Skiathos. The ensuing inquiry, however, established that the charts in use, based on a survey done in 1887, were " imperfect," and her officers were therefore acquitted of all blame. The damage to her bottom made it necessary for her to return home, and on 8th November she reduced to two-fifths complement at Portsmouth. On 22nd January, 1929, she recommissioned " as an independent command for further service in the Mediterranean," and subsequently she was ordered to succeed the *Queen Elizabeth* as fleet flagship. She sailed for Malta on 14th March, 1929, but experienced turbine trouble soon after reaching her station. Not until 18th November did she hoist the flag of the Commander-in-Chief, now Admiral Sir Frederick Field.

Warspite's second term as Mediterranean fleet flagship lasted only six months, for in May, 1930, she brought Sir Frederick Field home after he had turned over his command to Admiral Sir Ernle Chatfield*, and the flag was again transferred to the *Queen Elizabeth*. *Warspite* docked at Portsmouth, after which she, the *Barham* and *Valiant* all joined the 2nd Battle Squadron in the Atlantic Fleet. Our ship went out to Gibraltar each year for the combined exercises, but otherwise saw little of her former station for a time. It was while returning from Gibraltar to Portsmouth on 21st March, 1933, with *Valiant* astern that, in thick fog off the mouth of the Tagus, she was rammed on her starboard side by the Roumanian steamer *Peles*. Most of the damage sustained by the battleship was above water, and after building a temporary cofferdam round the

---

* Now Admiral of the Fleet Lord Chatfield, P.C., G.C.B., O.M., K.C.M.G., C.V.O., etc., 1st Sea Lord 21st January, 1933, to 6th September, 1938, and subsequently Minister for the Co-ordination of Defence.

damaged section she proceeded on her course. After being repaired *Warspite* rejoined the 2nd Battle Squadron in May, 1933. But her service with the fleet lasted only six months, and in December of the same year she " reduced to reserve " at Portsmouth. The reason was that the Admiralty had obtained approval to spend a considerable sum of money on entirely modernising certain capital ships.

By the naval limitation treaties of the 1920's Britain was not allowed to possess more than fifteen capital ships. The *Nelson* and *Rodney* (laid down 1922, completed 1927) had been the only new ships of that type built since the end of the war; and except for the five *Queen Elizabeths*, the five *Royal Sovereigns* and three battle cruisers the whole of the mighty Grand Fleet of 1918 had been scrapped. In the early 1930's stringent economy was still the order of the day in Britain; and for all that the rise of Hitler and Mussolini plainly indicated that the sands of peace were running out, the Admiralty knew full well that it was hopeless to press the government of the day to replace the ageing battle fleet with new construction. Not until the 1937 naval programme was approval given to start the capital ships which finally entered service during the second World War as the five *King George V* class. Meanwhile the Admiralty had to face the increasingly urgent problem of adapting the ships they were allowed to retain to the changed conditions of the new era then opening. This could only be done by completely modernising them. It was not a wholly satisfactory substitute for building new ships, but it had the advantage of costing less than replacement. This appealed to the politicians and the Treasury, and permission was therefore given gradually to take in hand the five *Queen Elizabeths* and the battle cruiser *Renown*. The modernisation had, of course, to be done within the terms of the naval treaties, which had limited capital ship displacement to 35,000 tons, even though it was already suspected that Germany and Japan were actively engaged in building ships in defiance of the treaty terms.[2]

The *Warspite*, now nearly twenty years old, was the first to be reconstructed. She was followed by the *Renown*, the *Valiant* and the *Queen Elizabeth*. The two latter ships did not complete until after war had broken out, and the *Barham* and *Malaya* were never taken in hand. The programme started in 1934 was thus never finished; but the reconstruction of the four ships actually completed was an outstanding success, and they all proved invaluable in the 1939-45 war. Rarely can new wine have been more successfully poured into old bottles, or money have been spent by a Navy to better purpose than in rejuvenating the *Warspite* and her sisters. It cost, in the case of *Warspite*, £2,362,000 —less than one-third of the cost of the *Nelson*, and far less than the later-built *King George V* class; and it gave the Navy what was virtually a new ship. It will be convenient now to summarise the work undertaken.

Firstly, the main propelling machinery was entirely renewed. The twenty-four Yarrow boilers were replaced by only six Admiralty-type boilers of modern design, capable of developing the same horse-power. The two original funnels were removed, and the boiler up-takes were led into one large funnel. This cleared her upper works to give room to mount the greatly increased anti-aircraft armament, and gave those weapons good arcs of fire. Completely new geared turbines were built for her by the Parsons Marine Engineering Company at Wallsend-on-Tyne. To protect the ship better against air attack the deck armour was increased to 5½ inches over the machinery spaces and magazines. The turret roofs were removed, and the 15-inch guns lifted out. Messrs. Vickers-Armstrong then modified the turrets in their Elswick-on-Tyne works*, to increase the maximum elevation of the guns from 20 to 30 degrees. This, combined with the design of a new projectile, increased the range of the big guns from about 23,500 yards to 32,000 yards.[3] The turret machinery, however, was left practically unaltered, and worked exceedingly well in the new conditions—no small tribute to those who had originally designed it. The secondary armament was reduced from the original eight 6-inch guns on each broadside to half that number, and two 4-inch twin anti-aircraft mountings were fitted above each 6-inch battery. Above her 4-inch guns, abreast the single funnel, two 8-barrelled multiple 2-pounder pom-poms (which the sailors quickly nicknamed " Chicago pianos ") were fitted on each side, and on the superimposed turrets *(each of)* *(B & X)* were placed two multiple 0.5-inch (4-barrelled) machine guns. It will thus be seen how the emphasis on anti-aircraft defence was greatly increased. She now carried no less than 1,394 tons of ammunition, of which about 1,000 tons was for her main armament.

To control the fire of the armaments entirely new equipment was supplied, embodying the experiences of the first war and of the intervening years. The " Admiralty Fire Control Tables " for the 15-inch and 6-inch guns were made by Messrs. Elliott in their Century Works at Lewisham, while the anti-aircraft fire control equipment came from the Crayford and Barrow works of Messrs. Vickers-Armstrong. All this complicated equipment was installed by Portsmouth dockyard in co-operation with the firms concerned. An immense amount of electrical machinery had to be added in connection with it, and the whole ship was entirely re-wired.

---

* It was in these works that *Warspite*'s turrets were originally built (see p. 89). The two firms of Sir W. G. Armstrong-Whitworth and Vickers had been merged in 1928 as Vickers-Armstrong.

* often referred to as 'multi-machine guns' or 'MM' or 'MMG' on ships' plans etc.

On the upper deck, abaft the funnel, a hangar was built to accommodate two Swordfish Torpedo-Spotter-Reconnaissance aircraft, and a catapult was fitted for launching them. Two electric cranes were added to hoist the aircraft inboard on recovery from the sea. The main functions of these aircraft were to carry out reconnaissance for the fleet, and to spot for their own ship's gunfire. Pilots, observers and maintenance crews from the Fleet Air Arm were added to the ship's complement when she re-commissioned.

The bridge structure was entirely re-designed, to meet the needs of a modern fleet flagship, and to carry the new control positions for all the many armaments. It will easily be realised, and is well shown by comparing the photographs taken in 1937 with those which showed her earlier form, how these changes entirely altered the appearance of the ship. For all that she was no longer in her first youth, she now had a modern and streamlined appearance.

To carry out this great programme Portsmouth dockyard first of all stripped the ship down to her bare hull, and then opened up a huge cavity amidships to remove the main machinery. When she was no more than an empty hulk the inner bottom was entirely rebuilt (the first time such work had ever been undertaken), the engine-rooms were sub-divided into eight compartments, and the boiler-rooms were divided longitudinally.[4] These measures strengthened the hull and greatly improved the watertight integrity of the ship. The opportunity was also taken to make permanent repairs to the hull damage suffered at Jutland, as was mentioned earlier.*

By the middle of 1936 the reconstruction had progressed far enough for the Admiralty to start appointing the specialist officers to the ship. The first sight they

* See pp. 134-135.

gained of her was not attractive, for she was then a rusty hulk, still with an immense cavity amidships, lying alongside a wall in a Portsmouth basin. But things were in fact beginning to move, and to move fast. It is always the case when building or refitting a ship that chaos appears for a long time to reign supreme; it seems that order will never return to her, and that she cannot possibly complete to her date. Then, quite suddenly, the various items are finished, the workmen remove themselves and all the paraphernalia of ship-building, the sailors thankfully start to clean up, and she regains a ship's identity.

In October, 1936, a formidable programme of trials was approved by the Admiralty, and soon afterwards she commissioned to carry them out. It should perhaps be explained that before the ship's officers take over the machinery and equipment for which they are to be responsible, trials are invariably carried out by the contractors in conjunction with officers from the Admiralty and the naval technical schools, in order to make sure that everything is working satisfactorily. The ship's officers are present at all these trials, and in their own interests they follow them very closely, but they do not carry any responsibility for the equipment until the day comes to sign the completion form stating that they are satisfied to take it over.

On 8th March, 1937, the reconstructed *Warspite* left the dockyard to start her trial programme. Four days later, when steaming at full power, the helm jammed at hard-a-starboard. It was at once plain that, although a new steering engine had been fitted, the capriciousness of her rudders still remained; but there was nothing that could be done about it at the time, and she went on to Plymouth for the rest of the programme. It was at least satisfactory that on 15th March she steamed eight hours at full power, with her engines developing over 80,000 horse-power, and made good a speed of 23.84 knots. On the 18th she returned to Portsmouth for her gunnery and aircraft catapult trials. These included firing each weapon at maximum elevation and depression, to test the mountings and the ship's structure. The rounds which *Warspite* fired from her 15-inch guns at their extreme range of some 16 miles nearly caused a bad accident; for in misty weather a large Royal Mail liner passed unseen across her line of fire at the critical moment, and two 15-inch shells fell close to her. This, as the liner's master reported, caused some understandable alarm among her 800 passengers. Luckily no damage was done; but the narrow escape of the liner showed once again, and not for the last time, that the battleship's wicked fairy had not been exorcised by the reconstruction, and was still capable of playing some unkind pranks on her officers.[5] Worse was to follow.

On 29th June she commissioned to full complement for service as Mediterranean Fleet Flagship under Captain V.A.C. Crutchley, V.C.* Her complement of officers and men, which had originally been 993, but had been steadily increasing during the last twenty years, was now 1,183 in peace and 1,218 in war.

On 5th July *Warspite* sailed for what should have been her acceptance trials. She was to have her final inspections a week later and then sail for Malta; for Sir Dudley Pound, the Commander-in-Chief, Mediterranean, was pressing for the arrival of his new flagship. But her wicked fairy decided otherwise. Captain F. H. W. Goolden, who had been in command during the trials, had told his successor that he was not happy about the ship's steering gear, and as the Admiralty's orders permit a captain to carry out what movements he likes during the final acceptance trial Captain Crutchley decided to impose a severe test on the

---

* Now Admiral Sir Victor Crutchley, V.C., K.C.B., D.S.C.

ship. He took her into "action" against an imaginary enemy at high speed, acting as though he himself was under air and submarine attack the while. This involved the use of full rudder, and it was while so turning that the helm jammed again.[6] This was, perhaps, not unexpected; but the wicked fairy did not reveal the full extent of her wickedness until the ship was going up harbour that evening.

Ominous grinding noises were then heard from one set of turbine gearing, the shaft in question was stopped and the ship went up harbour on only three propellers. Inspection revealed serious damage to the coupling between the turbines and the gearing, and expert opinion held that it must have been caused by some movement either of the hull or of the engines.[7] To repair the damaged couplings was fairly simple, but to find the cause of the trouble, and prevent it recurring, was much more difficult. In August another series of trials was started, and it was then discovered that the trouble only occurred when turning at high speed under full rudder, and that it could be prevented by slowing down the outer shafts. But it took from August, 1937, to January, 1938, many trips to sea, two dockings and the turning of innumerable circles to discover this. One can understand that Admiral Pound's feelings towards his recalcitrant flagship were, by that time, hardly such as to assure her a warm welcome to his fleet. Furthermore, an incident which meanwhile took place among her ship's company made matters worse than ever.

When *Warspite* re-commissioned her crew was drawn from Chatham depot, in spite of the ship being at Portsmouth. In those days such arrangements had sometimes to be accepted in order to preserve the drafting balance between the three naval depots; but the Admiralty always tried to avoid commissioning a ship at a different port

from her crew's home depot. The reason for the universal
dislike of such a practice was that it made it difficult for
the men to see as much as possible of their families during
their last weeks in England before going abroad for several
years. In *Warspite*'s case certain other circumstances, quite
outside the control of the ship's officers, added to the
inevitable difficulties produced by her crew having been
drawn from Chatham. In the first place the prolonged
trials with entirely new machinery and equipment, sometimes of uncertain performance, placed a very heavy strain
on the technical officers and their staffs. Something has
already been told of the engine-room department's troubles;
but the gunnery staff had its own worries, and in fact the
gunnery officer, fully supported by his captain, had refused
to take the ship over at the first " completion conference."
On the upper deck the commander was also unenviably
placed. The first executive officer appointed by the
Admiralty was suddenly exchanged to the Home Fleet
flagship, the *Nelson*. Commander D. H. Everett took over
a ship which he had to prepare to undertake the very
special responsibilities of a fleet flagship in what at first
appeared likely to be a quite inadequate time. It has been
told how the commander-in-chief was pressing for the
ship's arrival. To ask for the ship to be made to look like
a fleet flagship, what time dockyard or contractor's work
was proceeding all the time on board was to ask an impos-
sibility. It is probably true that the exceptionally heavy
demands led to the ship's company being driven hard;
but the British sailor never minds hard work—so long as
he understands the reason for it and gets the leave to
which he feels himself fairly entitled. It was over week-
end leave that trouble occurred, and the subsequent
inquiry established that a tiny minority of the men (in
fact, about half a dozen) had used the difficulties of the

period to stir up disaffection on the lower deck when it was announced that they were required to return from their last week-ends at Chatham by the usual hour of 7 a.m. on Monday morning. This meant leaving their homes late on the Sunday night.

At about 10 p.m. on 30th June, the day after the ship had commissioned to full complement, it was reported to the duty commanding officer that a meeting of an unlawful character was in progress on the mess-deck, and he informed the captain. Captain Crutchley assembled the men not yet turned in on the quarter-deck, and addressed them on their supposed grievance, and on the manner in which such matters should be represented. Next day the captain reported what had happened to the chief of staff to the Commander-in-Chief, Portsmouth. It seems likely that nothing more would have been heard of an incident which no one at the time regarded very seriously, had not the ship been delayed and had not one of the few trouble-makers communicated with a newspaper. Once that happened the Admiralty was bound to step in.

The upshot was that Admiral Sir Max Horton, then commanding the Reserve Fleet and later to become famous as Commander-in-Chief, Western Approaches, was ordered to conduct an inquiry. The report which the Board of Enquiry made to the Admiralty remains, of course, secret; but the ship's officers were bound to become aware of its general trend. A few of those who had been examined were commended for their actions; others were censured. The Admiralty's decisions were made known to the public at the end of August, when it was announced in the press that the handling of the situation (which had arisen in June) " could not be regarded as entirely satisfactory."[8] The commander, first-lieutenant and captain of marines were relieved, three ratings were discharged from the

Service and nine or ten were drafted to other ships.*
Commander G. B. Amery-Parkes succeeded Commander
Everett as Executive Officer, and everyone hoped that a
curtain of oblivion would be drawn over an unhappy
scene; for the urgency of the ship's departure had disappeared with the need to locate the cause of her machinery
troubles. But the incident and its repercussions were
bound to reach the ears of Sir Dudley Pound, whose out-
look towards his absent and mechanically recalcitrant
flagship was not thereby improved. It would have been
hard to devise a worse start to any ship's commission—let
alone a fleet flagship's. The wicked fairy temporarily had
the upper hand; but thereafter she was to lose ground
steadily, even though she did attempt to make several come-
backs; and she was finally exorcised, after nearly thirty
years of malign activity, in the blaze of glory with which
the *Warspite* covered herself in the second World War.

The postponement of the ship's departure actually had
the effect of giving her new company a far better chance
to settle down, to get the ship running smoothly, and to
take the first steps on the road towards fighting efficiency
than had at one time seemed possible.[9] It will therefore
be a convenient moment to say a little about the organisation and running of a ship such as *Warspite*. Of her total
war complement of 1,284, 28 officers and 452 men belonged
to the "Executive" or Seaman's branch. They and the
Royal Marines, who numbered five officers and 138
"other ranks," manned and fought the whole of the
the armaments. Of the remainder of her company, some
260 belonged to the engine-room department, whose

* (a) All the officers relieved from *Warspite* received new sea-going appointments a short while later, and Commander Everett earned distinction in the *Ajax*
at the Battle of the River Plate (13th December, 1939). He retired as a rear-
admiral after brilliant war service.

responsibility was of course the main and auxiliary machinery of the ship. Smaller departments included the torpedo-men, who maintained all the electrical equipment, the communication ratings (signalmen and telegraphists), the Fleet Air Arm, which had charge of the aircraft, and the paymaster's staff, who were responsible for feeding the ship's company, for keeping the ledgers in which all the officers' and men's pay accounts were recorded, and who also had charge of the large emporium of miscellaneous stores needed to keep the ship running. In *Warspite*'s case six months' supply of some 10,000 different items of stores, weighing in all nearly 400 tons, were supplied to her initially by the Admiralty's Naval Store Department.

It will thus be seen that there were three sides to the organisation of the ship. The first was concerned with training the crews of all the armaments, with maintaining the weapons in condition for immediate use, and with fighting them in battle; secondly, there was the engineering side, which moved the floating arsenal about the seas and supplied the steam, electric and hydraulic power needed to work all its machinery; while the third was the domestic side, which dealt with feeding, clothing and accommodating a community of over a thousand souls, and with the men's recreation and welfare. In battle, however, every man had his special station, from the director layer in the control tower who actually fired the 15-inch guns, to the Stores assistant, who might be handling cordite in a magazine instead of tinned herrings in the issue-room.

The seamen were organised in three divisions, called Fo'c'sle, Top, and Quarter deck (names descended from the era of sail), each of which was commanded by a divisional officer. They were responsible for the good order and cleanliness of their part of the upper deck and for their own men's mess-decks, and also looked after the welfare of all their men. Each of the seamen divisions manned one-quarter of the armaments, the other quarter being manned by the Royal Marines. The organisation of the ship in peace-time was thus the same as would be needed in war.

The senior lower-deck ratings, the chief and petty officers, were divided equally between the divisions. They had their own "enclosed" messes, which gave them a certain amount of privacy, and were served by "mess-men," who were junior ratings of the branch to which the mess belonged. This was a popular job, for it carried with it certain privileges, such as standing fast from most calls for the hands. The Leading Rates and junior men all messed in "broadside messes," which consisted of a scrubbed deal table, two benches, and a locker for crockery and cutlery. The whole of the ship's company except the master-at-arms, the head of the ship's police and the senior man of the lower deck, slept in hammocks—as did the two or three dozen midshipmen. In daytime the hammocks were lashed up into tight sausage-rolls and stowed in "nettings." In the evening each man slung his own hammock between two hooks fixed to the overhead deck-beams. To pass around the mess-decks at night one had to crouch nearly double, beneath serried rows of men sleeping like caterpillars in their winter cocoons. It is fashionable to-day to regard sleeping in a hammock as something of a hardship, when compared with a bunk; but the older hands may be forgiven for doubting whether there is really any foundation for this feeling. A well-slung hammock was warm in cold weather and could be laid or slung on deck if it was hot; and because it swung with the motion of the ship it certainly gave the occupant less disturbed sleep in rough weather than a bunk. Apart from the hammock and a share of his mess, each man had only a locker in which to keep his clothes and personal possessions. In spite of the small space allocated to him for his entire wardrobe the standard of smartness among the men was exceedingly high. Once out of working clothes they were always able to appear ready for shore in spotless "flannel" (the equivalent to a landsman's shirt), and well-pressed "Number 1 suit" with gold badges.

The feeding of the ship's company was, of course, a matter of the highest importance—and presented no small difficulty to the paymaster commander and his hard-worked victualling and galley staffs. The size (and the appetite) of the community to be fed, and the small space available in which to prepare and cook the food presented daunting problems. Keeping the dishes hot and distributing them to the messes before they were spoilt was scarcely less difficult, though the recent introduction of electrically heated cupboards in the galley servery and in all the enclosed messes improved matters in this respect. There was, however, no escape from the fact that cooking had to begin many hours before the meal was to be eaten, and an egg and bacon fried at 3 a.m. might well appear past its best by 7 breakfast.

After the 1914-18 war a system of "General Messing" was gradually introduced by the Admiralty throughout the fleet.[10] It replaced the custom whereby each mess took up its own rations, and the "cooks of messes" for the day (who were only seamen or stokers) prepared the dishes according to their fancy, took them to the galley for cooking and then recovered them at meal-times. Though many of the old-time sailors prided themselves on the skill with which they prepared and served the food, the system produced insuperable problems to the galley staff, who might be required to cook a score of different dishes for a like number of messes. It was not without some opposition from the fleet that this was replaced by the paymaster himself taking up in cash the sum of money laid down by the Admiralty as the equivalent to the earlier "standard ration" of food and "messing allowance," which each mess had formerly drawn for its own use.* The paymaster now decided the daily menu for the whole ship's company. The opposition to the scheme, which actually faded out quite rapidly, stemmed mainly from the fact that "General Messing" deprived the men of all individual choice of what they wished to eat; but it was rapidly shown to be far more economical and efficient, and once it was properly established there was never any likelihood of the fleet reverting to the older system.

The planning of this formidable task of catering for over 1,000 men lay with the paymaster's victualling staff. *Warspite*'s refrigerator space could contain about twenty tons of fresh meat and fish, while fifteen tons of vegetables and potatoes were carried in special upper-deck stowages. The flour store held fifty tons of flour, which was issued to the electric bakery as needed to bake bread daily for the entire complement. These supplies enabled fresh food to be provided for thirty days in the case of meat and fish, and for two or three weeks in the case of vegetables. About 150 tons of every conceivable type of tinned and dried provisions were also carried, so that should fresh supplies run out a balanced diet could be provided for a further 100 days.[11] Whenever the ship arrived in port replenishment with fresh food was one of the first tasks to be tackled. In a British naval base the greater part came from the victualling stores in the dockyard; but in foreign ports the paymaster had to meet his requirements by buying

---

* This "General Mess Allowance," which was 1s. 3.2d. per man per day in 1940, is to-day (January, 1957) 3s. 2.7d. The corresponding figures for the "Victualling Allowance" for officers are 1s. 5.5d. and 3s. 5.8d. The change of values which has come to pass is well shown by the fact that a 1 lb. tin of corned beef which cost 6d. in 1940 is now issued at 2s. 4d.

from ship chandlers or contractors. In peace-time it was rare for a ship to run out of fresh food, but in war, and especially on long-drawn operations such as Arctic convoys, this was by no means uncommon, and all ships carried about 14 days' supply of "hard tack" (mostly biscuit and corned beef) to meet emergencies.

About 1,000 gallons of rum, enough for the daily issue to be made for at least three months, was stored in the ship's spirit-room. It was issued neat to chief and petty officers, but for the junior ratings it was mixed with three parts of water and served out as "grog." The reason for this was that grog will not keep, and so the temptation to save up the ration was removed. Men who did not take up their spirits could draw an allowance of 3d. a day instead, and in the days when pay was very low it was common for married men to prefer the small increment of pay to the daily "tot."

Once a fortnight the entire ship's company was paid. The men stepped up to a table, at which stood the paymaster or one of his staff with envelopes containing the cash sums due to them. A writer called the men's names from the ledger and the amount each was to be paid, the men took off their caps and held them out, and on to them the Paymaster tipped the contents of the envelopes. Few men took the whole of their pay in cash on these occasions. Most of them were remarkably thrifty, and either allotted a large proportion of their earnings to wives or mothers, or left a sum in the ship's savings bank. The cash which they took on pay days was generally the bare minimum needed to meet their small mess accounts for extra supplies bought at the ship's canteen, to buy tobacco and clothing, and to allow them their occasional "run ashore." When *Warspite* recommissioned the basic pay of an able seaman was 3s. per day, and of a petty officer was 6s. This could be augmented by Good Conduct badges (3d. each per day), by qualifying for a specialist rate (3d. in the case of seaman gunner or seaman torpedo-man), and by the "grog money" already mentioned. To-day (1957) the equivalent earnings of an able seaman and petty officer are 17s. and 28s. respectively, and it may be felt that at last the country's seamen are receiving payment which represents the true value of their services.

Tobacco was issued fortnightly, generally at the same time as "slops," as the paymaster's clothing stores were called. The tobacco could be taken in the form of leaf, or in half-pound tins. It was of excellent quality and, being duty-free, it cost only 1s. 10d. per lb. This was one of the sailor's most valuable privileges, and it is even more so to-day when the duty on tobacco has reached astronomic heights. Though cigarette smoking was increasing, the older men looked on it with scorn, and themselves still made up their own "pricks" of pipe tobacco from the raw leaf—an art which has now almost died out. The "slops" were also of excellent quality, and extremely cheap. Tailoring or "jewing" firms soon established themselves in every ship, and made up serge or duck suits to the order of their messmates. The sailor took great pride in the cut of his jumper and the shape of his "bell-bottoms," and the "jewing" firms were expert at producing the tight waist line and close fit over the hips which their customers liked to show off on shore. Firms of cobblers, called "snobs," would also soon set themselves up, as would "tickler" firms, who made up tobacco into cigarettes for a small charge. Many of the long-service seamen were more than handymen; they were very fine craftsmen in rope, wire, canvas and other materials. No ship was long in commission before the results of their work began to appear in the parts of the ship which were their responsibility. Boats' crews took great pride in beautifying their boats with white duck cushion covers, tasselled curtains of duck and blue jean over the cabin windows, "turks heads" worked on to boat-hook staves and "coach whipping" on white cotton manropes—all kept spotlessly clean.

A visitor from the shore who came off to a ship such as *Warspite* by boat might, as he viewed her from a distance, think her lines more symbolic of strength than of grace; for she lay squarely in the water, and the severe horizontals of her decks met the vertical lines of the funnel and bridge superstructures unrelieved by any curves. He might also be surprised that she did not seem larger; but that illusion would be dispelled as soon as he climbed up the accommodation ladder to her vast quarter-deck, and saw the big guns of the after turrets reaching out over his head like a giant's fingers. Beneath him as he stood on the quarter-deck were five more decks, while he would have to climb up steel ladders to six others before he reached the compass platform. If he penetrated inside the ship alone he would quickly become lost, so we will provide a young midshipman as guide, to take him on a brief tour of the ship. The first impression after passing through one of the screen doors leading off the quarter-deck would be of an interminable succession of white-painted steel passages, all brightly lit, and with decks covered by "Corticene"— a heavy linoleum—scrubbed to a pale brown colour. Other passages join the ones he passes along, and at intervals steel ladders give access to the decks above and below him. Each companion-way is fitted with a heavy steel hatch, normally hooked back, but closed by chain and pulley in action. On the main deck the hatches are enormously heavy, of 5-inch-thick armour-plate. On other decks they are from one to three inches thick. The visitor is warned to mind his head, for there are many obstructions to catch the unwary, and to beware of barking his shins as he steps over the coaming which surrounds every hatch and doorway through which he passes. He would notice the steady whirring of the ventilating fans which keep the air fresh inside the ship, while the constant human traffic passing and repassing may make him feel as though he has entered a beehive, full of the hum of its ceaselessly moving and working inhabitants. The midshipman guide takes our visitor off the quarter-deck by the starboard screen door, above which is the ship's name in large brass letters and scrolls emblazoned with the "battle honours" won by her and her ancestors.* The guide discreetly hurries the visitor past doors which actually give access to the captain's and other senior officers' cabins. Then he sees an enormous piece of machinery stretching right across the ship—the aircraft catapult mechanism. On the outboard side he next passes the gun-room and warrant officers' messes, and as the guide is a midshipman he allows the visitor a brief glance into his own mess, in which about two dozen young gentlemen like himself live under the strict discipline of the sub-lieutenant. The space is mostly taken up by a long polished mahogany table, with a cushioned settee running along the ship's side. At one end is a sideboard with a trap-hatch giving access to the pantry, and at the other a couple of arm-chairs (not for use by junior midshipmen) face an electric fire. It is a small enough home for the numbers accommodated in it, but they are a noisy, happy community, and would probably be surprised if the visitor remarked on the austerity of the furnishings and the congestion in which the midshipmen live. The warrant officers' mess next door has rather more comfort and considerably less congestion, and the wardroom officers live

* See pp. 286-287 for *Warspite*'s battle honours.

on the other side of the ship in a still higher degree of comfort. Each officers' mess has its own oil-fired galley, and its own small staff of cooks and stewards. The system of messing varied in the fleet according to the preference of the officers. In some cases it was left entirely in the hands of a messman, but the custom of nominating an officer to feed the mess on lines similar to the men's General Mess system was fairly common.

Our visitor is next led through the starboard 6-inch-gun battery, and notices the casemates inside which the guns revolve. On the inner side he passes the drying-room for the men's clothes and the ship's bakery. Forward of the bakery are the enclosed messes belonging to chief and petty officers of various branches. Each has its own pantry fitted with electric hot-cupboards and sinks for washing up. The furnishing is similar to that of the gun-room, but rather more austere, and even these senior ratings live in a space which, by shore-going standards, is very congested. Forward of the messes, in the eyes of the ship, are the men's "heads" (or lavatories), divided according to the seniority of the ratings who use them. Only the most senior have the privacy of enclosed w.cs.

The visitor is next taken aft along the port side of the ship, past more enclosed messes, to the port 6-inch battery, where he is shown the men's canteen and the issue-room for provisions. The former, which is run by the N.A.A.F.I., is really a general shop in which luxuries not issued under the General Mess system can be bought, and all the day-to-day purchases of the community can be made. Prices are low, and the greater part of the profits is paid to the Ship's Fund, which is administered by the canteen committee and meets the needs of the ship for such items as games equipment. The visitor next passes the wardroom, returns briefly to the quarter-deck, and then follows his guide down on to the main deck where, right aft, are the admiral's quarters, the staff office and many of the officers' cabins. He notices where the armoured barbette of the after turret passes through the ship, and as he walks past it forward again he enters the armoured citadel which encloses all the ship's vitals. Here he has thick steel beneath his feet and on both sides of the ship outboard of him. Doors and hatches are heavier, and movement correspondingly more difficult. On this level he comes first to the Royal Marines mess-deck, which is traditionally sited between the ship's company and the officers' quarters, and then to the main mess-decks, occupied by seamen on one side and stokers on the other. Here live the great majority of the 1,200 souls aboard. The broadside messes vary only in size, which is decided by the space available for the scrubbed wooden table. They accommodate from twelve to twenty men, and at meal-times there is just room for them all to sit at the table. At the ship's side end of each table is fixed a locker for cutlery, crockery and " ready use " provisions such as tea, sugar and tinned milk. A " bread basket," until recently of scrubbed oak but now of white enamel, completes the simple furnishings. When not in use the tables can be slung from overhead brackets and the benches put aside with legs folded. The mess-deck is cleared in this manner daily for cleaning, and whenever the ship prepares for battle, in order to allow clear passages for traffic. In action the benches and tables may be used by repair parties to shore up damaged bulkheads and to stop holes. Fixed to the deck-beams overhead are the hooks from which the men's hammocks are slung at night. It is, perhaps, now—especially if the midday " dinner " has just been served—that the visitor would realise the severe austerity and acutely congested conditions in which the great majority of his country's sailors lived. The Admiralty makes, and is still making, constant endeavours to improve the conditions; but there can be no easy solution to the problem, because a warship has to carry very large numbers of men to steam her and to man her armaments, and fighting efficiency will always have to take precedence over comfort. Indeed, the ever-growing complexity of warship equipment must tend to make congestion worse. In *Warspite*'s case nearly 200 more men had to be accommodated inside the same hull after she had completed her modernisation in 1937.

After walking through the main mess-decks the visitor leaves the armoured citadel where the forward turret's barbette passes down through the ship, and then finds himself outside the comparatively spacious and beautifully equipped sick bay. After the mess-decks this seems like an oasis of tranquillity, and the few men occupying the comfortable cots probably show appreciation of the luxury which sickness has temporarily made their lot. The equipment of the operating theatre and dispensary would not be despised by a shore hospital. In action, this is, of course, the main station for dealing with casualties. Forward of the sick bay, and like it running right across the ship, is the main chief petty officers' mess, which is fitted out on similar lines to the enclosed messes on the deck above, already described. Lastly, in his walk along the main deck the visitor comes to the cells, where malefactors may be confined for a maximum of fourteen days under the captain's powers of summary jurisdiction. In a happy ship, such as *Warspite* was, they were generally unoccupied.

Below the main deck the visitor can no longer walk from end to end of the ship. The division into water-tight compartments makes it necessary to climb down ladders into the various compartments. Officers' cabins occupy the after part of the Middle Deck, and the men's bathrooms and dressing-rooms fill the whole centre section on both sides of the ship. All the different ratings and branches—chief and petty officers, seamen, stokers, marines and so on—have their own bath-rooms, and each has a small dressing-room next door to it. The bathrooms have about two dozen basins with hot and cold water laid on, and also showers. It is perhaps in this respect that there has been the greatest improvement in the amenities of warship life in recent years. Laundries were also being fitted in the fleet, and the old habit of each man washing his own clothes in a bathroom, or in a bucket on the upper deck on "make and mend" (i.e. half-holiday) afternoons was dying unmourned. Inboard of the bathrooms in *Warspite* were the compartments containing the men's kit lockers, and the main machinery workshops, where the engineers carried out the constant maintenance and repair work necessary to keep all the hundreds of machines running.

Below the middle deck the boiler- and engine-rooms occupy the whole centre of the ship, and our guide will probably take the visitor down to one of each of them by electric lift from the main deck. There he would see the steam generating plant which was the heart of the whole ship's life, and the huge turbines which propelled her 33,000-ton bulk through the water. In harbour only auxiliary machinery would be running, but take the ship to sea for a speed trial and the roar of the high-pressure fans supplying air to the boilers and the high-pitched whine of the fast-rotating turbines would produce a very different effect. The engineers then move quietly in among their whirring and pulsating monsters, glancing at a gauge now and then, adjusting a manœuvring valve to keep the revolutions constant, and obeying each telegraphed order or telephoned message from the bridge. The control of the whole gigantic plant seems to be done by a gesture or a nod from the engineer officer of the watch; for not a word can be heard unless one shouts into a man's ear. On the same level in the ship, in separate compartments, are the main dynamos, the hydraulic engines supplying power to the 15-inch turrets, the electrical switchboard, and the transmitting stations in which all the complicated fire-control equipment for the armaments is installed. Still lower, on the platform deck, are the telephone exchange, the magazines, the refrigerator space and wireless transmitter rooms; but the visitor will be exhausted from climbing up and down thirty-foot vertical steel ladders if his guide takes him down to more than a few of these. Finally, right at the bottom, on the hold deck, are the 15-inch shell-rooms and many of the oil fuel and fresh-water tanks.

Life in a warship in full commission continues uninterrupted by night as well as by day. Even while the majority are sleeping, others are keeping watch in the boiler- and engine-rooms, at the switchboards and dynamos, at the magazine keyboard, and on the quarter-deck. When at sea many more officers and men are, of course, keeping watches than when in harbour; but the process of relieving the watches in every position every four hours continues, day and night, winter and summer, in calm and in storm, in war as in peace. Though it is more subdued at some times than at others the pulse of a ship's life never stops beating until she pays off. In war the routine was adapted to the " degree of readiness " necessary at the time. If an encounter with the enemy was likely the whole ship might stay at Action Stations for hours on end, taking meals at the guns as opportunities occurred. Should some relaxation be permissible, the " second degree of readiness " might be ordered, in which case a proportion of each gun's crew was allowed to leave their action stations for brief periods for meals or other purposes. The usual war routine in dangerous waters was "Defence Stations," the third degree of readiness. Half the armaments were then manned in two watches, and this might be kept up for days on end. If air attack was more likely than surface action, the whole of the anti-aircraft armaments would be kept manned continuously, at the expense of the 6-inch low-angle weapons. In the lowest degree of readiness, called "Cruising Stations," the anti-aircraft armaments would be fully manned in four watches; but this was used comparatively rarely in the last war. Whatever the condition of the ship at the time of an emergency, the ringing of the alarm rattlers would bring every man, even those who had just completed an arduous four-hour watch, back to their action stations. The price of safety at sea is everlasting vigilance, exhausting though it is to maintain such a standard day and night, perhaps for weeks on end, and often in conditions of the greatest hardship and discomfort. None who fought at sea will ever forget the unceasing battle against fatigue; nor, if they ever saw it exacted, the price of relaxed vigilance. The threat of air as well as under-water attack in the last war increased the strain many times over, until the introduction of radar reduced the need to rely only on the human senses to give warning of danger. Moreover, on top of the strain of continuous watchkeeping at sea came the need to replenish with fuel, ammunition, stores and food as soon as the ship returned to harbour. That done she would, as likely as not, prepare at once for the next operation.

Assuming, however, that our *Warspite* was in harbour in conditions where no emergency was likely, the day would begin with "Reveille" at 5.30 a.m. This gave the men half an hour to lash up and stow their hammocks, wash and dress and be ready to fall in on the upper deck. The first muster of the day, generally taken by the commander, set the men to scrubbing decks. Then the armaments were cleaned and tested, and at 7.30 breakfast would be piped. Every day in harbour, at eight o'clock, the ceremonial hoisting of the colours took place, with a guard of Marines present and the band to play the National Anthem. Then the hands were called up again, leaving "cooks of messes" to clean the mess-decks for half an hour, while the final touches were given to upper-deck and boats. At nine o'clock inspection at "Divisions," followed by prayers, might take place, or the men might be detailed straight away for the forenoon's work. From then until "Dinner" was piped at noon the day's programme would be interrupted only by a ten-minute "stand-easy." Sections of the armament would be taken through their drill, classes of men training for promotion would be sent to instruction, other parties might be embarking stores, while any men not taken for special duties would work under their "Captain of Top." The framing of the whole intricate programme was always done the previous day by the commander in consultation with the specialist officers, and it was issued in typewritten sheets to all messes and notice-boards in the evening. Each man thus knew before he turned into his hammock what the next day held in store for him. Just before dinner the day's rum issue would be made with some formality to a representative of each mess who mustered at the large oak tub in which the grog had previously been mixed.

After the dinner hour "cooks of messes" again cleaned up down below, and then the day's programme was continued. At four o'clock tea would be piped, and half an hour later "Libertymen" for the shore would be mustered. In peace-time one watch, that is half the ship's company, would be given leave until seven o'clock next morning, provided that the ship was in a port where accommodation on shore was available. Chief and petty officers were allowed leave whenever their duties permitted, generally on three days out of four.

If an emergency arose or some work had to be done after the libertymen had landed, the duty watch or part of watch would be called up. But assuming that the " dog watches " (4 to 6 and 6 to 8 p.m.) passed quietly supper would be served at 7 p.m., and the day would close with commander's " rounds " at nine, followed by " pipe down " (i.e. lights 'out) an hour later. On undisturbed evenings the men generally passed the time reading or writing letters in their messes, playing cards or games, watching a cinema film or listening to the music broadcast over the ship's loud-speaker system.

In peace-time a great deal of trouble was taken, especially on foreign stations, to arrange games and recreation for the men. At the main bases cricket, football and hockey competitions, athletic sports, rifle and revolver shooting and many other team activities between different divisions or departments, or against other ships, took place almost continuously. They aroused great keenness. In more remote harbours, pulling and sailing regattas, or picnics in the ship's boats, replaced the organised games. The annual fleet regatta was the cause of intense rivalry, and every race was contested with a fervour rivalled only by the football competitions. Almost every ship had its dance band, and would give dances when in the main bases. Another most important element in a happy ship's life was the concert party. Its entertainments invariably produced remarkable talent, forward as well as aft, and some of *Warspite*'s pre-war concerts are still remembered for their songs, and for the satires on ship life and personalities they produced.

The great merit of all these manifold activities was, of course, that they drew the officers and men together. They were generally organised by committees, of which an officer was chairman and moving spirit; but in the various teams, or on the concert party stage, distinctions of rank were lost in the cause of the ship herself.

Such, in brief outline, was the framework of a big ship's life. Once settled down, the community sense was very strong, and the pride of the men in the performance of their own ship could be felt in all that they did. The great majority of the men were in those days long-service ratings. They had signed on for twelve years from the age of eighteen, after which they could extend their service for another ten years and receive a pension. The chief and petty officers were nearly all in their second term of service, and were the backbone of the ship's company. They were splendid characters, experts in their specialist trades, and deeply versed in every aspect of the naval service and of life at sea. When war came many of them were called to continue on active service, regardless of the fact that their time of discharge had passed. They may thus have served as much as thirty years in the Navy. They played an immense part in the training of the flood of reservists and of " hostilities only " men who entered during the war; and anyone who then served with a ship's company, perhaps three-quarters of whom had never been to sea before, will acknowledge the debt which the country owes to those long-service men. It is indeed a matter of deep concern to a nation whose life and safety still depend on the sea that the sweeping social changes brought about since the war seem to be leading to the disappearance of the long-service naval man. His like will not be reproduced quickly, and the lack of such men may yet prove a disastrous handicap.

It was the 5th January, 1938, when *Warspite* finally sailed for Malta. She stopped for only two hours at Gibraltar, and then hastened east. On the morning of the 14th she steamed up the Grand Harbour. She was allowed only a fortnight to complete her working-up firings and exercises, but they went very well. By the early days of February she was fast becoming a ship of which all on board were proud; for it was obvious that she was not only smart but efficient.

None the less, while working up, she had another very lucky escape, comparable to that from which she was saved during gun trials in the Channel a year earlier. After anti-aircraft firings had been completed and the ship's head turned towards Malta harbour, the towing aircraft flew overhead again with the target. A very junior midshipman at one of the multiple pom-poms then opened fire of his own accord. The gunnery officer leapt for the cease-fire bell, but warned the captain that the stream of two-pounder shells then in the air would probably land in Malta. He was, in fact, correct, but instead of descending in the crowded city of Valletta they merely bombarded a rifle range on which a platoon of the Green Howards was exercising. There was no damage, and a visit of apology to the colonel of the regiment closed—or nearly closed—the matter.[12]

On 6th February the commander-in-chief boarded his new flagship for the first time, inspected the ship's company and then addressed them, or, more accurately, he dressed them down about their recent conduct. Admiral Pound was plainly angry with the *Warspite*; but if his speech caused some indignation forward and aft, it also made everyone, determined to show the admiral that he was quite wrong about themselves. They accordingly proceeded to set about that task with a will. It took about a year, but in the end it was triumphantly accomplished, and before he hauled his flag down Admiral Pound was as proud of his flagship as any member of her company.

Early in March *Warspite*, now a fully-fledged fleet flagship, sailed for the combined exercises. After a brief visit to Oran, for the commander-in-chief to call on his French colleague, she and all the Mediterranean Fleet met the Atlantic squadrons at Gibraltar. About a fortnight's intensive exercises followed. The problem investigated that year was the defence of British shipping—soon to become all too topical—and the First Sea Lord (Admiral Sir Ernle Chatfield) came out for part of the time.

It was the Mediterranean flagship's turn to give the entertainment after the exercises, and *Warspite*'s officers had long been preparing for the occasion. They produced a musical review called "What is the Delay?" satirising the frequent postponement of their own arrival on the station. Though perhaps rather uncharitable to the dockyard which had coped with her problems, it caused immense amusement to the audience from the two fleets assembled in Gibraltar's transformed coal-sheds.

From Gibraltar she briefly visited the French Riviera, and then returned to Malta in mid-April. Meanwhile the clouds of war were gathering over Europe, for Hitler's troops had marched into Austria on 11th March. Whilst high-level discussions and planning, involving the commander-in-chief and his staff, were almost continuous, the fleet, by constant firings and exercises, strove to put the final touches to its efficiency.

On her next return to Malta *Warspite* had to undergo as severe a test of her fighting efficiency as could be devised in time of peace; for the Admiralty had ordered that she was to carry out a prolonged firing with her main armament, to test all the new equipment fitted during her refit under conditions approaching as nearly as possible to actual battle.

On 28th August Admiral Pound took most of the fleet to sea off Malta for the purpose. *Warspite* had, of course, been training hard for the firing for some months. The "enemy" consisted of two high-speed battle-practice targets towed by light cruisers at about twenty knots, with complete freedom of manœuvre. The ill-fated *Hood* steamed ahead of the main body of the fleet, sighted the "enemy" and briefly engaged. *Warspite* catapulted her spotting aircraft in this phase. Then Admiral Pound deployed the battle squadron at about 15 miles range, and the flagship opened fire. The first salvos, fired at about 21,000 yards, fell just over the target, and a good air report at once corrected the range.* From then on, for forty salvos, *Warspite* hardly ever stopped hitting. The first target was quickly shot away, so she shifted to the second "enemy", and at once began to score hits on it as well. Meanwhile a towing aircraft represented a bombing attack, and was engaged by the anti-aircraft armaments. After about half an hour's "battle" it was obvious which side had "won." Admiral Pound was delighted, and himself attended the lectures on the results given to the ship's company. From then on there was no looking back for *Warspite*—only forward to greater deeds and services.

Next month, September, she sailed for Greece, but as Hitler's threats against Czechoslovakia became more and more violent, all cruises were cancelled and the fleet concentrated at its war base of Alexandria. Everyone in the

* *Warspite's* air observer in this practice was Lieutenant-Commander W. L. M. Brown, who was later to serve the same ship brilliantly in a similar capacity at the second battle of Narvik and in the action off Calabria. (See pp. 202 and 213-216.)

fleet then believed that war was imminent, and was ready
for it. Morale was never higher. The Admiralty mobilised
the whole Navy, and the Cunard liner *Aquitania* arrived
with the officers and men needed to bring all the ships'
complements up to war strength. They had travelled overland to Marseilles, and then been rushed on by sea, to
arrive just when the fleet was fusing all its shell and putting
the final touches to its readiness for war.

The night before the Munich agreement was signed
(30th September, 1938) a short conference was held in the
admiral's charthouse. If war with Italy and Germany was
declared that night, as was widely expected, the fleet would
sail at once and appear off Tobruk at dawn to bombard
the port. Admiral Pound was giving the enemy no chance
to get in the first blow. Then came the signing of the
agreement. There was no sense of relief in the fleet, for
everyone felt that it would only postpone the inevitable
clash. When the terms on which peace had been bought
were known sorrow, even anger, were the predominant
sensations. To mitigate the impact of what was certainly
an anti-climax, and was soon to be shown as a tragedy,
Admiral Pound decided to hold the fleet regatta at once
and in Alexandria. Thus was that superb fighting machine,
the Mediterranean Fleet, denied for another year the
chance to show the dictators its quality, ordered to unfuse
its shell—and to get out its pulling boats. *Warspite* won
that regatta, but the fruits of a victory which was greatly
coveted in normal times, then had a bitter taste about
them. When it was over she sailed to Cyprus, to Haifa,
back to Egypt and then to Malta—for the last Christmas
of peace.

At first the fleet programme for 1939 followed the
pattern of earlier years—a winter cruise to the east, and
then the combined fleet exercises. One more visit was

paid to the Riviera, and then the fleet concentrated again at Alexandria. With the likelihood of war constantly increasing, many of the fleet's base stores were being put afloat and shifted from Malta, which in the opinion of the Army and Air Force could not be successfully defended against Italian air attacks. In consequence of this the fleet was now much more in Egypt, and the central Mediterranean saw less of it. None the less opportunity was taken to dock and refit every possible ship while Malta's facilities were still available.

In June Admiral Pound was recalled to become First Sea Lord in succession to Sir Roger Backhouse, who was seriously ill. On the 6th the whole fleet went to sea to give the commander-in-chief a fine farewell. He steamed through the lines in *Warspite*, flying his flag for the last time. At sunset that evening it was struck, and next morning the flag of Admiral Sir Andrew Cunningham was hoisted. In July the new commander-in-chief took his flagship to Istanbul on an official visit.[13] The warmth of the reception given to the Royal Navy left no doubt about where Turkish sympathies really lay; but in those anxious days it was dangerous for small, ill-armed nations to show too clearly their dislike of the dictators. We could not supply the arms and equipment needed to enable the Turks to defend themselves, and it was therefore not surprising that when war came they remained neutral. In spite of very hot weather the sailors enjoyed themselves enormously. Admiral Cunningham told the First Sea Lord that 300 of them made short work of 1,200 bottles of beer at a party given by the ambassador, and that the appearance of a troupe of lightly-clad dancing girls " all helped to make the party go."[14] The *Warspites* were not to enjoy any more such parties for a very long time.

From the Bosphorus the flagship called at Cyprus,

carried out a bombardment practice with the rest of the battle squadron, and then returned to Alexandria. On 24th August news of the Russo-German pact was received and, so writes one of *Warspite*'s officers, " we then knew that war was inevitable."[15] Most of the wives and families still on the station were therefore sent home. At the beginning of September the 1st Battle Squadron held its annual pulling regatta, and it was finished on the day that war was declared. *Warspite*'s log mentions the regatta—but not the war. "The sailors," wrote the commander-in-chief, " are in great fettle. We are naturally champing at the bit out here, but trying to keep patient."[16]

British patience with the trickery and treachery of the dictators had finally run out. At last a new and more determined spirit was making itself felt at home. *Warspite* and all her fleet had been ready for it for months. That day, 3rd September, a "Most Immediate" signal was received from the Admiralty. It read: "Commence hostilities at once with Germany."

CHAPTER SEVEN

From Alexandria to Narvik
and Back Again
September 1939-July 1940

" The risk which had been accepted in sending a battleship into such confined waters was abundantly justified
by the devastating effects of the *Warspite*'s 15-inch
gunfire."

> " *The War at Sea*," Vol. I
> (*The second battle of Narvik*)

As LONG as the attitude of Italy remained in doubt the
Admiralty had to keep powerful forces in the Mediterranean, galling though it was for our ships to have only
a watching role to play. In spite of the French Navy
having accepted responsibility for the western basin, Italian
superiority over Admiral Cunningham's fleet, especially in
cruisers, destroyers and submarines, was so great that it
appeared to be well within their power to challenge British
control of the eastern basin successfully.* Moreover, in
southern Italy and Sicily, as well as along the African
coast in Tripolitania and Libya, Italy possessed many well-
placed air bases, and such great strength in bombers and
fighters that the weak Royal Air Force in the Middle East

* The comparative British and Italian strengths in September, 1939, were as
follows:

	Battleships	Aircraft Carriers	Heavy Cruisers	Light Cruisers	Destroyers	Submarines
British ..	3	1	3	3	26	10
Italian ..	2	Nil	7	11	61	105

would be very hard put to it to meet its wide responsibilities. Another serious threat to our position lay in the Italian naval and air forces stationed in Eritrea, very close on the flank of the narrow but vital shipping lane up the Red Sea to the Suez Canal. Once the Mediterranean was closed to through traffic, and it was recognised that this would be inevitable if Italy declared war, all our troopships and supplies would have to come out by the Cape of Good Hope and pass up the Red Sea to the Egyptian unloading ports. If that route were cut our position in Egypt was bound to become untenable.

Though the strategic situation in the Mediterranean appeared difficult, even dangerous, it made no difference to the determination of the British commander-in-chief to adopt a vigorous offensive from the very beginning. He knew the fighting spirit of his fleet, and that it was trained to the highest pitch of efficiency. All he asked was the chance to show what it could do. The backbone of his fleet was the 1st Battle Squadron (*Warspite*, *Barham* and *Malaya*), and the aircraft carrier *Glorious*. They were supported by three heavy and three light cruisers, and by three flotillas of destroyers. From 11th to 16th September Admiral Cunningham cruised to the west of Crete with his main strength; but nothing happened. Most of October also passed quietly in patrolling the eastern basin and exercising off Alexandria. Meanwhile the Home Fleet was faced with grave difficulties in carrying out its traditional duties of watching the Northern passages to the Atlantic, enforcing the blockade of Germany, dealing with U-boats and protecting our Atlantic shipping against raiders. On paper the Commander-in-Chief, Admiral Sir Charles Forbes, possessed considerably superior strength; but whereas all the principal German warships were modern, fast and well armed, many of the British ships were survivors from the

1914-18 war, and few had even been thoroughly modernised.
Moreover, operations in the stormy northern waters soon
found their weak places, and the tale of defects and weather
damage quickly began to mount. In those days, when air
reconnaissance was in its infancy, it was easy for German
warships or disguised raiders to creep up the Norwegian
coast, and then make their way out on to the trade routes
by the Iceland-Faeroes passage, or by the Denmark Strait between Iceland and Greenland; while the fast and powerful
battle cruisers *Scharnhorst* and *Gneisenau* could, by choosing
their moment carefully, strike at the weak ships of the
Northern Patrol and then elude our searching forces. The
initiative in all such operations was bound to rest with
the Germans. Their intelligence service was, at that time,
far superior to our own, and they could strike where and
when they chose, forewarned with accurate information
regarding British dispositions and movements.[1] Finally it
was soon obvious that a large number of U-boats (actually
39) had taken up positions at sea well before war was
declared, ready to attack our merchant shipping or to lay
mines off our bases.

As long as Admiral Forbes's fleet was based at Scapa
Flow in the Orkneys it was well placed to cover the cruisers
patrolling the northern passages, and to watch the exits
from the North Sea to the Atlantic. But on 14th October
the battleship *Royal Oak* was sunk by a U-boat inside the
fleet's main base, whose dangerous insecurity was thus at
once demonstrated. This is not the place to discuss the
many causes which contributed to this lamentable state of
affairs.[2] For our purposes the important point is that the
inadequacy of Scapa's defences forced Admiral Forbes to
abandon his chosen base, and to work from southern
harbours which were much farther from the waters where
his ships might at any moment be needed. Next it became

known that two German *Deutschland*-class pocket battleships were at large and preying on our shipping. Strong forces had to be detached to cover our convoys, to protect the focal points at which the trade routes converged, and to hunt for the raiders. It was plain that the Home Fleet was not strong enough to meet all the demands now falling on it. Reinforcements could only come from the Mediterranean, and as it was by that time fairly plain that Italy intended to sit on the fence, to reduce Admiral Cunningham's strength was the natural thing to do. On 27th October the First Sea Lord had signalled that as the Home Fleet would have to work from the Clyde instead of Scapa for some time, it was essential to have four battleships with long-range guns at home. " This," said Admiral Pound, " necessitates *Warspite* joining the Home Fleet. . . . Regret the necessity to take your fleet flagship." " Losing her," replied Admiral Cunningham, " is a blow, but not unexpected."[3] She sailed next day for Malta, where she was given a quick docking, and then hastened on to the west, leaving the commander-in-chief's flag flying ashore at Malta. On 6th November she reached Gibraltar, and was at once ordered to Halifax on ocean escort duty. Only battleships could protect our convoys adequately against surface raiders as powerful as the German *Scharnhorsts* and *Deutschlands*, and the Admiralty was now using them widely for such purposes. The new policy was completely successful, and several convoys were saved solely by the presence of one battleship.[4] *Warspite*, however, was destined to make only one Atlantic crossing with a convoy—and that one, as will be told shortly, was suddenly and dramatically interrupted.

She encountered repeated and violent gales on the way to Halifax, and made a slow passage. Not until 14th November did she berth there, in a snow blizzard. Four days later she sailed again to the east with convoy HX. 9 of thirty ships. Apart from familiar trouble with a jammed helm, the first three days passed quietly. Then, on the evening of 23rd, the Armed Merchant Cruiser *Rawalpindi*, which was on patrol in the Denmark Strait, reported being attacked by what she erroneously believed to be a pocket battleship. Actually both the German battle cruisers *Scharnhorst* and *Gneisenau* were out on a foray against our patrol lines. The *Rawalpindi's* signal at once set in motion the whole Admiralty and Home Fleet machinery designed to intercept enemies engaged on operations of a type which we had always anticipated.[5] Admiral Forbes took the main body of the fleet from the Clyde north-east towards the Norwegian coast to catch the enemy when he returned home, and cruisers were sent to watch each of the several alternative routes he might take. On the afternoon of 24th *Warspite*, then far out in the Atlantic, was ordered by the Admiralty to leave her convoy and steer to the N.N.E. She was, in Captain Crutchley's words, "hooked on to the left wing of the British searching forces most skilfully."[6] A gale delayed her on the 25th, but two days later she passed through the Denmark Strait between Iceland and Greenland. If the enemy ships were bound for the Atlantic they would probably try to break out that way, and it was natural that the Admiralty should send a battleship to block the exit. *Warspite* then steered east, passing to the north of Iceland, and used her catapult aircraft to search the seas whenever the weather was suitable. While she was scouring these far northern waters a remarkable incident took place one night on *Warspite's* bridge, when she was about on the 70th parallel. Captain Crutchley's bearded face was suddenly lit up by St. Elmo's fire.* It

---

* *Chambers's Encyclopedia* says of St. Elmo's Fire that it is "the popular name for a continuous electrical discharge which may occur in thundery weather

looked as though a spotlight had been turned on to him out of the surrounding, all-pervading darkness; and it gave him an ethereal, biblical appearance. Though he remained totally unaware of what had happened, the ship's company was deeply impressed.[7]

From Iceland *Warspite* swept towards the Faeroes, and then turned south down the west coast of Scotland. Nothing except our own forces was sighted. The enemy actually slipped through our patrol lines in very bad weather, close to the Norwegian coast on the 26th November; but the fleet's searches went on until the end of the month.

On the 3rd December *Warspite*, which had been ordered to Portsmouth, was met by screening destroyers. Next day, however, Admiral Forbes's flagship, the *Nelson*, was seriously damaged by a magnetic mine laid off Loch Ewe by a German U-boat, and the Admiralty thereupon diverted *Warspite* to Greenock, where she anchored that same day. If disappointment was felt that no action had taken place, at least the long search had been a valuable experience to her crew; but the drastically sudden change from Mediterranean sun to the borders of the Arctic Ocean may well have produced some nostalgia for the station she had so recently left. Three days later the commander-in-chief hoisted his flag in *Warspite*. Within just over a month she thus had the unusual distinction of serving as flagship to both the main fleets.

For the next three months the Home Fleet worked from the Clyde, and spent a large proportion of its time cruising in northern waters to cover our patrols and blockading vessels, and to protect our Norwegian convoys

---

or during and after snowstorms from elevated points such as the masts of ships. . . . It takes the form of a faint glow or brush of light, pink or bluish in colour, and may be accompanied by a slight rustling or fizzing sound." No one on *Warspite's* bridge noticed, however, whether the captain was "rustling or fizzing."

and those bringing Canadian troops across the Atlantic against attack by German surface ships. On 27th February, 1940, King George VI came on board *Warspite* while she was in the Clyde, and inspected her company. It was his first visit to the ship since 1927, when as Duke of York he had boarded her at Malta on his way back from Australia, and the first time the reigning monarch had inspected her since King George V had done so during Cowes Week in 1924.*

By March, 1940, the defences of Scapa Flow had been sufficiently strengthened for the fleet to return there, and on the 9th Admiral Forbes, whose flag had now been transferred from *Warspite* to the *Rodney*, arrived there. *Warspite* herself joined the commander-in-chief at the base on the 16th, and three days later she sailed once again with the main body of the fleet to cruise to the north of the Shetlands. Though the German heavy ships had several times shown activity, and had actually sailed to attack our Norwegian convoys in February, no action rose out of all this arduous steaming by the Home Fleet.

Meanwhile tension was rising in the North Sea, for the British Government was anxious to stop the shipment of iron ore from the Norwegian port of Narvik to Germany by the sheltered waters of the "Inner Leads," and to tighten its control over the waters off the coast of Norway, which the enemy was constantly using to pass warships, disguised raiders and blockade runners in and out from the Atlantic. Early in April it was decided to mine certain points off the Norwegian coast to force enemy traffic to leave territorial waters; but the Germans were also watching the situation in Scandinavia, and had long since prepared very careful plans for a surprise invasion of Denmark and Norway. On 8th April, while the British minelaying

* See p. 157.

plan was in course of execution, Hitler struck. Six groups
of warships sailed to land troops at various Norwegian
ports from Oslo in the south to Narvik in the north.[8]
Almost complete surprise was achieved and, for all that
the risks were serious, the enemy quickly achieved success.
It is with the German group sent to attack Narvik that
we here are primarily concerned. It consisted of the two
battle cruisers *Scharnhorst* and *Gneisenau*, which were to
cover the whole operation, and of ten large modern
destroyers carrying 2,000 troops to seize the port. The
latter arrived at the entrance to Vestfiord on the evening
of the 8th, and met no opposition to their progress up the
fiord to Narvik.* Early next morning they overwhelmed
the Norwegian defences and disembarked their troops.

Meanwhile the *Renown*, flagship of Vice-Admiral W. J.
Whitworth, commanding the battle cruiser squadron,
encountered the two German battle cruisers off Vestfiord.
She fought a skilful action with her more powerful and
faster adversaries, and damaged the *Gneisenau*; but her
efforts made no difference to the rapid success of the
German plan. After the German ships had broken off the
fight and disappeared in a snow squall, Admiral Whitworth
patrolled off the mouth of Vestfiord; for it was not yet
known that a powerful enemy naval force carrying troops
had passed up the fiord to Narvik about twelve hours
earlier.

The main body of the Home Fleet had sailed from
Scapa late on the 7th when intelligence indicated that unusual
enemy movements were in progress, and steered to the
north-east at high speed. *Warspite* had already sailed from
the Clyde for the Mediterranean, but she was promptly
diverted by the Admiralty to join Admiral Forbes. The
aircraft carrier *Furious* was also sent north from the Clyde,

* See Map 4.

but such was the haste with which all forces were ordered to sea by the Admiralty that the carrier had no time to embark her fighter aircraft, and this deprived the fleet of their protection at a critical time.[9] The *Warspite* joined the rest of the fleet at 7.30 a.m. on the 10th. A short time later she had her first taste of action, when German dive-bombers attacked unsuccessfully. Compared with the ordeals which she was to undergo later, this was a trifling skirmish; but it was none the less a valuable initiation for her air defence crews.

During the forenoon of the 9th indications that German forces had arrived at Narvik became strong, and Admiral Forbes therefore ordered Captain B. A. W. Warburton-Lee, commanding the 2nd Destroyer Flotilla, who was patrolling off Vestfiord under Admiral Whitworth, to proceed up the fiord and prevent enemy troops landing. This order led to the first Battle of Narvik, fought off the port in the early hours of 10th by five British destroyers against double that number of larger and more heavily armed German ships. By attacking at dawn, Captain Warburton-Lee achieved surprise and sank two destroyers; but when he was withdrawing fresh enemies appeared and turned the tables on him. The fight ended in the British destroyers *Hardy* and *Hunter* being lost, and in the former the gallant flotilla commander was killed; but they inflicted heavier losses (two destroyers and six merchant ships sunk, and two other destroyers damaged) on the enemy, and the battle can justly be claimed as a British success even if it fell short of a victory.[10]

The Admiralty and the Commander-in-Chief now made plans to finish off the German ships left at Narvik. On the 12th dive-bombers from the *Furious* attacked them, but the weather was very bad and no damage was done. *Warspite* was with the main body of the fleet covering the aircraft carrier, and when it was known that the air attack had failed, Admiral Forbes decided to send her and nine destroyers up the fiord next day. The 12th April was a Saturday—the day which is traditionally devoted by the Navy to cleaning ship. On this occasion a slight amendment was made to the commander's daily orders to meet the new circumstances. The routine order to " clean up mess-decks and flats " was altered to read " clean up mess-decks and fiords."[11]

Admiral Whitworth transferred his flag from the *Renown* to *Warspite* that night, and the whole force assembled inside Vestfiord about 100 miles from Narvik early on the 13th. By noon the battleship was well inside the fiord, with three destroyers ahead of her and three on either bow.* Her aircraft had been catapulted and at once performed excellent service. " I doubt," wrote Admiral Whitworth in his report, " if ever a ship-borne aircraft has been used to such good purpose." First she reported two enemy destroyers close ahead of the flagship. Then she flew right to the head of the fiord, bombed and sank U. 64, but was herself slightly damaged by the U-boat's gunfire. Next the Swordfish flew back down the fiord and reported that a destroyer, actually one of the two she had seen earlier, was taking up a position in a creek whence her torpedoes might be used with deadly effect. The aircraft's crew were indeed a remarkably successful team. The captain and observer (Lieutenant-Commander W. L. M. Brown) reported all the enemy ships quickly and correctly, the pilot (Petty Officer Airman F. C. Rice) sank the U-boat, and the telegraphist (M. G. Pacey) got all the enemy reports through to the flagship.†

---

* See Map 4. The British destroyers were the *Icarus, Hero, Forester, Cossack, Kimberley, Foxhound, Bedouin, Punjabi* and *Eskimo.*

† The same air crew did excellent service later in the action off Calabria. See pp. 213-216.

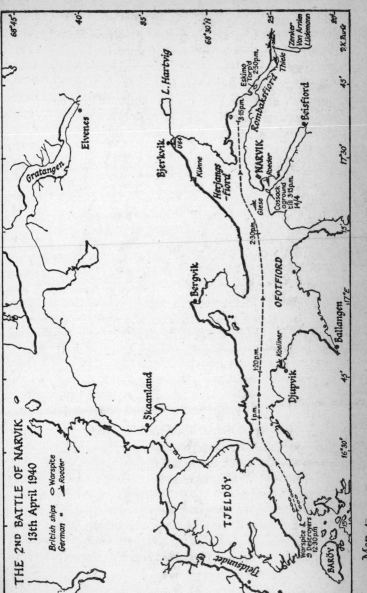

THE 2ND BATTLE OF NARVIK
13th April 1940

British ships ○ Warspite
German " ▲ Roeder

68°45'
40'
35'
63°30'N
25'
20'

Gratangen
Elvenes
L. Hartvig
Bjerkvik
U64
Herjangs-fiord
Künne
NARVIK
Roeder
Giese
Cossack aground till 3.15p.m. 14/4
3.15p.m.
Eskimö
Torpd
2.50p.m.
Rombaksfiord
Thiele
Zenker
Von Arnim
Lüdemann
P.K. Parls
Beisfiord

2.30p.m.

Bergvik

Skaanland

TJELDÖY

1.20p.m.

Koellner

Djupvik

OFOTFIORD

Ballangen

17°30'
45'
17°E
15'
16°30'

Warspite &
9 Destroyers
12.30 pm

1p.m.

Tjeldsundet

BARÖY

Map 4

Immediately the last report was received from the aircraft, the leading British ships trained their guns in the direction of the destroyer, and when the enemy came into view they overwhelmed her with their fire. It was at this target that *Warspite* fired her main armament in earnest for the first time since the Battle of Jutland in 1916. By 2 p.m. the force was off Narvik itself and a hot action was being fought with the German destroyers. *Warspite* engaged whenever a target could be seen through the smoke and haze of the destroyer battle. Her aircraft continued to keep the British ships posted about the enemy's movements, and thus aided in pursuing them right up to the head of the fiord, where the last German ships were destroyed. Lieutenant-Commander W. W. Fitzroy, who was the ship's air defence officer, and therefore had a grand-stand view of the proceedings, records his impressions as follows :

" As we passed into the narrows at the end of the long fiord I remember thinking that it was like a forward rush in rugger. We belted along at high speed, with the destroyers doing magnificent work ahead of us. The roar of our 15-inch guns reverberated from the steep, snow-covered sides of the fiord, but the explosions of the enemy torpedoes when they hit the rocks were even greater. Fortunately the enemy was prevented from firing across our track, and all the torpedoes ran parallel to us and so missed. Tall columns of smoke soon marked the positions where the big German destroyers had met their end, and we passed quite close to one beached or burning wreck after another. After the battle was over Captain Crutchley jutted his beard out, removed his pipe from his mouth, and said to Admiral Whitworth, ' Just like shelling peas, sir.' "[12]

Eight large German destroyers and a U-boat were lost to the enemy that afternoon, at the cost of damage to only two British ships, the *Cossack* and the *Eskimo*.* Though the strength ultimately thrown in by Admiral Forbes was overwhelming, the dash and determination of the British destroyers had been splendid and, in Admiral Whitworth's words, " the cumulative effect of the roar of *Warspite*'s 15-inch guns reverberating down and around the high mountains of the fiord, the bursts and splashes of these great shells, the sight of their ships sinking and burning around them must have been terrifying [to the enemy]." It had been a fine success, gained, moreover, at a time when things were going badly for the Allies on land in southern Norway.

Petty Officer Daniel Reardon, who was gunner's mate of A Turret in *Warspite* on that day and was later seriously wounded in the same ship in the Battle of Crete, has left a vivid account of the second Battle of Narvik as he saw it :

" *April* 12*th*-13*th*, 1940.

" It is one of those dark nights when men have to be very careful changing the watch, for the deck is frozen and one false move and it's over the side and nobody knows. So the guns' crews prefer to remain at their action stations and sneak a few minutes' sleep there. Hallo ! The ship is stopping ! What's happened ? A blue light flickers just alongside, and then we are under way again. The news soon spreads—an Admiral has come aboard. Next a messenger calls to

---

* The German ships, all of 1,625 tons and armed with five 5-inch guns and eight torpedo tubes, were : *Georg Thiele, Hans Lüdemann, Hermann Künne, Diether von Röder, Wolfgang Zenker, Erich Giese, Erich Koellner* and *Bernd von Arnim*.

tell all us Gunner's Mates to report to the Gunnery Officer. His orders are short and sweet—we are going up to Narvik to-morrow and everything must be on a split yarn. Back to our stations, and plenty to do now. Fuses to be set to non-delay (only light enemy ships believed there), first-aid gear checked, fresh water provided and all the thousand and one other little things that can make or mar good shooting.

" There is very little sleep left in us now; everyone is wondering what to-morrow will bring. At last it is daylight, and the watch is being called to Day Defence stations. One young seaman puts his head out of the top manhole and soon bobs down again. 'Looks as though we are in the money—you ought to see the destroyers we have with us.' So out we troop and have a look. Nine destroyers. Someone must be making a fuss of us. We have our breakfast and carry on with the usual routine, cleaning and preparing. We are passing some land now, and it looks very snow-covered and forbidding. An early dinner to-day, before going to Action Stations. My own crew are on the fo'c's'le for a smoke, some wag rolls a snowball and one of B Turret's crew gets it in the neck. This is the general signal for a snow fight between the two turrets, when 'Action Stations' sounds. . . . Our gun-house crew is soon correct and so are the shell-room and magazine crews. We report to control and the Turret Officer tells me I can load. We hear the order repeated to the men down below, the cages come up with a thud, and out go the rammers. We can feel that we have increased speed as the ship has begun to vibrate. Heavy explosions shake the ship, and we hear that the destroyers are attacking a submarine. Suddenly comes the order ' Salvos,' and the right gun comes to the ready. Then 'Enemy in Sight' and the sight-setters chant the ranges. It is just like a practice shoot. Our guns are nearly horizontal, so the range must be short. Then the 'ding ding' of the fire gong, the right gun moves a little, comes steady and there is a 'Woof' which rocks the turret. The left gun is now at the ready, and fires while the right gun is re-loading. B Turret, firing over our heads, blows away our 'blast bags' and the turret fills with smoke—like London on a November night. The turret officer calls out, 'Tell the crew we have hit a destroyer and she is burning nicely.' Good work, boys, keep it going. Steady firing now. Then the trainer reports, 'Blimey, another one has got it,' and the news is passed to the men below. You can hear them cheer. Down in the machinery space the O.A. (Ordnance Artificer), his face covered with oil and sweat, grins and holds up his thumb. Hydraulic pressure is O.K. Sixteen rounds from each gun so far. The salvos now aren't going so fast, because the different targets sink or blow up. After a while 'Check fire' is ordered and the ship seems to be stopping. 'Crews may go on top of turrets,' and up there it is a sight—burning and sinking enemy ships all around us, and our own destroyers searching into every little corner that might hide something. . . . We return to our action stations, and the Turret Officer and I make out our report as we steam down the fiord. Nothing special in it—just that everyone did their job from the youngest to the oldest. Thirty-two rounds fired by each gun, and no salvos missed. One of the crew in the turret cabinet had a tea kettle on the electric radiator, and every time the fire gong went he lifted it off to stop it being spilt. Wounded from the destroyers are next brought aboard; some are beyond help and are buried at sea that night. Now we *Warspites* know we shall carry on as we have started."[13]

On the afternoon of the battle a large German reconnaissance aircraft came over the mountains very low, and it was obvious that she had seen what was happening. Heavy reprisals were therefore expected from the air, and all *Warspite*'s gun crews stood to in readiness; but nothing happened. The battleship stayed on in Vestfiord for a time, as Admiral Whitworth's flagship, in support of the combined expedition sent from Britain to capture Narvik. This proved a difficult task, for we then had little of the specialised equipment needed for an assault from the sea, the country was still under deep snow, no properly organised base was available, and the Germans held command of the air.[14] On 24th April, *Warspite* and other ships went up the fiord again, and bombarded the enemy defences and the port of Narvik in the hope that heavy shelling would persuade the enemy to surrender. Weather conditions were once more very difficult, and it was impossible to judge the effects of the three-hour bombardment. The Germans in Narvik did not, however, surrender, and the place was not actually captured until 28th May. *Warspite* left for home immediately after the bombardment, for the increasingly hostile attitude of Italy had made it essential to reinforce the Mediterranean Fleet once again, and the Admiralty was collecting ships for Admiral Cunningham from various stations. On 27th April, while she was briefly in home waters, Captain Crutchley was relieved by Captain D. B. Fisher. The author of this history happened to meet the former in London and, avid for news of the ship and of the recent fighting, asked how things had gone. The captain's first remark was: " I've discovered a new use for a beard. It stops the snow getting down one's neck!"

On the same day that Captain Fisher took over command, *Warspite* sailed from Scapa for Greenock, embarked stores, and left three days later for Gibraltar. She sailed unescorted on a circuitous, evasive route far out in the Atlantic. "We are doing our best to scratch up a fleet for you in the Eastern Mediterranean, but it is not easy," wrote the First Sea Lord on 29th April. "*Warspite* is being sent to Gibraltar, but the question whether she can get through to the eastern Mediterranean depends on the situation. . . . I know you will be glad to be getting a fleet of some kind again, even if it is rather a second-rate one as regards the age of the ships."[15] The commander-in-chief answered urging "that *Warspite* should be sent to Alexandria as soon as possible," and she actually arrived on the 10th May after an uneventful, if anxious, passage through the Mediterranean. Next day she re-hoisted Admiral Cunningham's flag. "You must be very glad to find yourself back again in *Warspite*," wrote Admiral Pound. "I have not envied you in the last eight months, but I do now,"[16] he added rather wistfully, perhaps remembering his former flagship, and regretting the exchange to the heavy responsibilities of his office. The same day, 20th May, Admiral Cunningham wrote: "We are now all collected at Alexandria . . . *Warspite* is in good order, but badly wants docking."[17] She was actually taken in hand at once for repair of the blast damage she had done to herself at Narvik, and was the first war-damaged ship to be dealt with by the Alexandria base. By 24th May she was completed and ready for service. On 11th June Italy declared war, and the following day the commander-in-chief took his whole fleet to sea to sweep the central Mediterranean and seek the enemy. No one knew the deficiencies of the fleet better than Admiral Pound. "There are," he wrote, "so many things we should have liked to have kitted you up with before the crash ... more destroyers, more submarines, more minesweepers, and in particular more fighter aircraft. ...." He ended his letter "With the very best of good luck, and supreme confidence in what you will do."[18] It was not long before Admiral Cunningham found opportunities to show how well placed that confidence was. "I feel," he wrote on the day before Italy declared war, "that the only way we can make the Italians think a bit ... is to move a strong portion of the fleet into the central Mediterranean. ... The force I propose will be *Warspite*, *Eagle* and *Malaya*. ... I am sure *Warspite* and *Malaya* are equal to anything the Italians will produce. ... We are practising furiously." Then, after the fleet's return "from our first tour of the central Mediterranean," he told the First Sea Lord that "On the whole it was a curious experience. I expected to spend most of the daylight hours beating off bombing attacks. Actually the battle squadron never saw a plane. This is most encouraging at first sight."[19] The commander-in-chief's expectations were, however, to be fulfilled very accurately the next time he took the fleet to sea, and the quiet which had prevailed throughout his first operation was soon shown to have been only a lull before the storm.

Then, on 22nd June, came the fall of France. The succeeding weeks were as critical and anxious as any period in British history; for not only was the homeland most seriously threatened, but the Army, recently rescued from Dunkirk, was so deficient in equipment as to be practically unarmed; and the loss of the French Fleet was bound to throw a tremendous strain on the Royal Navy, especially in the Mediterranean. Though the morale of Admiral Cunningham's fleet never wavered, these anxieties were aggravated for his officers and men by the knowledge that their families and homes were under air bombardment, and by the infrequency of the mails, which now had to be sent out by the long Cape route.

In London the withdrawal of the Mediterranean Fleet was meanwhile being discussed, but Admiral Cunningham argued very forcibly that it should not be carried out. "I feel," he ended his letter on the subject to the First Sea Lord, "that we can keep the Italians pretty well engaged."[20] But his first, and extremely difficult task, was to secure the immobilisation of the French squadron left marooned at Alexandria by its country's surrender—and if possible without bloodshed. On 4th July, after long and patient negotiations, that was accomplished, and the commander-in-chief was then ready to carry out his next plan, which was to bring two convoys, a fast one of three ships and a slow one of four, from Malta to Alexandria with urgently needed stores and men.[21] He intended to cover the movement by sweeping into the central Mediterranean with practically his whole strength, and by appearing close off the Italian coast he hoped to provoke an action with their fleet. The commander-in-chief divided his ships into three forces. Five 6-inch cruisers and one destroyer, commanded by Vice-Admiral J. C. Tovey, formed the first. The second consisted of the fleet flagship, escorted by five destroyers, while the third comprised the battleships *Royal Sovereign* and *Malaya*, the carrier *Eagle* and ten destroyers under Rear-Admiral H. D. Pridham-Wippell. All three forces sailed from Alexandria on the evening of 7th July and steamed to the west. Meanwhile a patrol line of submarines had been stretched across the central Mediterranean to report enemy movements. Early next day one of these submarines signalled the presence of an Italian squadron, which included two battleships, about half-way between Taranto and Benghazi, steaming south. Aircraft from Malta were directed to watch this force. The indications that the Italian fleet intended to intervene in the operation now in train received some confirmation when many contacts were made by our destroyers with enemy submarines. That same day, the 8th, very persistent high-level bombing attacks by Italian aircraft took place against Admiral Cunningham's fleet; and they continued with scarcely a break for the next five days. Many of the attacks were unpleasantly accurate. The *Eagle* and *Warspite* were generally selected as the principal targets; but only one ship—the cruiser *Gloucester* —was actually hit. The *Eagle* had precisely two Gladiators with which to defend the fleet, and although they were flown most gallantly and to some effect, the main burden of defence fell on the ships' own anti-aircraft guns. They fired thousands of rounds during those days, and if they did not bring down many aircraft they certainly forced them to keep at a good height, and probably succeeded also in disturbing the bomb-aimers. The Italians claimed fantastic successes from their bombing, and even published an air photograph of " a British battleship on fire," which, on being scrutinised, proved to be the *Royal Sovereign* steaming her best speed and belching smoke.[22] This caused much amusement in the fleet.

The next report of the Italian surface forces came from our reconnaissance aircraft during the afternoon of the 8th. It placed two battleships, six cruisers and a number of destroyers 200 miles from Benghazi steering slightly west of north. Next they were signalled steering east, which caused Admiral Cunningham to deduce that they were covering the passage of a convoy of their own to Libya. He therefore postponed the sailing of his own merchant-men from Malta, and hurried on himself in order to get between the Italians and their base at Taranto. Actually the admiral's assumption was nearly correct, for the Italians were returning home after having successfully escorted an important convoy to Benghazi.

At daylight on the 9th the British fleet was some 60 miles to the west of the south-west corner of Greece with the cruisers leading, *Warspite* and her escort in the centre, and the slower battleships and *Eagle* about eight miles astern of her. Air reports placed the enemy some 145 miles ahead, and the composition of the Italian fleet was now reported more correctly. It consisted of two *Cavour* class (12-inch) battleships, six 8-inch and ten 6-inch cruisers and thirty-two destroyers. In battleships Cunningham was therefore superior on paper, but the slowness of the *Royal Sovereign* and *Malaya*, and the fact that their guns could only shoot to about 23,500 yards compared with *Warspite*'s 32,000, made his superiority more theoretical than real. In cruisers and destroyers he was greatly outnumbered. That afternoon the *Eagle*'s torpedo-bombers were sent to attack the enemy battleships, but an alteration of course prevented the striking force finding them, and an attack on an enemy cruiser was unsuccessful. By 2.15 p.m. the commander-in-chief had gained the position he was seeking between the enemy and Taranto, so he altered more to the west. Contact was now imminent. In *Warspite* the expectation of engaging an enemy battle squadron for the first time had aroused high hopes. The *Malaya* and *Royal Sovereign* were struggling to come up with her, but were still a long way astern.* At 2.47 the *Orion*, on the cruiser screen, sighted the enemy; but it was her sister-ship the *Neptune* (Captain R. C. O'Conor) which signalled the first report of an enemy battle fleet since Commodore Goodenough's *Southampton* had sighted Scheer's High Seas Fleet at Jut-

* See Map 5.

land,* and the first such report to be made in the Mediterranean since Nelson's days. About half an hour later the Italians opened fire. The western horizon now seemed to be alive with enemy warships, all of which concentrated their fire on Admiral Tovey's cruisers. Their position was for a time unenviable, but they were saved by *Warspite* coming into action at 3.26. In face of her 15-inch salvos the Italian cruisers turned away under cover of smoke. Firing temporarily died down until 3.50, when *Warspite* sighted the Italian battleships and at once engaged the leading one. A few minutes later she obtained an unmistakable hit amidships on her target. The damage that this hit caused to the *Giulio Cesare* was, in fact, considerable. Apart from wreckage among the light armaments on her upper deck, she had four boilers put out of action and suffered 115 casualties. Her speed was temporarily reduced to 18 knots. The tactical consequences were quickly observed from *Warspite*; for the enemy at once made a large turn away. As we had previously captured the Italian naval codes we were now able to read their admiral's signal to his destroyers to cover his retirement with smoke. Our aircraft watched, with some amusement, the confusion which this manœuvre caused in the enemy's ranks.

There next took place a confused action between the British cruisers and destroyers and the enemy light forces, which were covering his battle squadron's retirement. The Italian flotillas fired torpedoes, all of which missed, but one of their 8-inch cruisers received several shell hits. The smoke-screen was, however, effectively laid, and his light forces darted in and out of it, firing a few rounds and then disappearing again. This made them exceedingly difficult targets to hit. *Warspite* and *Malaya* both joined briefly

* See p. 116. Captain O'Conor, one of the most brilliant of the younger generation of naval officers, was lost when the *Neptune* was mined off Tripoli in December, 1941.

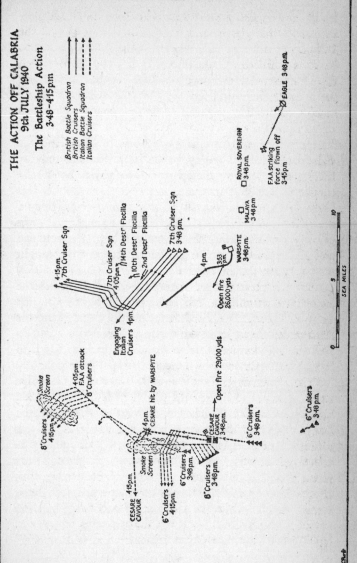

THE ACTION OFF CALABRIA
9th JULY 1940

The Battleship Action
3·48–4·15 p.m.

British Battle Squadron
British Cruisers
Italian Battle Squadron
Italian Cruisers

4·15 p.m. 7th Cruiser Sqn
7th Cruiser Sqn
4·05 p.m.
10th Destr Flotilla
14th Destr Flotilla
2nd Destr Flotilla
7th Cruiser Sqn 3·48 p.m.

Engaging Italian Cruisers 4 p.m.

4 p.m.
3·53 p.m.
Open fire 26,000 yds
WARSPITE 3·48 p.m.

ROYAL SOVEREIGN 3·48 p.m.

MALAYA 3·48 p.m.

FAA striking force flown off 3·45 p.m.

EAGLE 3·48 p.m.

SEA MILES
0   5   10

8" Cruisers 4·15 p.m.
Smoke Screen
4·05 p.m. FAA attack
8" Cruisers
4 p.m. CESARE hit by WARSPITE
Open fire 29,000 yds
CESARE hit by WARSPITE
CESARE CAVOUR 3·48 p.m.
CESARE CAVOUR 4·15 p.m.
Smoke Screen
6" Cruisers 4·15 p.m.
6" Cruisers 3·48 p.m.
6" Cruisers 3·48 p.m.
6" Cruisers 3·48 p.m.
8" Cruisers 3·48 p.m.
6" Cruisers 3·48 p.m.

Map 5

in the fight, but little damage was done on either side. Gradually the enemy drew away to the west behind the smoke, and by 4.50 all firing had ceased. Admiral Cunningham suspected, quite correctly as it turned out, that the enemy would try to lure him over a submarine ambush, and he therefore declined to enter the area covered by smoke. Instead he decided to work round to the north of it.

By 5 p.m. not an enemy ship was in sight, and the Calabrian coast was clearly visible from *Warspite*, only 25 miles away. Our aircraft reported the enemy to be making for the Straits of Messina at high speed, and when his high-level bombers renewed their attacks they distributed their loads with a pleasant impartiality against their own ships as well as ours. The angry signals from the Italian admiral which this provoked were decoded with delight in the British flagship.

When it became clear to Admiral Cunningham that the enemy had no intention of renewing the fight he turned towards Malta. He cruised to the south of that island for the next 24 hours, while the destroyers entered harbour to fuel. The two convoys from Malta had meanwhile sailed to the east under their own escorts, and early on 11th July the main body of the fleet followed. Once again our ships were subjected to heavy and persistent bombing attacks. The ordeal which *Warspite* underwent is shown by the fact that during the forenoon of the 12th her officers counted no less than 300 bombs dropped around her in twenty-two attacks; and on one occasion two dozen heavy bombs fell close along her port side simultaneously with another dozen off her starboard bow, all within 200 yards of the ship. Yet neither she nor any other ship suffered any damage. For *Warspite* it was the beginning of a period which the air defence officer remembers as consisting of

" Bombs, bombs and bombs ! " " Yet," he continues, " surprisingly few ships were hit. . . . In my memory I can only reach back to the sounding of alarm bells, to the whine of the forced-draught fans as the ship rapidly increased speed, and to the wide swathes of bombs as they crossed and re-crossed the fleet. Action Stations, Defence Stations and, much more rarely Cruising Stations [the lowest degree of readiness]. One after the other, day in, day out. On one occasion, in an interval between air attacks, a tired bridge messenger accidentally tripped up, and shot a jug of scalding cocoa down the back of my neck. My roar of pain coincided with the ' Air Raid Red ' alarm bells. Captain Fisher turned round and said to me, ' We seem to be rather noisy in our closing-up to-day, A.D.O.' "[23]

The flagship and part of the fleet, together with the fast convoy from Malta, arrived safely back in Alexandria on the 13th July. The other two battleships and the *Eagle* followed a day later, and on the 15th the slow convoy also made port safely under a separate escort.

So ended a successful operation. The " Action off Calabria " on 9th July, 1940, though indecisive, appears to-day to have had more important results than could have been realised at the time ; for it undoubtedly established a moral ascendancy over the Italian Fleet, and it set the pattern for many future encounters. Furthermore, it had shown the enemy that, even if our fleet was inferior in numbers, speed and gun-power, it could still command the central Mediterranean, and under Admiral Cunningham's determined leadership would certainly do so again. Nor can the tactical confusion during his retirement, and the poor co-ordination shown by the Italian Air Force's attacks on their own ships have afforded the enemy any comfort. True they had got back to harbour with only a battleship and a heavy cruiser damaged; but a chance to achieve a big result had certainly not been seized.

On our side much was owed to *Warspite* herself. It was her long-range support which brought relief to the hard-pressed cruisers; and it was she who " by hitting the *Cesare* in the ribs at 26,000 yards," caused the enemy battle squadron to retire. But the operation had shown Admiral Cunningham that to enable him to force a decision against a superior enemy who was reluctant to fight he badly needed more, and more modern, ships. He told the First Sea Lord that he " must have one more ship (besides *Warspite*) that can shoot to a good range"[24], that the old battleships were more of a handicap than a source of strength to him, that he needed 8-inch as well as 6-inch cruisers; and that perhaps the most valuable reinforcement of all would be a modern carrier with an armoured flight deck, able to provide fighter protection for the fleet. " But," he characteristically ended, " don't think I am discouraged. I am not a bit . . . on the bright side I do not think we need expect anything very dashing from the Italian Fleet."[25]

CHAPTER EIGHT

From Calabria to Crete
July 1940 - May 1941

> " Sir—We have taken and destroyed all the Spanish
> ships and vessels which were upon this coast, the
> number as per margin."
>
> *Captain George Walton of H.M.S. 'Canterbury'*
> *to Admiral Sir George Byng, 6th August, 1718*

> " Five ships of the enemy fleet were sunk, burned or
> destroyed as per margin."
>
> *Admiral Sir Andrew Cunningham's despatch on*
> *the Battle of Matapan, March 28th, 1941*

AT THE end of July, 1940, the Mediterranean Fleet was
once more at sea, this time to cover a convoy from the
Dardanelles. Early next month *Warspite* was briefly docked,
and then she repainted herself in camouflage colours. On
16th August Admiral Cunningham was off again with his
main strength, and bombarded the fortifications of Bardia
at dawn next day. *Warspite* used her 6-inch as well as her
15-inch guns at the shore targets, while her 4-inch were
helping to beat off air attacks. Alexandria was now being
bombed fairly frequently. The proximity of the Italian
desert airfields and the weakness of the defences of the fleet
base meant that the ships could get little rest in harbour,
for their anti-aircraft guns were constantly in action at
night.

For all the handicaps which Admiral Cunningham had
to overcome—the age, even obsolescence, of many of his

ships, the enemy's superior strength, his own lack of effective fighter cover and the insecurity of his bases—the period which followed the first trial of strength off Calabria was one of great achievements. During that time the Mediterranean Fleet, aided certainly by Admiral Somerville's Force H working from Gibraltar, established so complete an ascendancy over the Italians that Malta was kept adequately supplied, occasional convoys were run straight through to Alexandria, the enemy's communications to North Africa were harassed and his Navy was several times severely handled. By the early days of 1941 it was plain to the Germans that Italy was cracking under the pressure of the Mediterranean Fleet and the Army of the Nile. They acted promptly, and sent firstly the Luftwaffe and the Afrika Korps, and later the U-boats to "prop up Italy." In this purpose they were temporarily successful, and their success brought its supreme trial to Admiral Cunningham's command. But in the summer of 1940 there were no such portents in the sky, and the fleet was working with ever-rising vigour to achieve the victory over Italy which appeared to be just around the corner.

At the end of August *Warspite* and the fleet sailed again to command the central and eastern Mediterranean during a composite operation to pass strong reinforcements (including *Warspite*'s newly-reconstructed sister *Valiant* and the modern carrier *Illustrious*) through to Admiral Cunningham, to cover the first of the long series of convoys to Malta from the east, and to carry military and air reinforcements to the island from the west. The Italian fleet put to sea, but made no attempt to intervene. On the morning of 2nd September, when *Warspite* was within sight of Malta, the reinforcements from Gibraltar joined the commander-in-chief. That evening the flagship was again bombed unsuccessfully. "It was around this time," writes her air defence officer, "that I am said to have reported to the command position 'Formation bearing Red 30 is friendly.' A short time later one of the air look-outs reported: 'Friendly aircraft Red 30. Friendly bombs released!' The story spread from the directors to the transmitting stations, to all the gun positions and so around the whole ship—to everyone's delight. But in all these actions it seemed to me that it was like playing hockey against a much faster opponent. Sometimes it was hard to find the ball."[1]

The strengthened fleet now returned to the east, passing north of Crete to give the *Illustrious* a first chance to show her mettle by attacking enemy installations on Rhodes. On the morning of the 5th all ships were safely back in Alexandria. Apart from damage to one merchantman, not a casualty had been suffered.

The next operation began in the small hours of 29th September, and again had as its main object the passing of military and air reinforcements into Malta. *Warspite*, *Valiant*, *Illustrious*, *York*, the 3rd and 7th Cruiser Squadrons and destroyers took part. The carrier operated her aircraft almost continuously, and the fighter cover she provided, helped by the ships' guns, defeated all air attacks; but the flagship was narrowly missed by one salvo of bombs, and also by four air torpedoes. On the 30th enemy warships were reported about sixty miles away to the north-west, and Actions Stations was ordered; but the Italians withdrew in the face of such strength, and after endeavouring till after nightfall to cut them off from their bases, Cunningham turned east again. A practice shoot was carried out off Alexandria, and late on 2nd October the fleet returned briefly to harbour.

A week later Cunningham sailed to pass convoys to and from Malta once again, and to try to tempt the Italian fleet to battle. His four battleships, two carriers, six cruisers and sixteen destroyers made a brave array. The light forces fuelled in Malta, while the main body of the fleet cruised to the south of the island all the afternoon of the 11th. Though this trailing of his coat did not bring the fleet action desired by the commander-in-chief, Italian light forces were encountered by the cruisers, and three of their destroyers were sunk. On the way back the carrier-borne fighters dealt with all bombing attacks, and the Fleet Air Arm dive-bombers attacked the island of Leros in the Dodecanese; but on the 14th the cruiser *Liverpool* was torpedoed and badly damaged. *Warspite* and other ships stood by the cripple while she was taken in tow, and early on the 16th she got back to Alexandria—during an air-raid. Captain Fisher remembers how he had to lead the fleet up the Great Pass into harbour while all navigation lights were extinguished—" a very tricky affair."[2] The operation had been wholly successful, and *Warspite*'s track chart clearly shows how Cunningham's great concourse of ships had held complete control of the eastern and central basins from 8th-16th October during the passage of the two convoys.

On the 28th of October, Mussolini made his unprovoked attack on Greece, thus bringing Britain a new ally, but also adding to the fleet's responsibilities. Next day reinforcements sailed for Crete, covered by the fleet; for it was intended to establish a naval base in the excellent harbour of Suda Bay, and to build airfields on the island. Unhappily the acute shortage of equipment from which all the services were suffering made these desirable developments all too slow. After only four days in harbour Cunningham sailed again on 6th November. More reinforcements, including the *Barham* and two cruisers, were on their way from Gibraltar to join him, supplies were again being passed into

Malta from the east and from the west—and, best of all, the commander-in-chief was now able to carry out a long-cherished plan to attack the main Italian base at Taranto with the torpedo-bombers from his two carriers. Covered and protected by the fleet's main strength, twenty-one Swordfish took off from the *Illustrious* on the evening of the 11th from a position 180 miles south-east of Taranto. The attack was completely successful and the Italian battleships *Littorio*, *Duilio* and *Cavour* were severely damaged and sunk at their moorings.[3] Though the first two were raised about six months later and repaired, the *Cavour* took no further part in the war. The balance of power in the Mediterranean had been transformed at a blow, and one happy consequence was that a fortnight later a convoy of three ships (two for Malta and one for Alexandria), and two more cruisers for Admiral Cunningham's command, were passed straight through from Gibraltar. A powerful proportion of the fleet, including the flagship, came west from Alexandria to meet the reinforcements. On the 26th *Warspite* anchored in Suda Bay to land a commando she had embarked, and then steered for Malta. She met the ships coming from Gibraltar, and returned to Alexandria with them. Once again our command of the central basin had been convincingly demonstrated.

In the early hours of 16th December Cunningham sailed to call briefly again at Suda Bay and then to bombard the Albanian port of Valona, which the Italians were using to supply the army against which the Greeks were putting up such a valiant resistance. It was a bold plan to enter the Adriatic with heavy ships, only some 100 miles from Taranto, and it was the recent success of the Fleet Air Arm attack on that base which made it possible. From Suda Bay *Warspite* steamed up the west coast of Greece past the Ionian Islands she had known so well in peace—

Zante, Cephalonia and Corfu. Memories of regattas at Nava-
rino or Argostoli must have stirred in the minds of her
older hands as she sped past them, darkened, on her un-
friendly errand. At 1.15 a.m. on 19th she and the *Valiant*
opened fire, and *Warspite* delivered fourteen salvos of 15-inch
shells into the port and on the airfield. Surprise was complete, and there was no reply to the crashing explosions
on shore. About a score of Italian aircraft were wrecked.
Then Admiral Cunningham went south again, and on
20th *Warspite* entered Grand Harbour, Valletta, for the
first time since she had called there in October, 1939, on
her way to Halifax.* It was a stirring encouragement to
the Maltese to see the flagship in Grand Harbour once
again, even if the former cynosure of the fleet was now
dazzle-painted, scarred with rust and her guns blistered
from recent use. The people gave Admiral Cunningham
and the whole ship's company an enthusiastic reception
wherever they went in the island. The commander-
in-chief found "the base as effective as when war
broke out, and far better defended against air attacks or
invasion "[4]; but he realised that, in spite of all that had
been accomplished in recent months, serious deficiencies
still existed.

Embarked in *Warspite* at that time was the representative
of America's Associated Press, Mr. Larry Allen. He had
gained a great name by his fearlessness under bomber
attack and his irrepressible humour in all circumstances.
On the one evening the ship spent in Malta Captain Fisher
and a party of officers took the reporter ashore to play
bowls in the Junior Officers' Club—the scene of many hila-
rious reunions in peace-time. Mr. Allen wrote his report on
the evening in his best A.P. style (for circulation only in the
ship). It ended: "Malta's gayest night in months ended

* See p. 196.

with a score in liquidity, rather than numerals. The results
—four cases of beer liquidated, six bottles left, smuggled
on board in violation of ship's regulations."[5] Early on the
22nd, after this brief interlude of gaiety, *Warspite* slipped
out of Grand Harbour, and Christmas Eve found her back
in Alexandria once again.

The flagship's first action of 1941 came very early in
the New Year when, on 2nd January, she carried out
another 15-inch bombardment of Bardia in support of the
advancing Army of the Nile*; but her next operation,
which started before the year was many days older, made
it plain that the halcyon days of 1940 were over, and that
severe trials lay ahead. On 6th January a fast convoy bound
for Malta and Greece left Gibraltar. Admiral Cunningham
sailed next day to pass two merchantmen to Malta, to
bring out empty ships from the island, and to meet and
support the convoy from Gibraltar. The full strength
from both ends of the Mediterranean was thrown in for
these important movements. The passage of the convoy
and warships from the west went well until the morning
of the 10th, when they were met by Admiral Cunningham off
Malta with *Warspite*, *Valiant*, *Illustrious* and other ships
from Alexandria. He had, however, been shadowed by
enemy aircraft continuously, ever since leaving his base,
and that afternoon very heavy air attacks took place. They
were of a far more dangerous nature than had previously
been experienced in the Mediterranean, for Hitler had just
moved an entire "Flieger Korps" of the German Air
Force (about 150 bombers) to Sicily to support his Italian
allies.[6] *Warspite* was hit a glancing blow by one bomb
right on her starboard anchor, but it did her practically
no damage. The enemy concentrated mainly on the
Illustrious, which quickly received six hits. She limped into

* See Map 6. (pp. 232-233).

Malta after dark. We will quote the entries in *Warspite's* log for these hectic hours:

10th January, 1941

0805	*Bonaventure* [light cruiser] in action with two destroyers. One sunk, one escaped.
0830	*Gallant* [destroyer] hit by torpedo.
1128	Fulmars [Fleet Air Arm fighters] shot down one shadower.
1222	Fired barrage. One torpedo dropped.
1228	Attacked by 30-40 Stukas [German dive-bombers] and CR.79s [Italian high-level bombers]. Opened fire. Two or three hits seen on *Illustrious*. Noon position 36°01' North 13°04' East.
1316	Near miss on starboard bow damaged paravane chains and starboard anchor.
1328	Opened fire with 4-inch at high-level bombers. Attack not pressed home.
1336	Ceased fire. *Illustrious* and two destroyers detached to Malta.
1618	Port 4-inch opened fire. Attacked by Stukas.
1625	Ceased fire.
1700	Malta in sight.
1715	Five aircraft in sight. Opened fire 4-inch and pom-poms.
1730	Ceased fire.

The air attacks continued next day, when the cruiser *Southampton* was sunk and the *Gloucester* damaged. Though the object of the operation was accomplished the cost had been heavy, and Malta was now under the lash of the Luftwaffe. On 23rd the damaged *Illustrious* slipped out of Grand Harbour and reached Alexandria safely two days later. The fleet " cleared lower deck " to cheer the carrier's arrival. "How proud we felt," wrote one of *Warspite's* officers, "when the *Illustrious* eventually reached Alexandria, badly damaged but by no means disabled. She had certainly gone through a very rough time." "Well," wrote Admiral Cunningham philosophically after these severe trials, "we have had a set-back; but we have been in the same position before, and I have no doubt we shall overcome our present difficulties."[7]

On the night of the last day of January the destroyer *Greyhound*, when leaving Alexandria harbour, rammed the *Warspite* and damaged her slightly. Her ship's book contains the entry that the collision was "dealt with by local action," and one cannot but feel that the commander-in-chief's generous solution was a happy one; for the *Greyhound* was soon to be sunk off Crete, where her captain, Commander W. R. Marshall A'Deane, lost his life in most gallant attempts to rescue survivors. Emergency repairs were done to *Warspite's* damaged bulge compartments.

The check received in January made no difference to Cunningham's determination, and early next month he was again in the central basin.* Though he swept to within sight of Cape Spartivento (on the "toe" of Italy) no opposition was encountered, and no air attacks took place; but Malta was still under heavy bombing, and magnetic mines were being dropped in the Suez Canal to block that life-line of all our forces in the Middle East. At the end of February *Warspite* was briefly docked at Alexandria.

Meanwhile the German threat to Greece was becoming plain, and early in March we started to send reinforcements there from Egypt. This greatly added to the strain on the fleet, and invited reprisals against our convoys running to

* See Map 6.

and from Piraeus. No surprise was therefore felt when, on 25th March, Cunningham received indications that a sortie by the Italian fleet was likely. He was determined to do all he could to encourage such a purpose, but at first cleared the eastern basin of our shipping so that the enemy's blow should fall on air. The light forces under Vice-Admiral H. D. Pridham-Wippell were sent to the south of Crete to await developments, and on the evening of the 27th the main body of the fleet—*Warspite*, *Valiant*, *Barham*, the carrier *Formidable* (which had recently come through the Suez Canal to replace the damaged *Illustrious*) and nine destroyers slipped quietly out of harbour; for at noon that day an R.A.F. flying-boat had reported enemy forces steering towards Crete.

·All the next night Cunningham steered to the north-west. At dawn on the 28th air searches were started, and very soon the *Formidable*'s aircraft and the light forces both reported the enemy. At 8.30 the battle squadron raised steam for full speed, and Cunningham set course to support Admiral Pridham-Wippell, who was hotly engaged with the much superior enemy. The *Formidable*'s striking force was sent to attack the battleship *Vittorio Veneto*, but did not succeed in hitting her. Though the situation remained obscure until later in the day the Italian fleet actually consisted of the one battleship and of two cruiser squadrons of five and three ships respectively. The enemy reports sent by our forces were, of course, being intercepted in the Admiralty, where the situation was being anxiously watched. "As I am dictating this," says a letter from the First Sea Lord to Admiral Cunningham, "you are chasing the Italians to the southward of Crete, and we are hoping to hear that your striking force from the *Formidable* and from Crete may be able . . . to slow the Italians up enough for you to get on terms with them."[8] There can be few

better examples of " two minds with but a single thought,"
for that was exactly what Cunningham was trying to do.
By 12.30 p.m. Admiral Pridham-Wippell had rejoined the
commander-in-chief with all his ships unscathed, and it
was plain that the whole Italian fleet had turned west
again. It was then about sixty miles away, and prospects
of catching it were not good—unless the carrier's torpedo-
bombers could damage and slow down the enemy. The
pursuit thus entered its second phase.

We will now leave the opposing forces temporarily,
and take the reader on to the admiral's bridge of *Warspite*.
This was placed just below the compass platform, from
which the captain navigated and fought the ship. It consisted only of a narrow space of deck on each side of the
ship, joined by a covered passage at the forward end. In
the centre was the charthouse, where staff officers kept the
plot of our own ships' and the enemy's movements continuously up to date. From the admiral's bridge a very
poor view was obtained—especially ahead—the direction
in which Admiral Cunningham was most wont to look.
With his staff and assistants around him the narrow space
was also very congested; but so was the captain's compass
platform, where all the controls for the ship's many armaments were situated. Immense trouble had been taken over
the design of *Warspite's* new bridge structure in 1936-37,
and Portsmouth dockyard actually built it first in wood to
enable the best solution to be reached; but it would be
idle to pretend that the final design satisfied, or could
satisfy, all interested parties. Many of their needs were
indeed fundamentally conflicting, and the design finally
accepted was in fact a bundle of compromises. Whenever
the fleet was at sea Cunningham—or " A.B.C.," as he was
everywhere known—used to spend most of his time on
the admiral's bridge. If enemy forces were about he

would pace up and down the narrow space, *always on the side nearer to the enemy*. His staff called this "the caged tiger act," and knew their commander well enough to recognise the sign, and to keep clear except on urgent matters. Always the steady pacing showed his impatience to get at the enemy. When action was imminent the admiral would go up to the compass platform, and manœuvre the fleet from there. This added to the already severe congestion; but there was no other place whence he could see the enemy and his own ships too. This was, of course, long before the days of automatic radar plots. On the morning of 28th March, then, the admiral was as usual on his bridge, pacing up and down on the starboard side, receiving the flood of enemy reports, assessing the situation and glancing occasionally at the plot. His one object was to catch the enemy main force, and he knew that he could only do that if the torpedo-bombers reduced its speed. Accordingly a series of attacks was made from the *Formidable* and from the shore base at Maleme in Crete during the afternoon. At 3.10 p.m. one torpedo hit was obtained on the battleship, and she slowed down. Hopes rose on the admiral's bridge; but soon it was plain that the fleeing enemy had again picked up speed. At 4 p.m. Cunningham therefore sent his light forces ahead to gain visual touch, and launched another air striking force.

One of *Warspite's* aircraft had been catapulted early in the afternoon for gunnery spotting purposes in the event of a fleet action, but the other was held back in case an urgent reconnaissance requirement should arise. At 5.45 this aircraft, whose observer was Lieutenant-Commander A. S. Bolt, was sent to clear up the uncertainty regarding the composition and movements of the Italian fleet. Three-quarters of an hour later Bolt gave the admiral the first really accurate reports he had received. The Italian com-

mander-in-chief (Admiral Iachino) later expressed his
envious admiration of the accuracy of these reports; for
he himself was still totally unaware that the British battle
squadron was at sea, let alone in hot pursuit of his force.
At sunset (about 7.30 p.m.) a last torpedo-striking force
attacked through the intense fire of the concentrated array
of Italian ships. The heavy cruiser *Pola* was hit and came
to a stop. An hour later the Italian commander-in-chief
sent back the *Zara* and *Fiume* (heavy cruisers) and a division
of destroyers to aid the cripple.

As darkness fell with the fleeing enemy still eluding his
grasp, Cunningham had to decide whether to accept night
action, with all the attendant risks and uncertainties. It is
probable that by 8 p.m. he had actually made his own
mind up, but he went through the formality of asking his
staff for their opinions. They, as was their duty, pointed
out the dangers, and one of them remembers " A.B.C."
answering : " You're a pack of yellow-livered skunks.
I'll go and have my supper now, and after supper see if
my morale is higher than yours."[9] The light forces were
now closing the enemy, and the battle squadron coming up
in support. At 9 p.m. Admiral Pridham-Wippell reported
passing close to a stopped ship, and the commander-in-
chief, who had now gone up on to the *Warspite*'s compass
platform decided to investigate.

He turned the battle squadron 40 degrees to port
together, and made for the position in single line ahead at
twenty knots. The *Valiant* had the only radar set in the
battle squadron, and at 10 p.m. she detected the stopped
ship eight miles away to port. It was a dark night, with
no moon. The big guns were all trained on the port bow
and " in tense readiness the great ships held on towards
the enemy."[10] By 10.20 the range was four and a half miles,
and the only destroyer on the port bow was told to clear

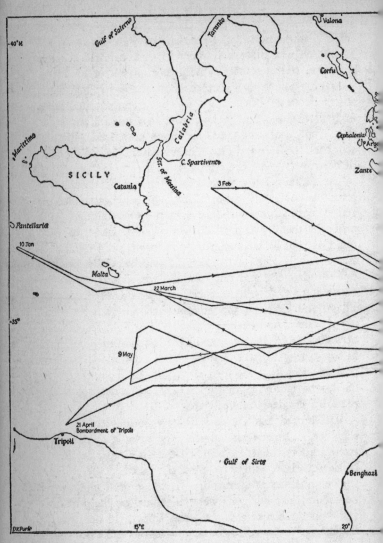

Map 6

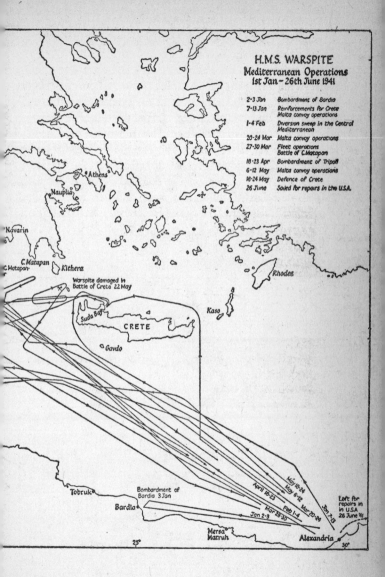

H.M.S. WARSPITE
Mediterranean Operations
1st Jan – 26th June 1941

2-3 Jan	Bombardment of Bardia
7-13 Jan	Reinforcements for Crete Malta convoy operations
1-4 Feb	Diversion sweep in the Central Mediterranean
20-24 Mar	Malta convoy operations
27-30 Mar	Fleet operations Battle of C.Matapan
18-23 Apr	Bombardment of Tripoli
6-12 May	Malta convoy operations
18-24 May	Defence of Crete
26 June	Sailed for repairs in the U.S.A.

Athens

Nauplia

Navarin

C. Matapan
C. Matapan

Kithera

Rhodes

Warspite damaged in Battle of Crete 22 May

Suda Bay

CRETE

Kaso

Gavdo

May 18-24
May 6-12
April 18-23
Jan 7-13

Feb 1-4

Mar 20-24

Tobruk

Bombardment of Bardia 3 Jan

Mar 27-30

Left for repairs in in U.S.A 26 June '41

Bardia

Jan 2-3

Mersa Matruh

Alexandria

25°

30°

the line of fire with a curt "Get to hell out of it." As he closed Cunningham handled the battle squadron as though it was a division of destroyers. He first turned to the south-west, bringing the ships into quarter-line. Suddenly the Chief of Staff (Commodore J. H. Edelsten*), who was looking out on the disengaged bow, sighted darkened ships steering a course to cross ahead of the battle squadron; and he gave the first "alarm."† The turrets were actually already swinging round in that direction, and for the next few seconds the silence on the flagship's bridge—broken only by the lap of the ship's wash and the hum of her machinery—was eerie. It was a perfect example of the good

* Now Admiral Sir John H. Edelsten, G.C.B., C.B.E.
† See Map 7.

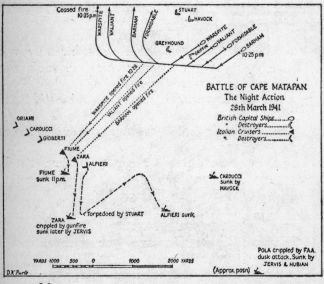

BATTLE OF CAPE MATAPAN
The Night Action
28th March 1941
British Capital Ships..........
"   Destroyers..............
Italian Cruisers................
"   Destroyers.............

Map 7

234

drill and strict discipline which alone can prevent confusion in a night encounter. Then the various control
positions reported that they could see the targets, and that
their armaments were " ready." Next came the captain's
order to open fire. Just before the ringing of the 15-inch
fire gong brought the blinding flash and shattering con-
cussion of the first main armament broadside, the destroyer
Greyhound illuminated the targets with her searchlight. They
were identified unmistakably as Italian heavy cruisers.
Cunningham had meanwhile altered to starboard to bring all
guns to bear, and told the *Formidable*, for her own safety,
to haul out of the line. The enemy ships, which were
the *Zara* and *Fiume*, "stood out like haystacks" to an observer on *Warspite*'s bridge ; yet they were caught totally
unprepared, with their guns trained fore and aft. Here
are the entries in *Warspite*'s report for these dramatic
minutes :

10.25.30	Sighted three cruisers and two destroyers 10 degrees on starboard bow. [Actually two cruisers and four destroyers.]
10.26.30	Altered course to 280° to open " A Arcs " on port side.
10.26.40	Alarm Port. [The targets were then fine on port bow.]
10.27.12	Searchlights " Target." [Trained on the enemy and ready.]
10.27.15	15-inch guns " Target."
10.27.25	Starshell guns " Target."
10.27.30	6-inch guns " Target."
10.27.45	*Greyhound* illuminates with searchlight.
10.27.55	Open Fire.
10.28.00	First 15-inch broadside. Range 2,900 yards. Six guns fired, five or six hits. The enemy

burst into vivid flame from just abaft the bridge to the after turret.

10.28.10	First 6-inch salvo.
10.28.40	Second 15-inch broadside, eight guns, mostly hit. The ship now a mass of fire.
10.28.50	Shift one ship left.
10.29.18	Third 15-inch broadside at new target. Range 3,500 yards. Mostly hit. The ship burst into flames.

Enemy destroyers were then engaged by *Warspite's* main and secondary armaments. In all she fired forty rounds of 15-inch armour-piercing shell and forty-four rounds of 6-inch high explosive.

On the compass platform the first 15-inch broadside brought an astonished ejaculation from Captain Fisher: " Good God, we've hit her." This delighted " A.B.C.," all the more for the fact that his flag captain had himself been a distinguished gunnery officer. Another of *Warspite's* officers remembers that "In some ways the battle resembled a peace-time night exercise, with the battle squadron perfectly in station and so much noise and flash that one could do nothing more than concentrate on the dials and pointers that concerned oneself."[11] Such were the fruits of the training in night-fighting by heavy ships, which we had constantly practised ever since the Battle of Jutland had driven home the need.*

There is actually some controversy over which ship fired at which target during those hectic minutes. Admiral Cunningham and others who were with him are certain that *Warspite* first fired at the leading ship, and then shifted to the second one, leaving her first target to the *Valiant*; but Captain Fisher remains convinced that he engaged the

* See p. 139.

targets in the reverse order. It does not much matter. Both were quickly demolished, while the destroyers finished off the damaged *Pola* and sank two of the Italian destroyers which were with the *Zara* and *Fiume*.* At midnight Cunningham gave his scattered forces a rendezvous for daylight on the 29th to the south of Cape Matapan, the loom of whose light was sighted from *Warspite* at 4 a.m. He was intensely relieved when, on arriving there, all twelve of his destroyers hove in sight; for he had seen one of them, the *Havock*, apparently straddled by a 15-inch salvo from *Warspite* during the battle, and felt sure she had been sunk. To give the fleet the results of the action as soon as possible, the flagship hoisted the signal: " General from C.-in-C. Mediterranean. *Zara, Pola* and *Fiume* sunk." The search for the enemy battleship was then resumed, but in vain; for she was safely shepherded out of Admiral Cunningham's reach during the night. On the way back to harbour *Warspite* passed through the previous night's battlefield, where she noticed " the smell of burnt-out ships," and sighted rafts around which our destroyers were picking up survivors. Attacks by German bombers did no damage, and on the evening of 30th the fleet re-entered Alexandria.

The ships in port gave the victors a tumultuous welcome, and the world at large regarded the destruction " of three of the enemy's fast, well-armed and armoured cruisers and two destroyers for the loss of only one air-craft " as a substantial success.[12] In terms of tactics the battle brought to Admiral Cunningham the advantage of having eliminated three of the only Italian heavy cruisers whose armour protection was sufficient to keep out the 6-inch projectiles of his own cruisers. But in terms of strategy the results were much more far-reaching; for the

* See Map 7.

heavy losses suffered that night off Cape Matapan, and the narrow margin by which their damaged flagship escaped back to harbour, were a severe shock to the Italian Navy. The direct consequence was that they made no further attempt to interfere with the passage of our reinforcements to Greece, nor did they venture forth again when the time came for the Mediterranean fleet to evacuate our soldiers from the mainland and from Crete. Though the escape of the *Vittorio Veneto* marred the completeness of the victory, and prevented the commander-in-chief from feeling wholly satisfied over the result, it cannot be doubted that, had the battle not been fought and won, the hazardous evacuations which were so soon to tax his fleet to the limit might well have been made impossible.

On the last day of March Captain Fisher " cleared lower deck " and addressed his ship's company, and on the next day a Thanksgiving Service was held throughout the fleet.

Shortly after Matapan things began to go very badly for the Army of the Nile, depleted as it had been by the decision to send as much strength as possible to Greece, and faced as it now was by Rommel and the German " Afrika Korps." The enemy's rapid advance on land aroused grave misgivings in London over the arrival of reinforcements and supplies at Tripoli, and heavy pressure was applied by the Prime Minister for the Navy to block the port. Admiral Cunningham did not like the idea, and considered that the proper answer was for light forces and submarines from Malta to attack the enemy convoys at sea, and for the R.A.F. to bomb the port. However, he finally agreed to take his whole fleet into those dangerous waters to bombard Tripoli, and to use the opportunity to pass convoys into and out from Malta.[13] On 18th April he sailed for these purposes, fuelled at Suda Bay and then steamed west. Contrary to expectations there were no serious air attacks on the outward journey, and at three minutes past 5 a.m. on 21st April (three minutes late on the planned time, after having come 1,200 miles), *Warspite* opened fire with 15-inch and 6-inch guns to the light of flares dropped by *Formidable*'s aircraft. Her targets were the main quay and shipping in harbour. The shore defences were taken completely by surprise, and it was twenty minutes before the coastal batteries answered. At 5.24 the fleet reversed course and continued the bombardment. Twenty minutes later "Cease Fire" was ordered, and Cunningham set course for Alexandria at twenty-one knots. The weight of explosive thrown into the enemy base by the whole fleet was some 530 tons, to which *Warspite* contributed 135 15-inch and 106 6-inch shells. The wear on her guns must by this time have been getting serious; and no one could say when an opportunity could be found to replace them. Though the bombardment certainly appeared spectacular and probably had some moral effect, we now know that only one ship was sunk in the harbour, and although much damage was done in the town the military installations suffered little. By noon on the 23rd all ships had returned to Alexandria safely. "In spite of the immunity on this occasion," wrote the commander-in-chief, "I do not consider . . . that the results justified hazarding the whole . . . fleet in mined waters and exposed to potentially heavy air attacks at such a distance from its base."[14]

Meanwhile the German attack on Greece had started on the 6th, and it soon became plain that the Navy would have to rescue the survivors of our outnumbered expeditionary force. On 16th April at a conference between Admiral Cunningham, General Wavell and Air Marshal Longmore on board *Warspite*, the decision was taken to evacuate our troops. Two days later the fleet sailed to carry out the bombardment of Tripoli already described, and did not return until the 23rd. Between 24th and 30th April 50,732 men (about 80 per cent of those carried to Greece) were brought away by the cruisers and destroyers of the fleet and by lightly-armed transports, or escaped in requisitioned small craft. The Italian Navy, shaken by its recent experiences off Cape Matapan, made no attempt to interfere. German bombers caused some losses to our light forces and transports, but they were not disproportionate to the results achieved. By 4th May the fleet was re-assembled in Alexandria for a brief period of rest; but the omens for the future could hardly have been worse, for Crete was now seriously threatened, and whereas the powerful German Air Force had many bases near at hand, the R.A.F. had few airfields on the island, and was desperately short of every type of aircraft.

Never was pressure on the fleet as heavy as during these months of April and May, 1941. Apart from the continuous problems of supplying Malta and the Army's forward bases at Tobruk and other ports in Egypt and Cyrenaica, it had to interfere with enemy traffic to Africa, it had just defeated the Italian fleet off Cape Matapan, bombarded Tripoli and evacuated Greece. Now an even more difficult task awaited its hard-driven ships. But before that crisis arose it still had to steam west once more, to take part in an operation to pass four fast merchantmen with urgently needed tanks for the Army straight through the Mediterranean. Once again Admiral Cunningham had to use his full strength. He sailed in *Warspite* on 6th May, took the opportunity to pass two convoys into Malta, met the ships from Gibraltar off the island on the 8th, and then set course for Alexandria. Heavy air attacks took place on the night of the 10th, but the terrific barrage put up by the fleet prevented accurate bombing, and no damage was done. On the 12th all forces were safely back in their base. Only one of the tank-carrying merchantmen was lost. In the course of this operation *Warspite*'s sister-ship and her nearest rival for historic fame, the recently reconstructed *Queen Elizabeth*, and two new cruisers joined the Mediterranean fleet. Never were reinforcements more welcome, for almost at once Cunningham had to send his light forces to watch the northern approaches to Crete to prevent any sea-borne landings. Thus was the stage set for the Battle of Crete.

On 20th May the enemy opened the attack with very heavy bombing, followed by glider and parachute landings. Admiral Cunningham had temporarily shifted his flag ashore at Alexandria, the better to co-ordinate his fleet's work with the other services, and Rear-Admiral H. B. Rawlings had hoisted his flag in *Warspite* in command of the 1st Battle Squadron. When the attack started she, the *Valiant*, one cruiser and ten destroyers were covering the light forces working close inshore, from a position about 100 miles west of Crete. "What a difference some air support would have made," writes a *Warspite* officer; "For we were fighting almost within sight of enemy-held airfields. We could see a great arc of Ju. 52 troop-carriers approach-ing to land Germans in Crete, but were helpless."[15] The cruisers and destroyers, however, totally defeated an attempted sea-borne invasion of Crete on the night of 21st-22nd May; but as soon as each day dawned our ships came under very heavy air attacks. Throughout the 21st *Warspite*'s log is a record of almost continuous bombing. At daylight on the 22nd two of the three groups of light forces were about to join *Warspite* and the rest of the sup-porting ships. The third group of cruisers and destroyers, which had swept into the Ægean, was withdrawing under intense bombing, and was nearly out of ammunition. Admiral Rawlings learnt of this group's predicament, and at once moved east in support. At 1.32 p.m., just as junction was being effected in the Kithera Channel, formations of aircraft were seen approaching from either beam. The ship was about to engage when three fighter-bombers (Me.109s) suddenly "appeared through smoke bursts 2,000 yards ahead at an altitude of 800 feet, making a shallow dive on the ship." The captain put on full port wheel, two bombs fell 50–100 yards clear and did no damage; but the third one hit the ship on the starboard side of the forecastle deck, and burst right on the starboard after 4-inch gun. It was probably a 500-lb. semi-armour-piercing bomb, and the damage it caused was severe. A dangerous fire was started in the starboard battery, and all four 6-inch guns were put out of action; the starboard forward 4-inch A.A. twin mounting was blown completely overboard, and one boiler-room had temporarily to be abandoned. One officer and thirty-seven men were killed or died of wounds, and thirty-one men wounded. While smoke and flame were still rising from her torn decks, and more bombs were dropping all around, Admiral Rawlings quietly remarked to the captain: " I wonder which dockyard in America you will be sent to for repairs."[16]

The ship's Executive Officer, Commander Sir Charles Madden*, has left a vivid account of that afternoon's events :

" In the early afternoon we were standing in to the north-west of Crete, to provide anti-aircraft support for the cruisers. It was a clear, blue Mediterranean day.

---

* Now Rear-Admiral Sir Charles Madden, Bart., C.B. His father was Jellicoe's Chief of Staff at Jutland, commanded the Atlantic Fleet after the 1914–18 war (see p. 155), and then became First Sea Lord.

The ship was at Action Stations and I was stationed in the Upper Conning Tower, listening through the voice-pipe to what went on on the bridge. I heard the report: 'Hit starboard side amidships' and left the U.C.T. to investigate. As I reached the back of the bridge I saw dense smoke coming from the starboard 4-inch battery. On reaching the upper-deck level it was apparent that one 4-inch mounting had gone overboard completely, and that the other was at an angle. There was a huge hole in the deck between the two mountings from which smoke and flame were pouring out.

"I then went down to the port 6-inch battery to see if fire parties were ready, and to try to get at the seat of the fire through the armoured door that connected the port and starboard 6-inch battery decks. I found the fire party lined up ready by this door, asked two ratings to enter with me, and told the fire parties to open the door and follow us in. We had great difficulty in opening this door and had to use a sledge-hammer. Finally it gave, to display a gruesome scene. The starboard battery was full of flames and smoke, in among which the cries of burned and wounded men could be heard. These were very unnerving and I remember thinking how accurate were the descriptions in C. S. Forester's books of the carnage on the gun-decks in Nelson's day. The flames seemed pretty fierce and I was doubtful if we would make headway against them. However, my two volunteers came either side of me with their hoses and we walked into the battery. To my surprise the flames, which I suppose were dying down, seemed to subside before us, and soon we had the fire parties following us and were putting out the flames as we advanced.

"I was soon joined by more fire parties coming

from the after end of the starboard battery, and felt confident that I could get the fires out, but was hampered by the continued cries of the burned men, which distracted the fire parties, who wanted to leave their hoses to assist their comrades. I therefore concentrated on administering morphia.

" About this time the smoke cleared in the hole in the deckhead, and I could converse with those on the deck above. I sent for all officers with morphia, and soon had several on the job, which became the main task as soon as the flames were out. As it was dark and wounded men were thrown in all directions amidst piles of ironwork and rubbish this was not easy.

" The hole in the upper deck was now clear of smoke, and through it we could see the deep blue sky and the next wave of attacking aircraft coming at us. The 4-inch battery being out of action made it seem unpleasantly quiet, until the pompoms started up, which caused a lot of the broken ironwork to fall about. I can remember the pompom bursts filling up the area of sky we could see and the aircraft still coming on, and some of the fire parties dropping their hoses to shake their fists at them.

" I now had plenty of officers to take charge in the battery and we were moving the wounded out, so I went down to the mess-decks under the battery. The port side was cleared for casualties, which were being laid out in rows. A surprising number of men had trickled along to look after their friends, and I had some trouble in reducing their number, as they were all being kind and helpful.

" I then went to the starboard mess-decks, where a fresh and unexpected scene of carnage greeted me. The armoured deck overhead, that of the starboard

6-inch battery, had been pierced by the explosion, the force of which had descended into a mess-deck where communication ratings off watch were resting. These, contrary to instructions, and because of the heat, were lightly clad, and there were heavy casualties from burns. The great amount of water we had pumped into the battery above to put out the fires had poured into the mess-deck, which was in parts knee-deep in water, thus adding to the confusion of scattered mess tables, lockers and bodies.

"When all was under control I went to the bridge to report. The calm, blue afternoon seemed unreal after the dark and smelly carnage below.

"I then busied myself with removing the dead. I made as I thought sensible arrangements for laying them out in one of the after flats, but had not counted on the strong feelings of the men, who insisted that they should all be taken to the chapel—a tortuous journey through the armoured 'dips.' Sorting the dead out and identifying them occupied most of the dog watches, and they were then sewn up in hammocks for burial. The stout Corporal of Marines who served so cheerfully in the Wardroom bar, volunteered for and personally led this operation throughout the next two days till we returned to harbour."

Warspite, with her fires out and temporary repairs completed, stayed with the fleet through the ordeal then in progress. Then, within sight of her, first the destroyer *Greyhound* and then the cruisers *Gloucester* and *Fiji* were sunk. Next day, the 23rd, Lord Louis Mountbatten's *Kelly* and her sister the *Kashmir* fell victims to the bombers. In the early hours of the 24th the damaged *Warspite* reached Alexandria and landed her wounded. Next day Admiral

Cunningham rehoisted his flag in her, and also addressed her company. The theme of his remarks was "You must not think you have finished—you've got to go on." On the 27th the decision was taken to evacuate Crete, and the battered survivors of the fleet rose to the occasion most heroically. About 18,600 men of the garrison of 32,000 were rescued, but at a terrible price to the Navy. In all two battleships and an aircraft carrier were damaged, three cruisers and six destroyers sunk and six cruisers and seven destroyers damaged. "But the effort made by the fleet had truly been magnificent."[17]

One of *Warspite*'s seriously wounded was that same Daniel Reardon, now a chief petty officer, whose account of the Battle of Narvik was quoted earlier. He lost a leg, and when Admiral Cunningham visited the injured in hospital he specially remarked Reardon's cheerful fortitude.[18] Perhaps we may also quote that gallant sailor's own account of his last thoughts about his ship. " 2nd Battle of Narvik, bombardments in the Western Desert, Malta convoys, Greek convoys, bombardments of Valona and Tripoli, the Battle of Matapan and now that of Crete," he wrote. "The team worked well, but now I am leaving them. Those who come after will carry on where we left off. My last look at Her is from a stretcher as we are being gently carried ashore. Famous old Lady! We who served in you will always have a weak spot for you!"[19]

Warspite was taken in hand at Alexandria for such repairs as would make her fit for an ocean passage; but she had a very narrow escape from further serious damage. During the night of 23rd-24th June there was a heavy air-raid, and a large bomb fell right alongside her starboard side and demolished a motor boat. "Well," remarked a sailor philosophically, "that's one less boat to hoist anyhow."[20]

Captain Fisher and others with him on the bridge were showered with water, mud, splinters and broken glass. Two days later she was escorted by destroyers to Port Said, whence she passed through the Suez Canal, and so said a temporary good-bye to the station on which she had served with such distinction. She could not then know that she, having seen the nadir of the fortunes of her fleet, would return to serve once more under Admiral Cunningham, and would then take part in its triumph. She passed by Colombo, Singapore and Manila to Honolulu, which she reached on 2nd August. There her crew enjoyed comforts and hospitality of a nature which they must almost have forgotten existed. Captain Fisher remarked on " the unbounded and spontaneous friendliness of every U.S.N. officer and enlisted man towards us." Enormous numbers of visitors came on board, and interest in her damage was intense. On 4th August she sailed for Esquimault, off which port she was met by two Canadian destroyers. She anchored there on the 10th, and at once sent a draft of 284 officers and men back to Britain. That evening she sailed under American escort for Seattle, and berthed there on the 11th at Bremerton Navy Yard. About half her officers and men then went home, some 600 being kept to help with the refit. Captain Fisher recalls " the excellent conduct of those remaining, largely due to every man being ' adopted ' by an American family and so being able to ' go home ' at night."[21] He himself and many of his officers toured America and Canada giving lectures on Britain's war effort.

The Admiralty wanted, of course, to give the ship as thorough a refit as possible while the opportunity offered. This meant sending out from England a large amount of equipment which could not be procured in the United States. Among other items, five of her 15-inch guns had to be replaced. This was a complicated affair, for the spare guns had been dispersed in England for greater safety, and the special " gun-sets " used for transporting these enormous weapons, weighing 100 tons each, by rail had to be located. Having brought the guns and the gun-sets together they had then to be moved to a seaport; and to spread the risk the guns were sent across the Atlantic in three different ships. It is a tribute to the Armament Supply Department that the whole complex organisation worked successfully. The guns arrived safely at Norfolk, Virginia, whence the Americans moved them on special railway trucks to the west coast. There " they were duly mounted, and *Warspite* was fit for service again."[22] But that did not happen until January, 1942, by which time the United States had become an Ally and Japan an enemy.

CHAPTER NINE

Eastern Fleet January 1942—
Mediterranean 1943

*" Operation well carried out. There is no question
when the old lady lifts her skirts, she can run."*
Admiral Sir Andrew Cunningham to ' Warspite,'
17th July, 1943

Warspite re-commissioned, still under Captain Fisher, at
Seattle on 28th December, 1941—exactly three weeks after
the Japanese attack on Pearl Harbour had transformed the
whole face of the war. Many new officers and senior ratings
had joined during the preceding weeks, but there was still
a good leavening of those who had served in her during
the previous commission. On 7th January she left the
hospitable shores of America, where she had been so
efficiently repaired and her men had been made to feel so
very much at home, and steamed to Vancouver Island to
work up efficiency. *Warspite* left Canadian waters on the 22nd
escorted by two R.C.N. destroyers, carried out target
practices, and then set course to the south-west. On 1st
February she crossed the " Line " with the usual cere-
monies, and five days later met and fuelled from a tanker
off Henderson Island. Any ship steaming west across the
Pacific is, of course, bound to miss a day on crossing the
International Date Line ; but few can be as lucky as *Warspite* was, and make Friday, 13th February, their *dies
non.* Sailors are a superstitious race, and it was a good

omen for her new commission. On the 20th she arrived at
Sydney, New South Wales. Once again, and for all the
ominous events then happening in Malaya and the East
Indies, her crew enjoyed lavish hospitality. She left for
Ceylon on 26th February; but the Japanese seem to have
known about her arrival in Australia, though not about
her departure. When their midget submarines attacked
shipping in Sydney on the night of 31st May-1st June,
1942, they claimed, with many lurid details, that *Warspite*
had been one of the targets attacked, and that she had
blown up.[1] Actually she was many thousands of miles
away, off East Africa, at that time; but the enemy plainly
attached great importance to her movements.

She carried out more target firings off Sydney, escorted
the while by Australian warships, and then set course
round the south of Australia for Fremantle. When, however, submarines were reported off that port she was
diverted back to St. Vincent Gulf, near Adelaide, and
there she completed with fuel, from another British tanker
sent to meet her. Destroyers from the Eastern Fleet met
the battleship when she was three days' steaming from
Ceylon, and on the 22nd March she anchored in Trincomalee harbour. Five days later Captain Fisher was
relieved by Captain F. E. P. Hutton, and that same day
Admiral Sir James Somerville, who had formerly commanded the famous Force H working from Gibraltar, and
was now Commander-in-Chief, Eastern Fleet, hoisted his
flag in her. Thus, in her twenty-eighth year, she once
again assumed her famous role as fleet flagship.

Just after *Warspite* reached Ceylon a ceremony which
concerned the ship took place in London. The Admiralty
had arranged that all major warships should be " adopted "
by British cities and institutions during the war, and the
sponsors thereafter took a special interest in " their " ship

and her crew. *Warspite* was adopted by the London Stock Exchange on 28th March, 1942, during " Warship Week " in Britain, and a bronze plaque was presented to the ship by the members of the Stock Exchange to commemorate the event. Many other generous gifts from her sponsors soon followed. When the plaque reached the ship her officers and men made a return presentation. Ever loyal to their Woodpecker, it showed that crest instead of the more orthodox Elizabethan cannon*; but the Lords Commissioners of the Admiralty, probably unaware of the ship's presentation, themselves sent a plaque to the Stock Exchange " to commemorate the adoption of H.M.S. *Warspite* "; and their plaque shows the cannon as the ship's crest[2]. It thus happens that to this day a visitor to Throgmorton Street may see two " Warspite " presentation plaques with two different crests on them— an inconsistency which those unaware of her history may find puzzling.

But to return to the Eastern Fleet, the early months of 1942, during which *Warspite* was steaming from Vancouver to Trincomalee were among the most anxious of the whole war ; for Britain was then having to face the onslaught of a very powerful and utterly ruthless enemy, what time her new ally had not yet begun to muster her tremendous fighting capacity, and had, moreover, lost a great proportion of her fleet in the treacherous attack on Pearl Harbour. Our heavy losses in the Mediterranean and elsewhere had destroyed the possibility of building up a balanced fleet for the Far East when, towards the end of 1941, that horizon had darkened; and the first embryo Eastern Fleet had met with utter disaster off Malaya on 10th December, 1941, when the *Prince of Wales* and *Repulse* were sunk by Japanese aircraft. Disintegration on land

* See p. 26.

and sea followed hard on the heels of that disaster. Malaya was lost, and on 15th February, 1942, Singapore surrendered. Resistance was continued from the Dutch East Indies, but the Battle of the Java Sea (27th February-1st March) eliminated the remnants of Allied maritime power in the theatre. Even before they had conquered Java the Japanese were rapidly spreading their tentacles along the islands to the east, threatening Australia. At the same time Burma was invaded, and, on 9th March, Rangoon fell. The peril to India and Ceylon and to all that lay west of them—including the oil of Persia and Iraq and the lifeline from Britain to the Middle East by the Cape of Good Hope—was all too plain. The Admiralty was meanwhile trying to scrape together a fleet which, based on Ceylon, could at least defend the Indian Ocean trade routes, even if it could not possibly act offensively against the Japanese Navy; but we were desperately short of every class of ship, and especially of aircraft carriers, and it was therefore inevitable that the fleet should consist mostly of old ships. Nor were its bases in any better state, for we had expected to be able to defend the Indian Ocean by holding Singapore.

At the time when he arrived at Colombo on 26th March Admiral Somerville was faced with an impossible situation. He had two large and one small carrier, five battleships (of which four were of the slow, unmodernised and vulnerable " R-Class "), two heavy and five light cruisers and a heterogeneous collection of some sixteen destroyers. With such a force he could not possibly fight the Japanese fast carrier striking force of five large fleet carriers with ample modern ships in support; and if he was unlucky he might very well lose the whole of his fleet, which was positively the last that Britain could send to the East. As soon as he had assumed command intelligence indicated attack on

Ceylon by precisely the force which Somerville had greatest reason to fear. Because of the insecurity of his bases at Colombo and Trincomalee he was working from a secret anchorage at Addu Atoll, some 600 miles to the south-west; but at the end of March he sailed to the waters south of Ceylon to try and meet the threat which faced him. His intentions were to avoid day attack by the Japanese carrier-borne aircraft, and to try to get in night torpedo attacks with his own. The chances of accomplishing both purposes were, however, plainly very slender. *Warspite* first met the other ships of her new fleet on the last day of March, just when these movements were in train, and throughout 1st and 2nd April they were all cruising to the south of Ceylon. Somerville had divided his fleet into a Fast Division (*Warspite*, the fleet carriers *Indomitable* and *Formidable*, and three cruisers), and a Slow Division comprising the four R-Class battleships, the small carrier *Hermes*, and the remaining cruisers. By 2nd April no signs of the expected attack had been received, and Somerville decided to replenish his ships with fuel and water at Addu Atoll. Just after he arrived there at noon on the 4th the enemy striking force was reported by our reconnaissance aircraft 360 miles south-east of Ceylon. *Warspite* and the fast division sailed as quickly as possible, leaving the slow division to follow. Somerville still hoped to get in a night torpedo-bomber attack on the retiring enemy.[3]

Colombo was actually attacked at dawn on Easter Sunday, 5th April, but the harbour had been cleared of shipping; and the defending fighters gave a good account of themselves. The damage was relatively small, but unhappily the heavy cruisers *Dorsetshire* and *Cornwall*, which had been detached by Somerville to Colombo on 2nd and were now hastening back to rejoin the fleet, were caught by the enemy bombers to the south of Ceylon, and both were sunk.

On the 6th the slow division joined his flag, but Somerville's anxieties were increased by reports from Ceylon that the enemy was moving still farther west—possibly to strike at Addu Atoll. He therefore decided that he must keep clear of his temporary base. Flying constant air searches, he finally approached the atoll from the west, and anchored there on the 8th. In fact, the Japanese temporarily withdrew eastwards after attacking Colombo, but on the day the Eastern Fleet reached Addu Atoll they struck at Trincomalee. There a good deal of damage was done, and the light carrier *Hermes* and two smaller warships were caught and sunk off the east coast of Ceylon next morning. Meanwhile other Japanese warships were sweeping our shipping from the Bay of Bengal. Though we may be thankful that the enemy carriers never found Somerville's main fleet, it seemed that British maritime power in the Indian Ocean was crumbling. Fortunately the enemy went back to his home bases after these attacks, and we were granted time to restore and rebuild the structure on which the fortunes of all Allied forces in the theatre so greatly depended. None the less the experiences of the early days of April, 1942, had been most ominous, and rarely in her history can Britain have been faced by so serious a threat to her control of the ocean routes.

After this escape *Warspite* went to Bombay to meet General Wavell, the Commander-in-Chief, India, and to carry him to Ceylon for conferences. Then, at the end of the month she sailed for Mombasa in East Africa, calling at Seychelles on the way. A new base was in process of creation at Kilindini in Kenya, and Somerville was determined at all costs to safeguard the vital convoy route from the Cape of Good Hope to Suez. By the middle of the

year the American victory off Midway Island had eliminated
for good the Japanese fast carrier striking force, the
defences of Ceylon had been greatly strengthened, and the
fleet was able to return there. Meanwhile Madagascar, with
its excellent harbour at Diego Suarez, had been occupied
by British forces, and in October *Warspite* called there.
Then she docked briefly at Durban.

From November, 1942, to May, 1943, Allied eyes were
mainly focused on North Africa, where in the former
month we had successfully carried out the first big combined operation of the war, and in the latter month we
finally drove the Axis forces out of Africa. One cannot
but regret that *Warspite* missed this turn of the tide on the
station to which she must have felt she really belonged.
In February the battleships of the Eastern Fleet sailed from
Kilindini to cover the passage of a great troop convoy,
including the " monster liners " *Queen Mary* and *Queen
Elizabeth*, which was carrying the Australian Division
back to their own country from the Middle East. Near
Addu Atoll the fleet closed the convoy and was about to
steam down the lines when a submarine contact was
obtained, and the destroyers were detached to hunt it.
No attack developed, and the troopships all went on safely
to their destinations, while the fleet refuelled and returned
to East Africa.

As the campaign in the Mediterranean moved from
one success to another, and the Indian Ocean remained
quiet, it was natural for the Admiralty to recall ships from
Somerville's command for service in the theatre where the
Allied offensive was gaining momentum. Many important
ships had already left when, in March, *Warspite* was ordered
home. She first docked again at Durban, and there Captain
H. A. Packer relieved Captain Hutton. It was a singularly
appropriate appointment, for the new Captain had been

the first Sub-Lieutenant of her gun-room in 1915-1917 and had also been her gunnery officer in 1926. On 16th March she sailed for Freetown, joining a returning troop convoy off the Cape ; and on the 29th she set course from Freetown for the Clyde. Captain Packer had been able to observe at first hand the whimsical ways of *Warspite's* steering gear, when she turned circles at Jutland. Now, just to remind him that the gremlin was still present nearly 30 years later and was still able to play pranks, she had another breakdown on the way home. On 10th May she berthed at Princes Dock—which she had guarded in the General Strike of 1926.* It was a month over three years since she had left her home waters, and for many of her company the ten days' leave now given was the first they had enjoyed since 1941.

In June she was back at Scapa, for the first time since she called there in April, 1940, on her way back from Narvik.† She was now earmarked to take part in the next big Mediterranean combined operation—the invasion of Sicily.

While *Warspite* had been serving in eastern waters important changes in the composition of the Allied navies, and in the duties assigned to the different classes of ship had been taking place. The vitally important role of the aircraft carrier in modern war had been powerfully demonstrated in the early days. The disablement of three Italian battleships in Taranto harbour on 11th November, 1940, had been entirely the work of British carrier aircrews‡ ; the catching and sinking of the *Bismarck* in May of the following year was only accomplished because the *Ark Royal's* torpedo-bombers had reduced her speed drastically ; it was the same type of aircraft from the *Formidable* which damaged the *Pola* and so brought about the Battle of Cape Matapan. These and many other successes to the new arm had been studied by the Japanese and Americans while they were yet at peace; and both those nations had developed their naval air arms into the spearhead of their fleets. When Japan saw her opportunity for aggrandisement at the expense of a desperately struggling Britain and an unready America, it was with her carrier aircraft that she struck at Pearl Harbour, and again at the weak British Eastern Fleet. But the Americans recovered quickly from the initial shock, and in April, 1942, it was the turn of their aircraft carriers to give the Japanese their first major set-back in the Battle of the Coral Sea. Then, in the following month, the decisive battle of Midway, in which the Japanese carrier striking force was totally destroyed by four score American naval aircraft, removed any lingering doubts there may have been regarding the decisive influence of the aircraft carrier on maritime war.

While these battles were being fought and won Allied plans to take the offensive, firstly in Africa and then in Europe, against Germany and Italy were taking shape. Our maritime strategy had passed out of the first, and inevitably defensive phase. In fighting resources and in trained men we were fast overtaking the initial advantage of the dictatorships, and the British and American governments intended once again, as so often in the past, to exploit to the utmost the greatest of all the benefits which maritime power confers—namely to take the offensive by landing their armies on the enemy-held coastline *at points of their own selection*. Thus by the middle of 1942 great emphasis was placed on " combined operations," and the plan to invade North Africa was taking shape. Our early attempts at such undertakings—in Norway in April, 1940, and against Dakar in the following September—had been costly failures. Among the causes were faulty command organisation, indifferent inter-service co-operation, inadequate planning and, above all, lack of specialised equipment and trained men; but the lessons had been well studied and applied, and two years later the prospects of success were vastly improved. In order to test the new equipment we had, however, carried out a large-scale raid on Dieppe in August, 1942; and it had failed with heavy losses among the troops who were flung ashore against a heavily defended coast. One cause of the failure was that the gun support provided from the sea was quite inadequate, and enemy strongpoints and gun positions were therefore not neutralised before the landings. The naval force commander and the responsible naval commander-in-chief both reported that if heavy gun support from a battleship had been forthcoming the result might have been very different. This was, in fact, a very old requirement in combined operations; but it seems to have been forgotten until the lesson was re-learnt off Dieppe.[4] Off Norway, Greece, Crete and in many other theatres we had learnt, at no small cost, that command of the air was an essential pre-requisite to combined operations in a modern war; and that need was well provided for at Dieppe. But it was perhaps not realised that command of the air could not alone ensure a reasonably safe landing on an enemy coast; and that persistent and accurate heavy gun bombardment was essential to put the enemy's defences out of action during the inevitably hazardous period of the actual landings. Hence, after the Dieppe failure, the formation and training of heavy bombarding squadrons became a matter of first importance in Allied plans; and by far the best ships available to meet the need were the battleships. In the Royal Navy shore bombardment had always been a recognised requirement, and all classes of ship had frequently practised it in peace-time. Now the technique had to be adapted to modern conditions, and in the North African landings it was applied with excellent effect. The destruction of enemy defences before the actual landings, and the neutralisation of strongpoints which subsequently proved troublesome to the Army were not the only requirements place on the large warships allocated to cover combined operations. They had also to protect the defenceless troop carriers and store ships from interference by enemy surface warships; and as long as the enemy possessed powerful squadrons, such as the Germans had built around the *Tirpitz* in north Norway and the Italians still possessed in the Mediterranean, it was necessary to defend our troop and mercantile convoys against their depredations.

To return now to *Warspite*, she spent the first part of June, 1943, exercising from Scapa and, in particular, carrying out bombardment practices. On 17th June she sailed for Gibraltar with part of the great fleet then being assembled for the assault on Sicily. She was once again allocated to the 1st Battle Squadron, but that famous force was now working from Gibraltar as part of Force H, and was commanded by Vice-Admiral Sir Algernon Willis.* On 23rd she anchored in Gibraltar and hoisted the flag of Rear-Admiral A. W. la T. Bissett†, Second-in-Command of Force H. At the end of the month she moved to Algiers. The assault was to take place on 10th July, and the initial function of *Warspite*'s squadron was to cover the landings against interference by the Italian fleet, which still possessed six battleships, and to support the Army by bombarding shore targets. For these purposes Force H was divided into three divisions, working from ports in North Africa, from Alexandria and from Gibraltar respectively. *Warspite*,

---

* Now Admiral of the Fleet Sir A. U. Willis, G.C.B., K.B.E., D.S.O., etc.
† Later Vice-Admiral A. W. la T. Bissett, C.B., C.B.E.

Valiant and *Formidable* were allocated to the Alexandria division, and on 5th July she arrived once more at the base she had formerly known so well, and from which she had last sailed to the east, a severely damaged ship, on 26th June, 1941.* She returned there, from the west, in fine fighting trim, and on 7th July sailed again with the rest of her division. What memories of sweeps in the central Mediterranean, of Malta convoys, of battles won and bombings endured in those same waters must then have stirred in the old lady's steel bosom! Early on the 9th she met the division from Oran (*Nelson*, *Rodney*, *Indomitable* and many cruisers and destroyers) 240 miles south-east of Malta. Captain Packer noted in his diary: "It was a fine sight—four battleships, two carriers and about two dozen destroyers. 'Guns' stood up on the bridge, looked around him and, with a chuckle, said '*Mare Nostrum*!'"[5] After dark that night the whole great array of warships set course so as to arrive off the assault area at daylight next morning, 10th July.

Zero hour for the landings was 2.45 a.m., two hours after the moon had set. It was a clear, dark night, with the wind blowing freshly from the north-west. *Warspite*'s initial position was about 90 miles from the shore; gun flashes and bomb explosions could be seen ahead of her, and the night sky seemed to be filled with aircraft. "The sailors on deck," noted her captain, "are all peering ahead, and if they talk at all, it is in undertones. There is awe around us."[6] There were no attacks on the covering ships that night, and at dawn *Warspite* was about 40 miles off Cape Passero, the south-east corner of Sicily. The ship's company who, of course, had no prior knowledge of Allied plans and intentions, had organised a sweepstake on the various alternative possibilities of the operation.

* See p. 247.

As the day progressed there were continuous air alarms, but no attacks developed. By the evening it had become apparent that the landings had succeeded, and that the British and American armies were making good progress. The covering force continued to patrol off Cape Passero ready, as General Eisenhower had signalled " to take care of anything the enemy is bold enough to send against you," until it became necessary to detach ships in relays to fuel in Malta. *Warspite* returned there briefly on 12th July, gave a few hours' leave to her Maltese ratings (who had not seen their families for four years), and then returned to her covering position. It had been the first visit to Malta by a British battleship since December, 1940.* The next two days passed in similar fashion, and disappointment at the failure of the Italian fleet to put in an appearance was becoming widespread. There were several submarine contacts, but the destroyers always leapt on them like foxhounds, and generally eliminated such enemies before they could do any damage. In the small hours of the 15th the aircraft carrier *Indomitable* was, however, struck by an aerial torpedo, and a few hours later a U-boat hit and damaged the cruiser *Cleopatra*. *Warspite* escorted the carrier back to Malta. While in harbour her captain visited Admiral Cunningham and vented his disappointment that no action had so far come the way of his ship. " Well," answered the commander-in-chief, " I can't get hold of the Italian fleet, tie them down and let you have a go at them." " No," answered the *Warspite's* captain, " but I'm told Sicily is the biggest island in Europe, and I'm sure we could hit it if told to go and bombard." " I doubt it," said Cunningham, who could never resist an opportunity for leg-pulling, " *Warspite* was always the worst gunnery ship in the Mediterranean in peace-time." " And in war? " asked the captain. "She never missed," said the admiral. "She's one of those . . . all right on the night shifts."[7] But Captain Packer's visit probably did achieve his purpose.

Early on the 17th *Warspite* and *Valiant* left Grand Harbour for the anchorage of Marsaxlokk on the south side of Malta, which the big ships were now using; but the *Valiant* fouled the anti-submarine defences and was firmly held in them. At 11.30 orders were received to come to half an hour's notice for steam, and at noon the battleships were told to sail at once and bombard Catania, before which the Eighth Army was held up. The orders stated that the bombardment was to start at 6.30 p.m., and was to cease exactly half an hour later. There was only just time to cover the distance, and the *Valiant*, although she had by now disentangled herself, had to be left behind. *Warspite* worked up to full speed, and although she had paravanes streamed was soon registering $23\frac{1}{2}$ knots. Then her steering gear suddenly jammed, she turned a sharp circle and narrowly missed one of her escorts. Precious minutes were lost changing over to emergency steering, but at 6.43 she passed through her initial position for the bombardment and opened fire at a range of about 13,000 yards. Once a minute she placed a 15-inch salvo on her target. "A great mass of smoke and dust rose up out of the town."[8] Enemy coastal batteries replied, but did not hit her. Submarine contacts were reported on both sides, and the escorting destroyers fired great patterns of depth charges to keep them down. Then three F.W. 190s skimmed close along the ship's side, but did no damage. At two minutes past seven the last salvo was fired, and *Warspite* turned south and increased again to full speed. Air alarms continued all night, and the A.A. guns were constantly in action; but by 7 a.m. on the 18th she was safely back in Marsaxlokk harbour, well satisfied with her achievement. Admiral Cunningham had doubtless been watching her reports with special interest, and sent the signal which heads this chapter. A short time later, when she had returned to Grand Harbour, he came aboard and inspected her ship's company. His former flagship always occupied a special place in " A.B.C.'s " heart.

Meanwhile the Allied armies had been making good progress on land, and on 16th August Messina was captured. Sicily had been cleared of enemies in thirty-eight days, Mussolini had fallen, and it was plain that Italian resistance was crumbling. The campaign now moved to the mainland of Italy, where substantial German reinforcements were arriving, and fierce resistance was expected. On 2nd September *Warspite* and *Valiant* steamed right up the Straits of Messina and shelled enemy gun emplacements south of Reggio as part of the preparations for the Eighth Army to move across to the mainland. Next day the Canadians landed at the scene of this bombardment, and met with no opposition—a fact which did not surprise *Warspite*'s captain. Later on Captain Packer and some of his officers flew from Malta to Reggio to inspect the results of her gunfire. The target had been a 6-gun battery, and although no direct hits had been scored there were seventeen heavy shell craters around the battery, and all the guns had been put out of action by blast and splinters. A local farmer and his small son, who had evidently watched the bombardment from a safe distance, turned up and described with many appropriate gestures and noises what had happened. " Marina-bom-bom-plonk-plonk," said the boy. " *Soldati* ? " asked the Captain. " *Soldati refugio*," answered the boy, making running-away gestures. Evidently the whole garrison had " refugioed " at once, and had never returned to the battery.[9]

There had always been friendly but keen rivalry between

the two battleships, and the trouble which *Valiant* experienced with her wireless communications during the Reggio operation produced some caustic comments in her sister ship. Later on, when the *Valiant* was testing her recalcitrant transmitter and suddenly came on the air with the remark "This is *Valiant*," the classic breach of security caused her rival particular delight.

The next big step by the Allies was to be the capture of Naples by an assault from the sea in the Gulf of Salerno : and on 7th September *Warspite* sailed from Malta with the rest of Force H to take part in that operation. The four battleships and two carriers steamed to the south of Malta and passed through the Sicilian channel, before setting course for the Bay of Naples. On the night of 8th-9th they were attacked by a strong force of torpedo bombers, and *Warspite* was narrowly missed ; but no damage was done.

Meanwhile negotiations for an armistice were in progress with the Italians. It was signed on 3rd September, but was not announced until five days later. Included in the terms was the surrender of the Italian Fleet, the main units of which were ordered to steam south from Genoa and Spezia. On the way German aircraft attacked and sank the battleship *Roma*, but on the morning of 10th September the remaining ships were met by the *Warspite* and other ships of Admiral Cunningham's fleet. This historic occasion is recorded in her log by the laconic statement :

"10th Sept. 0832. Italian fleet sighted."

In his diary *Warspite*'s captain recorded the scene more fully. "Presently they [the Italian ships] came in sight," he wrote. "It was in November, 1940, at the Battle of Spartivento, that I last saw those ships. Our feelings were queer. The Officer of the Watch, Curtis—a South African

—was mumbling to himself, 'To think I should be here to see this'; and I felt the same. As they took station astern of us the Padre said, 'It's somehow pathetic'; and Pluto (the ship's dog) raced up and down the fo'c's'le barking. We set off along the north African coast for Malta.... Off Bizerta the C.-in-C. came out in the destroyer *Hambledon* to have a look at his old enemies.... He signalled his pleasure at seeing his old flagship 'in her proud and rightful position at the head of the line.' "[10]

Next day Admiral Cunningham reported to the Admiralty that "the Italian battle fleet now lies at anchor under the guns of the fortress of Malta."[11] The commander-in-chief has described his feelings on that day, when his "wildest hopes of years back [were] brought to fruition, and my former flagship the *Warspite*, which had struck the first blow against the Italians three years before, led her erstwhile opponents into captivity."[12] To the ship which had so often sought for, pursued and engaged those self-same enemies the moment must have seemed the climax of her long life, pregnant with memories of another fleet surrender she had witnessed twenty-five years earlier,* and of the many trials she had since endured. From the captain down to the youngest boy on board deep emotions were stirred. At 10 a.m. on the 11th she secured in Grand Harbour, passing the *Vittorio Veneto*, her principal rival at Matapan, on the way in. Next day Admiral Bisset's flag was transferred to the new battleship *Howe*, and *Warspite* sailed again, this time as a private ship, to meet more of the Italian Navy. Among that contingent was the battleship *Giulio Cesare*, which she had fought and hit in the action off Calabria on 9th July, 1940.† The "old lady"

---

* See pp. 151-153.
† See p. 214. The Italian warships surrendered included five battleships, nine cruisers, fourteen fleet destroyers, nineteen torpedo-boat destroyers and thirty-five submarines. A complete list is given in Appendix F.

may reasonably have thought that the time when she might rest had now arrived; but if that is the case she was quickly disillusioned.

While the Italian Fleet was passing into captivity the assault took place in the Gulf of Salerno. Although the initial landings, carried out in the early hours of 9th September, were successful, the arrival of strong German reinforcements soon produced a critical situation. The American VI Corps was pressed back almost to its landing beaches, and there had been suggestions from its commander that it might be necessary to withdraw his troops and throw them in again on the left flank, where the British X Corps had made better progress. It was, as the British naval and army officers on the spot quickly pointed out, utterly impossible to carry out such a proposal in the middle of a battle. The issue must be decided where the troops then stood, and emergency measures were taken to give them every possible support from the sea.

On the afternoon of the 14th *Warspite*, in company with the *Valiant* and *Illustrious*, left Malta to return to Britain, where she was to refit before joining the forces preparing for the invasion of Normandy. But they had not gone far when, at 8 p.m., came a signal from the commander-in-chief ordering the two battleships to Salerno Bay at full speed. They hurtled through the Messina Straits at 23 knots, to arrive next afternoon, the 15th, off the landing beaches in the middle of an air attack. The gunnery officer at once went over to the American headquarters ship to get particulars of the targets to be engaged. At 5.52 p.m. *Warspite* opened fire on enemy positions with her main armament. Her Captain of Marines had been landed to spot for her, and her fire was extremely accurate. "The American troops," we are told, "were much impressed." The enemy now sent his utmost air strength against the bombarding ships, including aircraft fitted to operate his new wireless-controlled bombs. All the evening of the 15th, and all the following night *Warspite*'s anti-aircraft guns were in action as she steamed up and down outside the bay. Very early on the 16th she moved right inshore again, to the position she had occupied on the previous day. Soon after she arrived the fighter direction ship signalled to ask if *Warspite* could provide a copy of the Admiralty's report on the new type of German bomb. One of the secretaries at once typed the document, and it was sent over by boat; but this prescient act was not to save the ship.[13]

Just after 1 p.m. fire was opened on enemy traffic concentrations and ammunition dumps. Thirty-two rounds were fired, again with great accuracy. It must have been heartening to the hard-pressed soldiers to see the great ships steaming up and down only half a mile or so off-shore, their guns belching flame, to hear the 15-inch shells screaming overhead, and then to see the heavy explosions in the enemy lines. But *Warspite* was not allowed to have matters all her own way. At 2 p.m. she got under way after completing the bombardment. Shortly afterwards twelve fighter-bombers (F.W. 190s) attacked straight out of the sun, and were engaged by her anti-aircraft guns. These enemies did no damage, but if, as seems possible, their purpose was to divert the ship's attention from a more dangerous form of attack then developing, they succeeded only too well. At 2.30 p.m., only a few minutes after the fighter-bombers had disappeared, the ship's look-outs sighted what were at first thought to be three high-level bombers at about 6,000 feet. They were actually wireless-controlled bombs, whose controlling aircraft was far away overhead at about 20,000 feet. Here is Captain Packer's account of what followed:

" The three bombs when directly overhead looked like three very white mushrooms as they turned vertically down and dived for the ship at great speed. From the time of sighting to the time of the bombs' arrival was only some seven to ten seconds. The ship was making about ten knots through the water at the time, and in the congested area avoiding action was not possible—and would in any case have been ineffective. One bomb came straight for the ship and penetrated to No. 4 boiler-room, where it burst. A second bomb was a near-miss amidships abreast the bulge on the starboard side. It burst under water. This bomb had looked like missing by 400 yards, but about two-thirds of its way down it curved in towards the ship. The third bomb was a near-miss on the starboard side aft."

The 3,000-lb bomb which scored the direct hit penetrated right through six decks (total thickness 6¾ inches of steel) to her double bottom before exploding, while the near-miss made a long gash in her starboard bulge compartments. One boiler-room was completely demolished, and four of the other five were soon flooded. " The shock," says her report, " was very violent. It was at first thought that *Warspite* had broken her back, and that the mast would crash to the deck." All steam was lost, she could not steer, and her armaments were all temporarily out of action. At the moment she was hit the commander was broadcasting the results of the attack by the F.W. 190s, and a number of men were listening on the mess-decks very near where the bomb went through. They all escaped with a shaking, while another man, who was much farther away but had removed his anti-flash protection, was killed. " There was never," records one of her officers, " any question afterwards of compelling men to keep their anti-flash gear on, however trying the heat." The bosun was in the " heads " (lavatory) when the ship was hit, and could not get out. Afterwards he told how he said to himself, " Now, Bosun, pull yourself together. Unlock the door first."[14] " The situation," continues her captain's report, " was unattractive. The ship was heavily damaged: she could not steam . . . some 5,000 tons of flood-water had increased her draught by about five feet. She was only a few miles from Salerno and liable to air attack at any moment: radar was out of action: it was known that there were submarines in the area and only four destroyers were in company: Malta was some 300 miles away and the Polish ship *Slazak* reported that she had overheard the Germans preparing another air attack." Never in all her long career had she been in such a predicament, and it called for all her own vitality and all the determination of her crew to save her. Yet, astonishingly, she had only nine men killed and fourteen injured. Captain Packer prepared at once to be taken in tow, changed over to mechanical steering and called on the *Delhi* to provide anti-aircraft protection. By 4.15 the American tug *Hopi* had taken her in tow, and she was moving slowly out of Salerno Bay. Two more American salvage tugs soon arrived, and she then set course for the Straits of Messina at four knots, surrounded by screening destroyers and with the *Delhi* still keeping radar watch for her safety.

With no lights except battery lamps, and no fans or machinery running, the silence inside the ship was eerie. On the upper deck men rose to their feet, looking like so many spectral bodies in their anti-flash hoods, and manned the guns whenever one of the escorts opened fire. Then, when the firing stopped, they sank once again in silent exhaustion to the deck. With no forced ventilation the atmosphere inside the ship resembled that in a long-submerged submarine. There was no water to drink, only a strictly limited quantity of lemonade; and nothing but biscuit and corned beef to eat. The *Valiant* passed her during the night a few miles to the westward, in a blaze of tracer; but the enemy aircraft were searching too far to the south, and they never found the *Warspite*. The cruiser *Euryalus* next tried to tow her, but the wire soon parted and the tugs had to take over once more. A speed of four knots was maintained all that night, and by next morning her list had only increased to about 4½ degrees. Her diesel dynamos were now providing electric power, and this enabled the pumps to prevent the flood-water spreading. Two more tugs now joined, and although the towing hawsers parted many times, speed was gradually worked up to six knots. In the Messina Straits a salvage ship and a fifth tug added themselves to the *cortège*; but the southward current was so strong that all towing wires except one parted, and the water-logged ship went through the Straits broadside-on. Nor could she be pointed in the correct direction and given steerage-way until three tugs were towing ahead, one was lashed alongside on either quarter, and the salvage ship pulled backwards from astern.* Still her luck held, and German aircraft did not attack again. "After considerable trouble," wrote Captain Packer, "this journey was accomplished"—perhaps one of the classics of understatement. At 8 a.m. on 19th September she arrived in Malta once again. "*Belli dura despicio.*" Never had she lived up to her motto better.

It is always difficult to say at what precise moment the crisis of a battle was surmounted and which of several

---

* The ships which towed the damaged *Warspite* from Salerno through the Straits of Messina to Malta were the American tugs *Hopi, Moreno* and *Narragansett*, the British tugs *Nimble* and *Oriana*, and salvage ship *Salveda*.

factors contributed most to surmounting it. But the German records leave no doubt regarding the effectiveness of our air and sea bombardments at Salerno. " Our attack," states the enemy's War Diary, " had to stop . . . because of the great effect of the enemy sea bombardment and continuous air attacks " ; and Admiral Cunningham has stated that it was " the Naval gunfire, incessant in effect, that held the ring when there was danger of the enemy breaking through to the beaches."[15] Though *Warspite* had been grievously hurt, she and the other bombarding ships had made an important contribution towards resolving a dangerous situation.

After she had arrived in Malta Captain Packer left the ship, and Commander Hon. D. Edwardes, the executive officer, took command temporarily. On 1st November she started off on the long tow to Gibraltar. She was then drawing nearly forty feet, and her displacement had risen to about 39,500 tons. Four ocean rescue tugs—*Restive, Nimble, Oriana* and *Jaunty*—had charge of the tow, and four destroyers screened her. At the start she herself managed to steam at slow speed on one shaft, which helped the tow to reach a speed of seven knots ; but she very soon lost what little steam she could raise, and thereafter she was towed the whole way at about five knots. On the 3rd an A.-A. ship joined, and " fighter protection was at call and very prompt " while passing south of the enemy's air bases in Sardinia. Early on the 8th she secured at the detached mole at Gibraltar. The distance towed was 1,035 miles. On 12th November she entered the dry dock, where such repairs as were necessary to make her fit for the homeward passage were carried out. The Admiralty had no intention of allowing the " old lady " to rest.

On 10th December Admiral Cunningham, ever faithful to his former flagship, visited her to inspect the damage, and on the 28th she was undocked. Considerable changes took place among her officers and men while at Gibraltar, and she therefore had to carry out a short series of " working-up " practices before she was ready for sea. Two of her 15-inch turrets could not, however, be made serviceable at Gibraltar. In January she was about to sail when a signal came cancelling her departure. " The ship's company," records one officer, " thereupon sat down to eat mountains of fruit which they had bought to take home to their families." Not until 9th March did she actually leave Gibraltar, and that evening she joined a homeward-bound convoy. It thus came to pass that for the second time *Warspite* left the Mediterranean station severely damaged in battle. But whereas in 1941 she had sailed through the Suez Canal and thence east for America*, two and a half years later she left by the Straits of Gibraltar for Britain. The journey was uneventful. When she parted company with the convoy the commodore sent a signal to " thank her for the protection." " We did not disillusion him," writes one of her officers. After calling at the Clyde she sailed round the north of Scotland, in weather which seemed bitterly cold after months of tropical or Mediterranean sunshine, to Rosyth, where she was to be more permanently repaired. She anchored there on 16th March, and two days later Captain M. H. A. Kelsey† assumed command. Rosyth dockyard could, however, only restore one of the two defective turrets in the short time available before she was needed again, and for the rest of her life *Warspite* remained a three-turret ship.

Throughout April, 1944, she carried out exercises and firings off the Firth of Forth—which had for so long been her base while in the 5th Battle Squadron in the 1914-18

* See p. 247.
† Now Vice-Admiral M. H. A. Kelsey, C.B., D.S.C.

war*—and on 2nd May she steamed to Scapa. More exercises and firings followed, especially 15-inch bombardment practices, and by the end of May she was ready to play her part in the invasion of Europe.

*See pp. 107, 145.

CHAPTER TEN

Normandy & Walcheren to the End, January 1944—August 1947

"There is a saying in the Navy that wherever there is fighting to be done Warspite will surely be in it."

Montague Smith in the 'Daily Mail,'
7th June, 1944

CONSIDERING THAT numerous changes had taken place in her ship's company since she left Malta, and that many of her new men had never been to sea before, *Warspite* had all too little time to prepare herself for the invasion of Normandy, and she joined her force with only six of her eight 15-inch guns ready for action. Nor was any attempt made to restore the boiler-room which had been totally destroyed at Salerno. The "old lady" thus went right through the strenuous operations now to be described with a large caisson stuck on to her bottom below the damaged boiler-room. Yet on her next series of trials, on leaving Rosyth, she steamed twenty-one knots.

In the immense and critical undertaking of opening the "second front" in north-west Europe the Allied armies were faced with a task for which there was no parallel in history; for it was a frontal assault on beaches spread along about fifty miles of a very heavily defended coastline. For several years Germany had been constructing the network of defences which constituted Hitler's "Atlantic Wall." Strong concrete and steel emplacements had been

built in great numbers. Some protected the heavy batteries
which were intended to prevent close approach by warships; others concealed hundreds of single guns, mortars
and machine-guns, grouped in strong-points, and linked
by entanglements of barbed wire; while thousands of
land mines covered the beaches on which troops assaulting
the coast from the sea must land, and the exits from them.
Lastly the shore between the high and low water marks
had been hedged with an almost continuous belt of formidable steel obstacles, with mines attached to them.[1]

The task of the Navy was not only to land the Allied
armies at the selected points, but to neutralise the enemy's
defences during the landings and to support the troops
during their advance inland. To achieve these purposes
there had been planned the heaviest bombardment from
the sea and air that had ever been known. A thousand
bombers were first to drop many tons of bombs on the
selected part of the coast. Then powerful forces of heavy
warships were to open fire on targets which had been most
carefully chosen, and allocated to each ship; and while
this continued many destroyers and smaller vessels were to
move close inshore and silence the strong-points covering
the individual beaches. It had been proved earlier in the
war that air bombing could not silence heavy batteries in
their thick concrete emplacements. Only big naval guns,
with their high velocity at impact and accurate means of
control could acomplish this. It was, moreover, particularly important to neutralise the enemy batteries covering the open eastern flank of an assault in which more
than 6,000 ships and craft were to take part. For this
reason the most powerful of the bombarding forces was
allocated to that flank. It consisted of the battleships
Warspite and *Ramillies*, the 15-inch monitor *Roberts*, five
cruisers and fifteen destroyers under Rear-Admiral W. R.

Patterson*, and formed a part of Rear-Admiral Sir Philip Vian's† Eastern Task Force, which was to land and support the British assault forces in three sectors stretching from the River Orne in the east to the dividing line between the British and American Task Forces in the west.‡ The three British assault areas were called (from east to west) "Sword," "Juno," and "Gold," and *Warspite* herself was allocated initially to the "Sword" area, where the 3rd British Division and Commandos were to land on beaches between the mouth of the River Orne and the coastal village of St. Aubin.

On the evening of 2nd June *Warspite* sailed from Greenock for the English Channel, where she met the remainder of her force. On the morning of the 5th she was off the Eddystone Light, and that evening all ships assumed a high degree of readiness for the approach to the French coast. At 1.20 a.m. on 6th June (D-Day) she sighted the buoy marking the swept channel by which she was to approach the coast. Then says her report : "Force D, preceded by forty minesweepers, approached the coast of France." At 5.25 a.m. she stopped in her bombarding position about eleven miles to the west of Havre, and almost at once opened fire on an enemy shore battery at Benerville, which had injudiciously planted a few shells near her. She was thus one of the first warships to open fire on the enemy shore defences in operation "Overlord." At 5.30 a.m., about two hours before the assault troops were to touch down, the big guns roared out along the whole coastline of the assault, followed soon afterwards by the lighter weapons of the smaller ships close inshore.

---

* Later Admiral Sir Wilfred Patterson, K.C.B., C.V.O., C.B.E.
† Now Admiral of the Fleet Sir Philip Vian, G.C.B., K.B.E., D.S.O.
‡ See Map 8. There was a fourth area to the east called "Band" but no assault was to be made there.

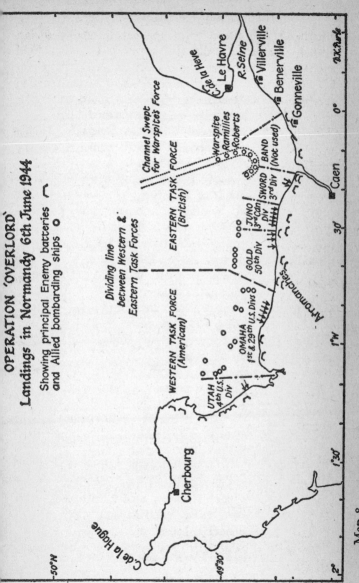

OPERATION 'OVERLORD'
Landings in Normandy 6th June 1944

Showing principal Enemy batteries ⌒
and Allied bombarding ships ○

Dividing line
between Western &
Eastern Task Forces

WESTERN TASK FORCE
(American)

EASTERN TASK FORCE
(British)

Channel Swept
For Warspite's Force

Cherbourg

C.de la Hague

UTAH
4th U.S.
Div

OMAHA
1st & 29th U.S.Divs

GOLD
50th Div

JUNO
3rd Can
Div

SWORD
3rd Div

BAND
(Not used)

Arromanches

Caen

o Warspite
o Ramillies
o Roberts

C.de la Hève

Le Havre

R.Seine

Villerville

Beneville

Gonneville

Map 8

Warspite herself had a very busy day, as the following extracts from her log show:

6th June, 1944

0530	Opened fire on enemy shore battery at Benerville. Three salvos fired "blind."
0545-0558	Bombarded battery at Benerville. [This battery was *Warspite's* principal target.] No spotting aircraft.
0604	Engaged twelve enemy destroyers at the mouth of the Seine. [Actually the attack was by three torpedo-boats, but a flotilla of patrol vessels was also in the offing. One torpedo narrowly missed *Warspite*.]
0612	Hit and sank one enemy destroyer. [A German patrol vessel was sunk off Havre at this time.]*
0612-0647	Bombarding Villerville coastal battery. Three hits obtained.
0733	First wave of assault troops touched down on beaches.
0738-0753	Bombarded shore battery at Gonnerville. Visibility poor. Spotting aircraft's tail shot away.
0755-0821	Bombarded battery at Villerville. Slight damage to ship from enemy return fire.
0821	Shifted billet.
0901-0938	Re-engaged Villerville battery.
0952-1012	Bombarded battery at Benerville.
1112-1200	Villerville battery again bombarded.
1219-1229	Bombarded Benerville battery.
1309-1335	Benerville battery re-engaged.

* The sinking of this ship is not credited to *Warspite* in the official records. None the less reliable observers at her radar saw a 15-inch shell hit, and the enemy disappear.

1315	Air-raid warning.
1440-1503	Bombarded concentration of enemy vehicles (tanks, lorries, etc.). Four hits on vehicles.
1520-1545	Bombarded German headquarters and shore battery. Knocked out 4-gun battery.
1551-1621	Bombarded Villerville shore battery.
1710-1814	Re-engaged Villerville battery, assisted by formation of aircraft.
2005	Air-raid warning.
2305	Came to with starboard anchor in eight fathoms [about four miles off-shore].

Although enemy batteries replied intermittently, and once straddled the ship, she received only slight damage. " By 9.30 a.m.," wrote Captain Kelsey, " the main batteries were silenced ; but they required periodic attention throughout the day." She actually fired seventy-three rounds of 15-inch at the Villerville battery, her principal target, and obtained nine direct hits. Mobile guns were " knocked out as the enemy brought them up to take the place of those already destroyed." Heavy and accurate bombardments from the sea such as this greatly assisted the assault forces, and enabled the Army to build up its strength rapidly. In spite of Hitler's boasted " Atlantic Wall," and in the teeth of all the German defences, by the end of D-Day the Eastern Task Force had landed nearly 133,000 men, over 6,000 vehicles and about 4,000 tons of stores and ammunition. Defence works on which the enemy had expended immense labour over several years had, in all but a few places, been swept away in as many hours by the combined naval, air and army assault of the Allies. In the British sector the leading troops were already six to eight miles inland.[2]

Warspite spent the next day, 7th June, in very similar

manner. Various "targets of opportunity" such as enemy
transport, guns and anti-aircraft batteries were engaged,
and an "area strong-point" was destroyed with twenty
rounds "fired blind" (i.e. without air or forward observer
spotting). In the afternoon she put eight salvos into
Benerville, and then, having by that time fired 181 rounds
of 15-inch high explosive and 133 of armour-piercing shell,
she returned to Portsmouth to replenish. She arrived at
Spithead in the early hours of the 8th, and moved up-harbour
in the afternoon. Next day she went across to the assault
area again. This time she was ordered to assist the Western
Task Force, as the American bombarding ships were
running out of ammunition. Captain Kelsey remembers
that "the German guns were mounted on a narrow neck
of the foreshore, with a marshy lagoon behind them, and
were extremely difficult targets. We were without air
spotting and the fall of shot was practically invisible to
the bombarding ships."[3] She none the less fired ninety-six
rounds to such good effect that the American force commander signalled to compliment her on her shooting. On
11th June she switched back to the "Gold" area, the
most westerly of the three British assaults, and at the
Army's request fired on enemy troops and tanks which
were concentrating in a wood, and threatening a heavy
counter-attack against the British 50th Division. This was
the occasion on which Captain Kelsey gave an order which
must be unique in the annals of British naval gunnery.
Sensing that as soon as his shells started to fall among the
enemy troops they would scatter outwards from the wood,
he ordered "Fifty rounds 15-inch rapid fire." "It did the
trick admirably," he writes, "as the increasing human
errors [in rapid fire] made the shells chase the German
vehicles outwards to the edge of the wood."[4] The general
commanding 50th Division signalled to her: "I want

those concerned informed [of] good shooting." That night she returned to Portsmouth to embark still more ammunition; but her guns were by this time wearing out again, and as the nearest replacements were at Rosyth, on the 12th she was ordered to proceed there to change them. She was routed up-Channel, and was the first capital ship to pass through the Straits of Dover since the German battle cruisers *Scharnhorst* and *Gneisenau* broke home from Brest in February, 1942. The German batteries on the French coast opposite Dover opened fire as she passed, and " the whole French coast was ablaze with their gun flashes." But British jamming of the enemy radar sets was highly effective, and *Warspite* ran the gauntlet of the coastal batteries in safety.

Early on the 13th, however, she or her escort exploded a mine under the battleship's port quarter when in the swept channel about twenty-eight miles east of Harwich. It may have been a magnetic or a pressure-operated mine— possibly one laid long previously which had escaped the repeated attentions of our sweepers, but was exploded by *Warspite's* large hull and deep draught. Be that as it may, her helm jammed, and she made a tight turn to starboard reminiscent of her gyrations at Jutland.* She then came to a stop with all four propeller shafts out of action, and a list of some six degrees. None of her crew was killed.

An hour later she was able to proceed on her starboard engines, and gradually worked up to seven knots. The Admiralty's first thoughts were to order her to the Tyne, but that idea was highly unpopular with the local authorities who feared that the great ship might sink in their river. She was therefore ordered to Rosyth, where she arrived under her own power, drawing forty-two feet aft, on the evening of the 14th. The new battleships *Anson* and *Howe*,

* See p. 124.

and other warships lying below the Forth Bridge all
" cleared lower deck " to cheer the injured *Warspite* as she
slowly passed. It was a heartening tribute to her long and
arduous service, and a remarkable repetition of the events
of 1st June, 1916, when, on her return, damaged and
listing, from the Battle of Jutland, she had been cheered
as she passed under the Forth Bridge to Rosyth.*

The problem facing Rosyth dockyard was how to get
the ship back into service quickly. In more normal times
the distorted shafts would have been " drawn " from the
ship and straightened in the machine shops; but that
process would have taken several months. It was therefore
decided to try and straighten them *in situ*, using " multitudes
of blow lamps and hydraulic jacks." " The result was,"
writes Captain Kelsey, " that we had one good shaft, one
fairly good one, and one very wobbly shaft. The fourth
one remained jammed solid."[5] By 11th August trials had
been " satisfactorily completed "; but on three shafts her
speed was now down to $15\frac{1}{2}$ knots. Though the old lady
was plainly becoming too arthritic any longer to " lift her
skirts " very high, she left at once for Greenock and for
further service.

Once again bombardment practices were carried out
off the west coast of Scotland, and on 24th August she
was back at Plymouth ready to strike again wherever she
might be needed.

On the 25th *Warspite* arrived off Brest, escorted and
screened by five destroyers, and opened fire at the extreme
range of her guns on coastal defences which were giving
trouble to the American Army. She fired 147 rounds of
15-inch high explosive and sixty-six armour-piercing shell
from a position north of Ushant, firing across that promon-
tory. The enemy batteries replied accurately, but she was

* See p. 134.

only hit by shell splinters. Next she re-appeared off Havre, and on 10th September bombarded German gun positions at her maximum range of about 32,000 yards, with the help of aircraft spotting. A troublesome coastal battery of three 6.7-inch guns was finally silenced, and other " targets of opportunity " were engaged.

Paris fell to the Allied armies on 25th August, Brussels on 3rd September, and next day the great port of Antwerp was captured. The Allies badly needed its use, to eliminate the long overland haul of the Army's supplies from ports in western France ; but the River Scheldt remained closed to their shipping because the Germans still held the fortified islands at the mouth of the estuary. A plan was accordingly made to capture the island of Walcheren by simultaneous attacks from land and sea.

In 1809 we had sent an expedition to this same island which fared so badly that it is chiefly remembered by the doggerel which pilloried the vacillations of the military and naval commanders.* But in 1944 the new technique of combined operations had reached its peak of efficiency, and the Walcheren expedition provided an example of the benefits to be reaped from bold planning and gallant execution. The plan was that while the Canadian Army attacked from the landward side, an assault force would be carried across the Scheldt to Flushing, and a frontal attack would be mounted from Ostend against West Kapelle, through a breach in the dyke protecting the western end of Walcheren Island made by our heavy bombers. It is with this last assault, made by Royal Marine Commandos, that we here are concerned ; for *Warspite* and two 15-inch monitors were allocated to the supporting squadron. She sailed from Portsmouth for Deal on 30th October, and next day set course for the entrance to the

River Scheldt. At 8.15 on 1st November she stopped in her bombarding position twelve miles from West Kapelle Light. Although the weather made air spotting and bombing impossible the Royal Marines went in most gallantly to the assault, and by 3rd November the German grip on the river mouth had been broken. *Warspite* engaged various enemy batteries and shore targets all day on 1st November, and then returned to Deal. These were the last of the hundreds of rounds fired at her enemies from her 15-inch guns.* She was at Spithead at the end of the year, when Captain M. H. Evelegh relieved Captain Kelsey. When the new captain was introduced to his officers he was astounded to learn that the president of the warrant officers' mess, Commissioned Gunner A. E. Cook, and several others of her officers had served in *Warspite* for four or five years. There were, in fact, also about twenty ratings, mostly belonging to the engine-room department, who had joined her when she commissioned at Portsmouth in 1937. It is doubtful if such continuity of service in one ship can be paralleled in modern times.

The old ship's life was now plainly drawing to a close. Her armaments and machinery had been driven so hard, and she had so often been damaged by the enemy that to make her fit for further service would necessitate a long and costly refit. Though Germany did not surrender until 8th May, 1945, by the beginning of that year it was plain that the threat to our sea communications in the west was no longer serious, and that having successfully transported the Army to Europe and kept it supplied from the start of the liberation campaign, the Navy's tasks were, so far as European waters were concerned, nearly completed. True a great fleet was being built up to join with the

* In the D-Day and subsequent bombardments *Warspite* fired about 1,500 rounds of 15-inch.

Americans in the Pacific, but in her thirtieth year *Warspite* was too full of the pains and discomforts of an ageing and injured body to be sent out to join that vigorous and youthful party. On 1st February the Admiralty sent a signal ordering her to pay off into reserve, and a fortnight later she was moved to the Reserve Fleet buoy off the Mother Bank at Spithead. She lay there until the last day of March, when the final entry in her log closed her long record of service and achievement.

The Admiralty had in fact made up its mind about her future even before she had shot her final bolt off Walcheren. On 9th September, 1944, it was recorded that she was " to be paid off into Reserve Category C. (the lowest category) on release from present duties." She accordingly spent the rest of 1945 " reducing to Category C." But before that year ended a ceremony took place in St. Giles Cathedral, Edinburgh, which ensured that at least one trophy from the ship would be cherished for posterity. On 27th September, when Admiral Cunningham was installed as a Knight of the Thistle in the presence of the King and Queen, he handed over *Warspite's* White Ensign to the Cathedral for safe keeping[6]; and by that full-hearted gesture the greatest of *Warspite's* flag officers, and the greatest British seaman of the Second World War, paid his final tribute to his old flagship.

On 31st July, 1946, as was mentioned at the beginning of this book, it was " approved to scrap " the ship. This decision meant that she was taken up Portsmouth harbour again, to be stripped of all the fittings which might be useful to other ships. A few of those who had served in her managed to obtain small trophies from the ship. Admiral Cunningham has one of her bells, and the name-plate which was fixed at the top of her starboard accommodation ladder now stands at the entrance to the

South African home of one of her former captains; several of her officers secured gun tampions with the woodpecker crest, and the two plaques mentioned earlier still commemorate her association with the London Stock Exchange*; but those scattered mementos are now almost all that remains of the great ship. And yet her spirit will surely live on, for in 1954 the Admiralty published a new list of "Battle Honours for H.M. Ships and Fleet Air Arm Squadrons."[7] There being no *Warspite* in the fleet at the time of publication she is not actually mentioned in it, but scrutiny of the "Fleet Actions, Campaigns, etc., for which a Battle Honour is awarded," suggests that when a new ship of her name is commissioned the following will be the honours that she will carry:

H.M.S. WARSPITE
BATTLE HONOURS AND CAMPAIGNS

21 June, 1596	Cadiz
25 July, 1666	Orfordness
28 May, 1672	Sole Bay
28 May and 4 June, 1673	Schooneveld
11 August 1673	Texel
19-24 May, 1692	Barfleur
13 August, 1704	Velez Malaga
10 March, 1705	Marbella
17-18 August, 1759	Lagos
20 November, 1759	Quiberon Bay
31 May-1st June, 1916	Jutland
10 and 13 April, 1940	Narvik
9 July, 1940	Calabria
28-29 March, 1941	Matapan

* See p. 251. When the ship was broken up the Admiralty offered to return the Stock Exchange's presentation plaque. It was accepted, and has been placed alongside the two presentations received from or on behalf of the ship.

20 May-1 June, 1941	Crete
September, 1940-June, 1942 ..	Libya
8 November, 1942-20 February, 1943	North Africa
10 July-17th August, 1943 ..	Sicily
9 September-6 October, 1943 ..	Salerno
6 June-3 July, 1944	Normandy
1 November, 1944	Walcheren

CAMPAIGNS

Atlantic	1939-45
English Channel	1939-45
North Sea	1939-45
Biscay	1940-45
Mediterranean	1940-45
Malta Convoys	1941-42

The long-drawn process of preparing her for the ship-breakers in Portsmouth dockyard was not, however, quite the end of her story, even though she had long since ceased to appear in the Navy List as one of His Majesty's ships. On 12th March, 1947, the tug *Volatile*, which was one of the oldest naval tugs and had helped to fetch back from the North Sea ships damaged in the Battle of Jutland, towed her equally aged compatriot out of Portsmouth to Spithead. There Metal Industries, Ltd., who had bought the hull for breaking-up, took her over. In April she left under tow for the Clyde with only eight men on board. She was " insured for the voyage for £150,000 "[8]— approximately the original cost of her 15-inch guns. On the way down-Channel very heavy weather was encountered. On 20th April her tow sparted and three days later she drove ashore on the Cornish coast in Mounts Bay. *The Times* reported her adventures thus:

"The battleship *Warspite*, which has been drifting off the Cornish coast since she broke a tow wire on Monday [20th April] went aground this afternoon [23rd April] on the rocks on the eastern shore of Mounts Bay. The latest news of her is that heavy seas have lifted her from the ledge on which she had grounded and driven her ashore at Prussia Cove, a more dangerous position.

"During the night the *Warspite* had drifted into Mounts Bay, where she dropped anchor about five miles off-shore. In the gathering gale of to-day which reached a force of 60 m.p.h. she ripped up her anchor and began drifting towards the rocks. Her two tugs could not hold her and the battleship, driven by the highest tide of the year, ran on to the rocks near Cuddan Point.

"The Penlee lifeboat, whose station is on the opposite shore of the bay, made her way through heavy seas to the *Warspite*, but the eight men on board the battleship refused to leave and the lifeboat returned to Newlyn harbour. Later, the lifeboat made a second trip to the *Warspite* and took off the battleship's crew."[9]

It was a last, splendid gesture of defiance. Finally on 29th August it was announced that "H.M.S. *Warspite* (how kind, if incorrect, to have given her the dignity of her former title at the end), the battleship now lying on the rocks in Mounts Bay, was sold yesterday to Bristol scrap merchants. The work of dismantling the battleship will begin on Monday, and is expected to last two or three years."[10] The final purchaser of the hull was actually The

Wolverhampton Metal Co., Ltd., and in September, 1955, their "*Warspite* Office" at Marazion wrote to the author as follows:

"The last few months have been a strenuous period, as we have been preparing to re-float the last section of *Warspite* inshore, and she has proved to be stubborn to the last. But we have succeeded in our efforts, and at last can say that the whole [hull] is almost certain to be recovered. . . . We expect to finish during 1956."[11]

It is therefore plain that about the time this book appears there will be nothing left of the seventh *Warspite*. She will then, in the words of one of her former petty officers, "have been pulled and burned to pieces by the hands of British workmen . . . doing what the enemy could not do."[12] Truly we are an unsentimental race.

THE OLD LADY

By *Admiral Ronald Hopwood, C.B.*

Noblesse oblige, no other choice remained,
   Pay homage, therefore, ye who pass her by,
   Last of a line of Royal ancestry
Whose roots were struck when Gloriana reigned.

For wellnigh three decades, from sea to sea,
   Remained she faithful in the hour of need
   To all the best traditions of her breed;
The breaker's yard no tomb for such as she.

Young in her heart, men saw her born anew,
   What time the name affection bred was won,
   An ancient dame who showed she still could run,
And teach the young ideas a thing or two.

She craves no pity, makes no plaint or boast,
　　Then leave her, rock and seaweed for her bed,
　　In peace, until the sea gives up its dead,
Soothed by the waves that wash her Island's coast.

And when your children gather round your knee
　　And ask her story, tell them, " It was hers
　　To win the love of countless mariners
By what she was, and taught them, too, to be."

THE END

EPILOGUE

*By Mr. E. A. Ogden, Chief Gunner's Mate
of H.M.S. 'Warspite,' 1937-39*

It was in May, 1954, whilst I was on holiday in Cornwall, that I found myself on the beach at Mounts Bay looking at the wreck of *Warspite*. Walking down the sands to the water's edge, and within a few yards of the remains of this "Great Old Lady," it was as though I was witnessing the end of a very dear friend. The shipbreakers were busy cutting her to pieces, and cranes were lifting the rusty steel into waiting lighters. "Dukws" were plying between the two halves of her and the beach. In my mind's eye I saw her again, as she was in peace-time, with her light grey paint shining, her spotless teak decks and ladders, the burnished gun muzzles, and her brass work flashing in the sunlight, the pride of her crew and the envy of the fleet, wearing the flag of Sir Dudley Pound, Commander-in-Chief of the Mediterranean Fleet; and I thought of her as she had been throughout the war when her sides were streaked with rust, her brightwork painted over and her decks no longer white; but her guns were still as well kept as ever, and they were always swinging round towards the enemy.

I know that all long-service naval men look back at one of their ships as the best they ever served in. To me, and I think to all men who were in her shortly before and during the war, I am sure that *Warspite* was that ship. She made a bad start to that commission, but the old lady seems generally to have done so. Once she settled down she was not only the smartest ship in the fleet, but the most successful. Whether it was at sports or in firing competitions no one ever touched her. She proudly wore "Proficiency Bands" on all 15-inch and 6-inch guns, and she was a very happy ship too, as anyone who went to her concerts or danced to her "Woodpeckers" band will remember. Captain Roskill was our gunnery officer and First Lieutenant then, and on his promotion was appointed Commander of the ship. Some used to think he made us do too many gunnery drills, but my remark was "Semper Strenuissima" (For Ever Striving); and when results appeared doubters saw why. It is known that no Capital Ship ever shot so well as she did, with her A.-A. and 6-inch as well as her 15-inch guns. The prolonged firing of forty salvos with the 15-inch done just before the war, when we scored a record number of hits at high-speed targets at long range, showed what she could do—and would do if war should come.

I feel very honoured that Captain Roskill has asked me to write the epilogue to his book and proud to think that I have served in such a wonderful ship. If even the best ships have to disappear in the end, I hope at least that the name will soon be revived. Then what is written here about the last *Warspite* will be an inspiration to the crew of the next one to try and do better. But I don't think they will!

APPENDIX A

Naval Building Programmes 1905-1913. Dreadnought to Royal Sovereign

Class and No. of ships, and Programme Year	Length (feet)	Beam (feet)	Displacement (tons)	Speed (knots)	Main Armament	Secondary Armament	Fuel
Dreadnought (1) 1905-6	490	82'	17,900	21	10-12-inch, 45 cal.	24-12 pdr., 5-Sub T.T.	2,900 tons coal
Bellerophon (3) 1906-7	490	82' 6"	18,600	20.75	10-12-inch, 45 cal.	16-4-inch, 3-Sub T.T.	2,650 tons coal
St. Vincent (3) 1907-8	500	84'	19,250	21	10-12-inch, 50 cal.	18-4-inch, 3-Sub T.T.	2,650 tons coal
Neptune (1) 1908-9	510	85'	19,900	21	10-12-inch, 50 cal. (Turrets re-arranged)	16-4-inch, 3-Sub T.T.	2,710 tons coal
Colossus (2) 1909-10	510	85'	20,000	21	10-12-inch, 50 cal.	16-4-inch, 3-Sub T.T.	2,900 tons coal
Orion (4) 1909-10	545	88' 6"	22,500	21	10-13.5-inch All on Centre line	16-4-inch, 3-Sub T.T.	3,300 tons coal
King George V (4) 1910-11	555	89'	23,000	21.7	10-13.5-inch	16-4-inch, 3-Sub T.T.	2,870 tons coal
Iron Duke (4) 1911-12	580	90'	25,000	21.25	10-13.5-inch	12-6-inch, 4-Sub T.T.	{ 3,250 coal 1,050 oil
Queen Elizabeth (5) 1912-13	600	90' 6"	27,500	25	8-15-inch	14-6-inch, 4-Sub T.T.	3,400 tons oil
Royal Sovereign (5) 1913-14	580	88' 6"	25,750	21	8-15-inch	14-6-inch, 4-Sub T.T.	Coal (converted later to 3,400 tons oil)

APPENDIX B

Captains of the 7th 'Warspite' 1915-1945

Name	Assumed Command	Relieved	Fleet
E. M. Philpotts	8.3.15	18.12.16	Grand
C. M. de Bartolomé	18.12.16	3.6.18	,,
H. Lynes, C.B., C.M.G.	3.6.18	17.1.19	,,
E. K. Loring	17.1.19	5.5.20	,,
F. Clifton-Brown, C.B., C.M.G.	5.5.20	4.5.22	Atlantic
R. N. Bax, C.B., A.D.C.	4.5.22	4.4.23	,,
R. M. Burmester, C.B., C.M.G.	4.4.23	2.9.24 (Paid off for refit)	,,
G. K. Chetwode, C.B., C.B.E.	6.4.26	4.8.27	Mediterranean
T. N. James, M.V.O.	5.8.27	7.11.27	,,
H. S. Monroe, D.S.O.	7.11.27	1.12.27	,,
J. F. Somerville, D.S.O.	1.12.27	1.9.28	,,
J. W. Carrington, D.S.O.	1.9.28	9.1.29	,,
A. H. Walker, O.B.E.	9.1.29	8.7.30	,,
C. A. Scott	8.7.30	6.9.30	Atlantic
O. H. Dawson	6.9.30	25.4.31	,,
St. A. B. Wake	25.4.31	2.8.32	,,
L. D. I. MacKinnon	27.8.32	15.12.33 (Paid off for refit)	Home
F. H. W. Goolden	24.2.37	1.5.37 (For trials)	,,
V. A. C. Crutchley, V.C., D.S.C.	1.5.37	27.4.40	Mediterranean Home
D. B. Fisher, C.B.E.	27.4.40	22.3.42	Mediterranean
F. E. P. Hutton	22.3.42	1.3.43	Eastern
H. A. Packer	31.3.43	12.10.43	Force H
Hon. D. Edwardes (actg. Capt.)	12.10.43	18.3.44	
M. H. A. Kelsey	18.3.44	29.8.44	Home
C. P. Frend	29.8.44	11.9.44	,,
M. H. A. Kelsey	11.9.44	30.12.44	,,
M. H. Evelegh	30.12.44	9.2.45	,,
G. F. Blaxland	9.2.45	15.3.45	,,
P. H. Calderon	15.3.45	26.7.45 (Paid off)	Reserve

APPENDIX C

Surrender of the German High Seas Fleet
18th November, 1918

BATTLESHIPS (9)	Friedrich der Grosse, König Albert, Kaiser, Kronprinz Wilhelm, Kaiserin, Bayern, Markgraf, Prinzregent Luitpold, Grosser Kürfurst
BATTLE CRUISERS (5)	Seydlitz, Derfflinger, Von der Tann, Hindenburg, Moltke
LIGHT CRUISERS (7)	Karlsruhe, Frankfurt, Emden, Nürnberg, Brummer, Köln, Bremse
DESTROYERS	49
SUBMARINES	20 (initially, but see note below)

Note: Under the terms of the Naval Armistice all other surface warships were to be concentrated in German Naval Bases to be designated by the Allies, and were to be paid off and completely disarmed. All existing German submarines were also to be surrendered.

APPENDIX D

British and Italian Fleets in the Action off
Calabria, 3rd July, 1940

BRITISH

BATTLESHIPS	..	..	..	Warspite
				Malaya
				Royal Sovereign
AIRCRAFT CARRIER		..	..	Eagle
8″ CRUISERS	..	..	..	Nil
6″ CRUISERS	..	..	..	Liverpool
				Neptune
				Orion
				Sydney
				Gloucester
DESTROYERS	..	..	..	16

ITALIAN

BATTLESHIPS	..	..	..	Giulio Cesare
				Conte di Cavour
AIRCRAFT CARRIER		..	..	Nil
8″ CRUISERS	..	..	..	Zara
				Pola
				Gorizia
				Fiume
				Bolzano
				Trento

APPENDIX D

6″ Cruisers   ..   ..   ..   *Savoia*

                                         Aosta

                                         Attendolo

                                         Montecuccoli

                                         Barbiano

                                         Giussano

                                             Abruzzi

                                             Garibaldi

Destroyers   32

APPENDIX E

British and Italian Fleets in the Battle of Cape Matapan, 28th March, 1941

BRITISH

BATTLESHIPS	..	..	..	*Warspite* *Barham* *Valiant*
AIRCRAFT CARRIER				*Formidable*
8″ CRUISERS	..	..	..	Nil
6″ Cruisers	..	..	..	*Orion* *Ajax* *Perth* *Gloucester*
DESTROYERS	..	..	..	13

ITALIAN

BATTLESHIP	..	..	..	*Vittorio Veneto*
AIRCRAFT CARRIER		..	..	Nil
8″ CRUISERS	..	..	..	*Zara* *Pola* *Fiume* *Trento* *Trieste* *Bolzano*
6″ CRUISERS	..	..	..	*Garibaldi* *Abruzzi*
DESTROYERS	..	..	..	13

APPENDIX F

The Surrender of the Italian Fleet
List of Ships in British control on 21st September, 1943

Class	Ships	Where
BATTLESHIPS (5)	*Vittorio Veneto*	Alexandria
	Italia	Alexandria
	Giulio Cesare	Malta
	Andrea Dorea	Malta
	Caio Duilio	Malta
CRUISERS (9)	*Luigi Cadorna*	Alexandria
	Montecuccoli	Alexandria
	Eugenio di Savoia	Alexandria
	Duca D'Aosta	Alexandria
	Garibaldi	Malta
	Abruzzi	Malta
	Pompeo Magno	Malta
	Scipiano Africano	Brindisi
	Attilio Regolo	Port Mahon
AVIATION TRANSPORT (1)	*Giuseppe Miraglio*	Malta
FLEET DESTROYERS (14)	4	Alexandria
	2	Algiers
	2	Malta
	3	Port Mahon
	3 (ex-French)	Taranto
T.B.Ds (19)	6	Malta
	4	Brindisi
	5	Taranto
	1	Palermo
	3	Pollenza (2 reported scuttled)

Class	Ships	Where
SUBMARINES (35)	21	Malta
	7	Taranto plus 4 midgets
	3	Crotone
	1	Brindisi plus 1 midget
	1	Bone
	1	Cagliari
	1	Proceeding to Colombo
CORVETTES (16)	7	Taranto
	5	Malta
	4	Brindisi
MINESWEEPERS	3	Malta
A/S VESSELS	9	Malta
MISCELLANEOUS	13	Malta, Brindisi, Taranto, etc.

MISCELLANEOUS
1 sloop, 2 Hospital Ships,
2 armed M/V's, etc.
Also 42 merchant vessels

APPENDIX G

REFERENCES

CHAPTER I

[1] Monson's Tracts, Navy Records Society, Vol. XXIII, p. 235.

[2] From a document printed in 1699 by Philip Raleigh, grandson of Sir Walter, which he had found among his grandfather's papers. See E. Edwards, *Life of Raleigh* (1868), Vol. II, pp. 146-156.

[3] Corbett, *The Successors of Drake*, pp. 433-434.

[4] Roskill, *The War at Sea*, Vol. I, pp. 324-5. (H.M.S.O., 1954.)

[5] *Dictionary of National Biography*, Vol. XXXIII, p. 145.

[6] Monson's Tracts, Navy Records Society, Vol. XXIII, p. 152.

[7] Sir William Laird Clowes, *The Royal Navy, a History* (1898), Vol. I, pp. 534-535.

[8] C. D. Penn, *The Navy under the Early Stuarts*, p. 173 *et. seq.* (Gieves, Ltd., 1920.)

[9] Roskill, *Op. Cit.*, pp. 169-204.

[10] Samuel Pepys' Naval Minutes. Navy Records Society, Vol. LX, pp. 241-2.

[11] Charnock's Naval Biography (4 vols., 1794), Vol. I, p. 63.

[12] *Naval Songs and Ballads*, Navy Records Society, Vol. XXXIII, pp. 65 and 72-75.

[13] Letter dated 29th September, 1666, from John Carlisle to the Secretary of State, Sir Joseph Williamson, preserved in Public Record Office State Papers, Domestic Series, Charles II (S.P. 29, Vol. 172, No. 74).

[14] Narborough's Journal. Navy Records Society, Vol. LXXXVI, p. 146.

[15] *Ibid.*, p. 378.

[16] *Ibid.*, Vol. LXXXVI, pp. 384-5.

[17] Charnock, *Op. Cit.*, Vol. I, pp. 106-8.

[18] Edward P. Powley, *The English Navy in the Revolution of 1688* (1928).

[19] Dartmouth MSS. (Historical Manuscripts Commission), pp. 238, 239, 245.

[20] *Ibid.*, Vol. XI, 5, p. 242.

[21] Charnock, *Op. Cit.*, Vol. I, pp. 106-8.

[22] *Ibid.*, Vol. II, p. 144.

[23] Gilbert Burnet, Bishop of Salisbury, *Own Times*, Vol. IV. Quot. Navy Records Society, Vol. XXXIII, p. xlv.

[24] Callender, *The Naval Side of British History*, pp. 128-9.

[25] Charnock, *Op. Cit.*, Vol. II, p. 144.

[26] J. Ehrman, *The Navy in the War of William III* (Cambridge University Press, 1953), pp. 383-391.

[27] A. T. Mahan, *The Influence of Sea Power upon History, 1660-1783*, pp. 187-9.

[28] Charnock, *Op. Cit.*, Vol. II, p. 414.

[29] J. S. Corbett, *England in the Mediterranean*, Vol. II, pp. 149-184.

[30] *Naval Songs and Ballads*, Navy Records Society, Vol. XXXIII, pp. 110-111.

[31] Roskill, *Op. Cit.*, Vol. I pp. 308-319.

[32] Laird Clowes, *Op. Cit.*, Vol. II, pp. 383-384.

[33] The Byng Papers, Navy Records Society, Vol. LXVII, p. 44.

[34] Life of Sir John Leake, Navy Records Society, Vol. LII, pp. 162-163.

[35] *Captain Loades' Journal*. Public Record Office (A.D.M. 51/4387). (The original spelling has been retained throughout these extracts, but punctuation has been inserted and abbreviations have been written out in full in modern English.)

[36] *Ibid.*

[37] Life of Sir John Leake, Navy Records Society, Vol. LII, p. 182.

[38] *Ibid.*, pp. 257-262, and Schomberg's *Naval Chronology*, pp. 122-3.

[39] The Byng Papers, Vol. I,

Navy Records Society, Vol. LXVII, p. 133.

[40] *Ibid.*, pp. 156-8.

[41] *Ibid.*, Vol. II, Navy Records Society, Vol. LXVIII, pp. vii, xvi, and 147.

[42] Laird Clowes, *Op. Cit.*, Vol. II, p. 514.

[43] *Warspite Journal*. Public Records Office, Admy. 51/4387.

[44] *Ibid.* for 3rd April, 1707.

[45] Laird Clowes, *Op. Cit.*, Vol. II, p. 525. Charnock, *Op. Cit.*, Vol. II, p. 387.

[46] Life of Sir John Leake, Navy Records Society, Vol. LIII, pp. 353-4.

CHAPTER II

[1] Roskill, *The War at Sea*, Vol. I, Appendix D.

[2] Callender, *The Naval Side of British History*, p. 144.

[3] Quoted. Callender, *Ibid.*, p. 145.

[4] Nicolas, *Letters and Despatches of Lord Nelson*, Vol. VIII, p. 149.

[5] Admiral Hercules Robinson, *Seadrift*, p. 237.

[6] Letters of Sir Thomas Byam Martin, Vol. II, p. 409 (Navy Records Society).

[7] James, *Naval History of Great Britain*, Vol. V, pp. 81-84.

[8] *Keith Papers*, Vol. III, p. 64. (Navy Records Society, 1955.)

[9] *Ibid.*

[10] *London Gazette*, 27th and 30th March, 1813, p. 628.

[11] *Ibid.*, p. 1149, and *Keith*

Papers, Vol. III (Navy Records Society, 1955.)

[12] Ralfe, *Naval Biography of Great Britain* (1828), p. 361.

[13] O'Byrne, *Naval Biography* (1869), pp. 172-3.

[14] *Ibid.*, p. 1156.

[15] *The Marine Society, a Short History* (Salisbury Press, 1952).

[16] 198th Annual Report of the Marine Society (1954), pp. 14-15.

[17] Lord Chatfield, *The Navy and Defence* (Heinemann, 1942), pp. 9-13.

CHAPTER III

[1] Proceedings of the Institute of Naval Architects, 1919. Paper read by Sir Philip Watts, 9th April, 1919.

[2] For detailed features of the *Dreadnought* the reader is referred to Government White Paper, Cmd. 3048 (1906).

[3] Institute of Naval Architects' Proceedings, 1919, p. 71.

[4] Data from *Warspite's* Ship's Book.

[5] *Western Morning News*, 26th and 27th November, 1913.

[6] Fisher to Beatty, 9th February, 1915. Quot. W. S. Chalmers, *Life and Letters of David, Earl Beatty*, p. 199.

[7] Bishop Carey, *Good-bye to my Generation* (Mowbrays).

CHAPTER IV

[1] W. S. Churchill, *The World Crisis*, Vol. III, Part I, p. 112.

[2] *Ibid.*, p. 110.

[3] Roskill, *The War at Sea*, Vol. I, Chapter XXVI.

[4] *Ibid.*, Vol. II, Chapter II.

[5] W. S. Churchill, *The Second World War*, Vol. I (1st Edition), pp. 364-5 and 550-2.

[6] Letter from Beatty to Jellicoe of 7th May, 1916. Quoted W. S. Chalmers, *Life and Letters of David, Earl Beatty*, p. 222, f.n.

[7] Corbett, *Naval Operations*, Vol. III, pp. 315-318.

[8] Rear-Admiral J. E. T. Harper, *The Truth about Jutland* (Murray, 1927), pp. 50-52.

[9] Rear-Admiral W. S. Chalmers to the author, Dec., 1955.

[10] *The Fighting at Jutland* (privately printed, 1921), pp. 135-6.

[11] Chalmers *Op. Cit.* p. 227

[12] *Ibid.*, p. 225

[13] *Ibid.*, p. 268.

[14] *Ibid.*, p. 222.

[15] W. S. Churchill, *The World Crisis*, Vol. III, p. 149.

[16] Papers of Admiral Sir Humphrey Walwyn.

[17] *Germany's High Sea Fleet in the World War*. English translation of *Der Krieg Zur See* (Cassell, 1920), pp. 142-3.

[18] J. S. Corbett, *Naval Operations*, Vol. III (Revised Edition, 1939), p. 341.

[19] *The Fighting at Jutland*, p. 137.

[20] Admiral Sir R. P.-E.-E.-Drax. Letter to the author, September, 1955.

[21] Chalmers, *Op. Cit.*, p. 283.

[22] *The Fighting at Jutland*, p. 138.

[23] *Etienne* (Commander Sir Stephen King-Hall), *A Naval Lieutenant, 1914-18* (Methuen, 1919).

[24] *The Fighting at Jutland*, p. 138.

[25] *Ibid.*, p. 139.

[26] Admiralty Narrative of the Battle of Jutland (H.M.S.O., 1924), p. 27.

[27] *The Fighting at Jutland*, pp. 139-145.

[28] Corbett, *Naval Operations*, Vol. III, p. 361.

[29] *Ibid.*, p. 359.

[30] Admiral Sir Herbert Packer to the author, June, 1955.

[31] *The Fighting at Jutland*, pp. 128-129.

[32] Corbett, *Op. Cit.*, Vol. III, p. 363.

[33] *Ibid.*, p. 366.

[34] Chalmers, *Op. Cit.*, p. 250.

[35] *Admiralty Narrative of the Battle of Jutland*, pp. 53-54. Compare Scheer, *Germany's High Sea Fleet in the World War* (Cassell, 1920), pp. 155-157, with this report to the Kaiser.

[36] Corbett, *Op. Cit.*, Vol. III, p. 378.

[37] Letter Admiral Jellicoe to Admiralty. Quot. Chalmers, *Op. Cit.*, p. 254, f.n.

[38] Admiral Sir R. Bacon, *The Life of Earl Jellicoe*, p. 289.

[39] Corbett, *Op. Cit.*, Vol. III (2nd Edition, 1939), p. 402 and Appendix J, which gives the text of the German signals de-cyphered in the Admiralty. They are not printed in the 1st Edition of *Naval Operations*.

[40] *The Fighting at Jutland*, p. 151.

[41] Vice-Admiral 5th Battle Squadron to *Warspite*, 5th June, 1916.

CHAPTER V

[1] Quot. Chalmers, *Life and Letters of David, Earl Beatty*, p. 348.

[2] *Ibid.*, p. 288.

[3] Admiral Sir Humphrey Walwyn to the author, August, 1955.

[4] *Ibid.* and recollections of Admiral Sir Herbert Packer.

[5] Chalmers, *Op. Cit.*, pp. 320-321. P. K. Kemp, *Nine Vanguards* (Hutchinson, 1951), p. 191.

[6] Sir Henry Newbolt, *Naval Operations*, Vol. V (Longmans, Green, 1931), pp. 149-159.

[7] Roskill, *The War at Sea, 1939-45*, Vol. I (H.M.S.O., 1954), pp. 483-490.

[8] Newbolt, *Op. Cit.*, pp. 164-177.

[9] *Ibid.*, pp. 230-231.

[10] *Ibid.*, pp. 184-194.

[11] *The Times*, 22nd November, 1918.

CHAPTER VI

[1] Rear-Admiral W. S. Chalmers to the author, June, 1955.

[2] Roskill, *The War at Sea*, Vol. I, pp. 57-58.

³ Information from the Captain, *H.M.S. Excellent*.

⁴ Information from the Constructive Manager, H.M. Dockyard, Portsmouth.

⁵ This incident was described in *Blackwood's Magazine* of June, 1949, under the title of "Near Misses."

⁶ Admiral Sir Victor Crutchley to the author, June, 1955.

⁷ Information from Rear-Admiral (E.) J. Breaks.

⁸ *Daily Mirror* of 26th August, *Daily Mail* of 27th August and *Daily Herald* of 28th August, 1937.

⁹ This section is derived mainly from the author's own service in *Warspite*.

¹⁰ Information from Director-General, Supply and Secretariat Department, Admiralty.

¹¹ Information from Director of Victualling, Admiralty.

¹² Incident described in *Blackwood's Magazine*, June, 1949.

¹³ Viscount Cunningham of Hyndhope, *A Sailor's Odyssey*, pp. 212-216.

¹⁴ Letter in Lord Cunningham's papers.

¹⁵ Captain W. W. Fitzroy to the author, November, 1955.

¹⁶ Letter in Lord Cunningham's papers.

² *Ibid.*, pp. 78-82.

³ Letter in Lord Cunningham's papers.

⁴ Roskill, *Op. Cit.*, Vol. I, pp. 374-376.

⁵ *Ibid.*, pp. 82-84 and Map 7.

⁶ Admiral Crutchley to the author, June, 1955.

⁷ Captain W. W. Fitzroy to the author, November, 1955.

⁸ Roskill, *Op. Cit.*, Vol. I, pp. 156-157 and Map 14.

⁹ *Ibid.*, pp. 170-171.

¹⁰ *Ibid.*, pp. 173-175 and Map 16.

¹¹ Captain W. W. Fitzroy to the author, November, 1955.

¹² *Ibid.*

¹³ Mr. D. Reardon to the author, June, 1955.

¹⁴ Roskill, *Op. Cit.*, Vol. I, pp. 190-194.

¹⁵ Letter in Lord Cunningham's papers.

¹⁶ *Ibid.*

¹⁷ *Ibid.*

¹⁸ *Ibid.*

¹⁹ *Ibid.*

²⁰ *Ibid.*

²¹ Roskill, *Op. Cit.*, Vol. I, pp. 298-299. I. S. O. Playfair, *The War in the Mediterranean and Middle East*, Vol. I, pp. 150-159. (H.M.S.O., 1954).

²² Playfair, *Op. Cit.*, p 151. fn (1).

²³ Captain W. W. Fitzroy to the author, November, 1955.

²⁴ Letter in Lord Cunningham's papers.

²⁵ *Ibid.*

CHAPTER VII

¹ Roskill, *The War at Sea*, Vol. I, pp. 19, 71, 87, 90, etc.

CHAPTER VIII

[1] Captain W. W. Fitzroy to the author, November, 1955.

[2] Admiral Sir Douglas Fisher to the author, August, 1955.

[3] Supplement to the *London Gazette*, No. 38023, of 22nd July, 1947.

[4] Roskill, *The War at Sea, 1939-45*, Vol. I, p. 304.

[5] Report in Admiral Fisher's possession.

[6] Admiral of the Fleet Viscount Cunningham of Hyndhope, *A Sailor's Odyssey*, pp. 302-305.

[7] Letter of 18th January, 1941, Lord Cunningham's papers.

[8] Letter of 21st March, 1941. Lord Cunningham's papers.

[9] Vice-Admiral G. Barnard to the author, August, 1953.

[10] Roskill, *Op. Cit.*, p. 430.

[11] Captain W. W. Fitzroy to the author, November, 1955.

[12] Supplement to the *London Gazette*, No. 38031, of 29th July, 1947. Roskill, *Op. Cit.*, pp. 430-431. Cunningham, *Op. Cit.*, pp. 326-337.

[13] Roskill, *Op. Cit.*, pp. 431-433. Cunningham, *Op. Cit.*, 341-345 and 346-347.

[14] Message of 22nd April, Lord Cunningham's papers.

[15] Captain W. W. Fitzroy to the author, November, 1955.

[16] Admiral Fisher to the author September, 1955.

[17] Roskill, *Op. Cit.*, p. 446.

[18] Lord Cunningham to the author, 18th April, 1955.

[19] Mr. D. Reardon to the author, 21st April, 1955.

[20] Captain W. W. Fitzroy to the author, November, 1955.

[21] Admiral Fisher to the author, 26th April, 1955.

[22] Mr. R. S. Lawson (Admiralty Armament Supply Dept.) to the author, 19th April, 1955.

CHAPTER IX

[1] S. E. Morison, *The History of United States Naval Operations in World War II* (Little, Brown), Vol. IV, pp. 65-68.

[2] Secretary, London Stock Exchange, to the author, 15th September, 1955.

[3] Roskill, *The War at Sea, 1939-45*, Vol. II (H.M.S.O., 1956), Chapter I.

[4] *Ibid.*, Chapter X.

[5] Admiral Sir Herbert Packer's "Warspite Captain's Record," lent to the author, 1956.

[6] *Ibid.*

[7] *Ibid.*

[8] *Ibid.*

[9] *Ibid.*

[10] *Ibid.*

[11] Viscount Cunningham of Hyndhope, *A Sailor's Odyssey*, pp. 562-565.

[12] *Ibid.*

[13] Lieutenant-Commander A. M. Jones to the author, October, 1955.

[14] *Ibid.*

[15] Supplement to the *London Gazette*, No. 38899, of 28th April, 1950.

CHAPTER X

[1] Major L. F. Ellis, *Victory in the West*. Official Military History (in preparation).

[2] *Ibid*.

[3] Vice-Admiral M. H. A. Kelsey to the author, September, 1955.

[4] *Ibid*.

[5] *Ibid*.

[6] Viscount Cunningham of Hyndhope, *A Sailor's Odyssey*, p. 656.

[7] Admiralty Fleet Order 2565/54.

[8] *Daily Telegraph*, 30th April, 1947.

[9] *The Times*, 24th April, 1947.

[10] *Ibid*., 29th August, 1947.

[11] The Wolverhampton Metal Co., Ltd., to the author, September, 1955.

[12] Mr. G. C. M. Pharoah to the author, 26th September, 1955.

INDEX

*The ranks shown against officers are those
which they finally attained*

WHEN THE MOON RISES

TONY DAVIES

A trainload of British prisoners of war steams
slowly through the Italian mountains.
Suddenly there is a screeching of brakes and
the sound of shots from the guards. Two
British officers have made the leap for
freedom...

Tony Davies's first escape bid ends in
recapture and transfer to a new camp in the
north. When he escapes again he and his
companions are faced with a 700 mile walk
along the spine of the Appenines to the Allied
beach-head at Salerno. The journey begins as
a schoolboy adventure: it ends as a terrifying
and deadly game of hide-and-seek where
the Germans hunt down the fugitives like
animals and courageous Italian peasants risk
their own lives to save them.

ESCAPE FROM THE RISING SUN
IAN SKIDMORE

'The oily dust fell everywhere, on hungry
stragglers searching for their units, on armed
deserters who roamed the streets searching fo
loot, on . . . fear-crazed men fighting their way
at the point of a gun or bayonet, pushing wome
and children aside . . . The dead lay in the
streets . . . but no one collected the corpses now

Singapore had fallen. The British Army, retreating
in disorder before the onslaught of the Japanese
shock-troops, had been told to surrender. One
man was convinced he could escape.

Geoffrey Rowley-Conwy seized a junk and sailed
for Padang. There he joined a group of fellow
officers for a desperate escape-bid in a dilapidate
sailing boat across the Indian Ocean to Ceylon.
1,500 miles of open sea swept by the fury of the
monsoon and patrolled by Japanese fighter plane
on the lookout for British survivors.

'One of the best and liveliest escape stories of
the Second World War . . . enthralling.'
Times Literary Supplement